MANAGEMENT
OF
INFORMATION
SYSTEMS

SECOND EDITION

MANAGEMENT
OF
INFORMATION
SYSTEMS

EDITED BY

Paul Gray
Claremont Graduate School, Claremont, California

William R. King
University of Pittsburgh, Pittsburgh, Pennsylvania

Ephraim R. McLean
Georgia State University, Atlanta, Georgia

Hugh J. Watson
University of Georgia, Athens, Georgia

SECOND EDITION

The Dryden Press
Harcourt Brace College Publishers

Fort Worth Philadelphia San Diego New York Orlando Austin San Antonio
Toronto Montreal London Sydney Tokyo

Acquisitions Editor	Richard Bonacci
Project Editor	Jon Gregory
Art Director	Beverly Baker
Production Manager	Ann Coburn
Photo & Permissions Editor	Steve Lunetta
Publisher	Elizabeth Widdicombe
Director of Editing, Design, & Production	Diane Southworth
Compositor	Maple-Vail

Address for Editorial Correspondence
The Dryden Press, 301 Commerce Street, Suite 3700, Fort Worth, TX 76102

Address for Orders
The Dryden Press, 6277 Sea Harbor Drive, Orlando, FL 32887-6777
1-800-782-4479, or 1-800-443-0001 (in Florida)

ISBN: 0-03-092685-8

Library of Congress Catalog Card Number: 93-071419

Printed in the United States of America

3 4 5 6 7 8 9 0 1 2   090   9 8 7 6 5 4 3 2 1

The Dryden Press
Harcourt Brace College Publishers

The Dryden Press Series in Information Systems

Arthur Andersen & Co./Flaatten, Mc-
Cubbrey, O'Riordan, and Burgess
Foundations of Business Systems
Second Edition

Arthur Andersen & Co./Boynton and Shank
*Foundations of Business Systems: Projects and
Cases*

Anderson
*Structured Programming Using Turbo Pascal:
A Brief Introduction*
Second Edition

Brown and McKeown
Structured Programming with Microsoft BASIC

Coburn
Beginning Structured COBOL

Coburn
Advanced Structured COBOL

Dean and Effinger
*Common-Sense BASIC: Structured Program-
ming with Microsoft QuickBASIC*

Electronic Learning Facilitators, Inc. Series
The DOS Book
The Lotus 1-2-3 Book
Stepping Through Excel 4.0 for Windows
Stepping Through PageMaker 5.0 for Windows
Stepping Through Windows 3.1
Stepping Through Word 2.0 for Windows
*Up and Running with Harvard Graphics 1.03
for Windows*
*Up and Running with PageMaker 5.0 for Win-
dows*
*Up and Running with WordPerfect 5.2 for
Windows*
*Up and Running with Quattro Pro 1.0 for
Windows*
*Up and Running with Microsoft Works 2.0 for
Windows*
*Up and Running with Lotus 1-2-3 Release 1.1
for Windows*
*Up and Running with Paradox 1.0 for Win-
dows*
Up and Running with DOS 6.0
Up and Running with Paradox 4.0 for DOS
*Up and Running with Microsoft Works 3.0 for
DOS*
*Up and Running with Excel 4.0 for the Macin-
tosh*
*Up and Running with Word 5.1 for the Macin-
tosh*
*Up and Running with PageMaker 5.0 for the
Macintosh*
*Up and Running with Microsoft Works 3.0 for
the Macintosh*
Working Smarter with DOS 5.0

Working with WordPerfect 5.0
Working with WordPerfect 5.1

Federico
WordPerfect 5.1 Primer

Goldstein Software, Inc.
Joe Spreadsheet, Macintosh Version

Goldstein Software, Inc.
Joe Spreadsheet, Statistical

Gray, King, McLean, and Watson
Management of Information Systems
Second Edition

Harrington
*Database Management for Microcomputers: De-
sign and Implementation*
Second Edition

Janossy
*COBOL: An Introduction to Software Engi-
neering*

Laudon and Laudon
*Business Information Systems: A Problem-
Solving Approach*
Second Edition

Laudon, Laudon, and Weill
The Integrated Solution

Lawlor
Computer Information Systems
Third Edition

Liebowitz
*The Dynamics of Decision Support Systems and
Expert Systems*

McKeown
Living with Computers
Fourth Edition

McKeown
Living with Computers with BASIC
Fourth Edition

McKeown
Working with Computers
Second Edition

McKeown
*Working with Computers with Software Tutori-
als*
Second Edition

McKeown and Badarinathi
*Applications Software Tutorials: A Computer
Lab Manual Using WordPerfect 5.1, Lotus
1-2-3, dBASE III PLUS and dBASE IV*

McKeown and Leitch
*Management Information Systems: Managing
with Computers*

v

McLeod
Systems Analysis and Design: An Organizational Approach

Martin
QBASIC: A Short Course in Structured Programming

Martin, Series Editor
Productivity Software Modules
  Disk Operating System (DOS) Windows 3.1
  Word Processing with WordPerfect 5.0 and 5.1
  Word Processing with WordPerfect for Windows 5.2
  Spreadsheets with Lotus 1-2-3
  Spreadsheets with Quattro Pro 4.0
  Database Management with dBASE III PLUS
  Database Management with dBASE IV
  Database Management with Paradox 4.0
  A Beginner's Guide to BASIC

Martin and Burstein
Computer Systems Fundamentals

Martin and Parker
Mastering Today's Software Series
Texts available in any combination of the following:
  Microcomputer Concepts
  Extended Microcomputer Concepts
  Disk Operating System 5.0
  Disk Operating System 6.0
  WordPerfect 5.1
  WordPerfect for Windows 5.2
  WordPerfect 6.0
  Lotus 1-2-3 (2.2/2.3)
  Lotus 1-2-3 (2.4)
  dBASE III PLUS
  dBASE IV (1.5/2.0)
  Paradox 4.0
  BASIC

Mason
Using IBM Microcomputers in Business: Decision Making with Lotus 1-2-3 and dBASE III PLUS (or dBASE IV)

Millspaugh
Business Programming in C for DOS-Bases Sysetms

O'Brien
The Nature of Computers

O'Brien
The Nature of Computers with Productivity Software Guides

Parker

Parker
Computers and Their Applications
Third Edition

Parker
Computers and Their Applications with Productivity Software Guide
Third Edition

Parker
Productivity Software Guide
Fourth Edition

Parker
Understanding Computers and Information Processing: Today and Tomorrow
Fifth Edition

Parker
Understanding Computers and Information Processing: Today and Tomorrow with BASIC
Fifth Edition

Robertson and Robertson
Microcomputer Applications and Programming: A Complete Computer Course with DOS, WordPerfect 5.1, Lotus 1-2-3, dBASE III PLUS (or dBASE IV) and BASIC

Robertson and Robertson
Using Microcomputer Applications (A Series of Computer Lab Manuals)

Roche
Telecommunications and Business Strategy

Simpson and Tesch
Introductory COBOL: A Transaction-Oriented Approach

Sullivan
The New Computer User

Swafford and Haff
dBASE III PLUS

The HBJ College Outline Series

Kreitzberg
Introduction to BASIC

Kreitzberg
Introduction to Fortran

Pierson
Introduction to Business Information Systems

Veklerov and Pekelny
Computer Language C

The Dryden Press Series in Information Systems

v

McLeod
Systems Analysis and Design: An Organizational Approach

Martin
QBASIC: A Short Course in Structured Programming

Martin, Series Editor
Productivity Software Modules
   Disk Operating System (DOS) Windows 3.1
   *Word Processing with WordPerfect 5.0 and
      5.1*
   Word Processing with WordPerfect for Windows 5.2
   Spreadsheets with Lotus 1-2-3
   Spreadsheets with Quattro Pro 4.0
   *Database Management with dBASE III
      PLUS*
   Database Management with dBASE IV
   Database Management with Paradox 4.0
   A Beginner's Guide to BASIC

Martin and Burstein
Computer Systems Fundamentals

Martin and Parker
Mastering Today's Software Series
Texts available in any combination of the
   following:
   Microcomputer Concepts
   Extended Microcomputer Concepts
   Disk Operating System 5.0
   Disk Operating System 6.0
   WordPerfect 5.1
   WordPerfect for Windows 5.2
   WordPerfect 6.0
   Lotus 1-2-3 (2.2/2.3)
   Lotus 1-2-3 (2.4)
   dBASE III PLUS
   dBASE IV (1.5/2.0)
   Paradox 4.0
   BASIC

Mason
*Using IBM Microcomputers in Business: Decision Making with Lotus 1-2-3 and dBASE
   III PLUS (or dBASE IV)*

Millspaugh
*Business Programming in C for DOS-Bases
   Sysetms*

O'Brien
The Nature of Computers

O'Brien
*The Nature of Computers with Productivity
   Software Guides*

Parker

Parker
Computers and Their Applications
Third Edition

Parker
Computers and Their Applications with Productivity Software Guide
Third Edition

Parker
Productivity Software Guide
Fourth Edition

Parker
*Understanding Computers and Information
   Processing: Today and Tomorrow*
Fifth Edition

Parker
*Understanding Computers and Information
   Processing: Today and Tomorrow with
   BASIC*
Fifth Edition

Robertson and Robertson
*Microcomputer Applications and Programming:
   A Complete Computer Course with DOS,
   WordPerfect 5.1, Lotus 1-2-3, dBASE III
   PLUS (or dBASE IV) and BASIC*

Robertson and Robertson
Using Microcomputer Applications (A Series of
   Computer Lab Manuals)

Roche
Telecommunications and Business Strategy

Simpson and Tesch
*Introductory COBOL: A Transaction-Oriented
   Approach*

Sullivan
The New Computer User

Swafford and Haff
dBASE III PLUS

The HBJ College Outline Series

Kreitzberg
Introduction to BASIC

Kreitzberg
Introduction to Fortran

Pierson
Introduction to Business Information Systems

Veklerov and Pekelny
Computer Language C

Preface

For most organizations, information is a resource. For some it is both a resource and a strategic weapon used to gain competitive advantage. The magnitude of the resource is underscored by the fact that most organizations spend at least 2 percent of their annual sales (not profits!) and leading-edge firms as much as 10 percent of their sales each year on information systems. Clearly, something important is going on here.

From the point of view of the organization, then, information systems are a large investment that require managerial attention if a proper return is to be gained. Many firms, however, have delegated this management task to the technical specialists in their computer shops. We contend that the management of information systems (MoIS) is not a task that can be left to the specialist, but one that is an integral part of the work of every manager.

This book is addressed principally to three groups of people:

- M.B.A. students who are interested in the management of information systems and recognize its importance to their future careers
- Undergraduate business students who are majoring in information systems
- Practitioners who are involved or interested in the management of information systems

Why MoIS Is Important to You

Business professionals and managers are continually involved with information systems. Typical interactions involve

- Managing the purchase and use of information systems or computers in your department
- Buying services from the information systems department or vendors for yourself, your department, or your company
- Making decisions about priorities and budget allocations in the development of new information systems as a member of a management steering committee
- Working with information systems (IS) professionals on specific tasks, such as project definitions, feasibility studies, and systems designs
- Assessing the potential of information systems to improve the position of your organization or company (that is, the strategic use of these systems) and determining the threat posed by the strategic use of information systems by your competitors
- Developing your own computer applications
- Managing IS professionals assigned to work for you

As you read the above list you will see that each interaction involves managerial as well as technical considerations. You will have to make judgments as to what information systems can and cannot do. You will have to recognize that information systems technology is changing continually, that organizational structures are being modified by the evolving nature of these systems, and that new ways of using information systems are being developed. All managers are faced with having to understand the potential and the role of information systems in this changing environment.

What We Expect You Already Know

The editors of this textbook assume that you have some personal acquaintance with computers and information systems. It does not have to be deep. Most of you will be able to use productivity software, such as a spreadsheet or word processing program, or you may have learned how to program computers in a high-level language. In short, you will find it much easier to understand the selections in this book if you feel comfortable with the computer and have had some experience with either a mainframe or a personal computer.

If you are an IS professional, you should be able to go to any of the articles of interest to you. The articles in each of the sections are organized in logical sequence, but they can be read in any order.

You will find it helpful to have had an introduction to the specifics of computer systems given in a course on information systems, but such a course is not a prerequisite. More important is that you have an understanding of how organizations are managed. Many of the principles discussed in this book for information systems are the same as those for managing other business functions, such as marketing, finance, or manufacturing.

How This Book Came to Be

Several years ago, the International Business Machines (IBM) Corporation became concerned with the state of understanding of MoIS, particularly among managers. IBM believed that future managers should be as conversant with managing information systems as they would be with managing any other functional areas of a firm. Therefore, IBM held a national competition in which it invited business schools to submit proposals for large grants. Of a total of 218 schools that competed, IBM chose 13 (Arizona, Claremont Graduate School, Georgia, Georgia State, Illinois, Indiana, Massachusetts Institute of Technology, Minnesota, Pennslvania, Pittsburgh, Rochester, Texas, and UCLA). Each grant school received $1 million in cash and $1 million in equipment and supporting software. They were given a charter to find ways of teaching about, and doing research on, the management of information systems.

As the IBM grant schools began their work, it became clear that while much folk wisdom, many rules of thumb, and scattered articles in journals and magazines on the subject had accumulated over time, there was no coherent, integrated, focused understanding of MoIS. The researchers also recognized that MoIS is a big subject that had to be organized and defined.

When we, each of whom had major responsibility for the IBM grant at our school, were approached with the idea of creating a book on MoIS, our universal response was that none of us individually knew enough about the whole subject to do it justice. However, we felt that if we could combine our knowledge and work intensively together, then we could create a framework for thinking about MoIS and collect the knowledge that had been accumulated thus far about MoIS. Because of the importance of disseminating such a framework quickly and the high quality of what was being written on specific subjects, we decided that this book of readings was the appropriate approach. The end product of our efforts was the publication of the first edition of this title in 1989.

About This Edition

We were pleased with the reception the first edition of the book received. It was adopted for use in many colleges and universities and added to the libraries of many practitioners. The information systems field, however, does not remain still. New technologies emerge, followed by a desire to employ them effectively. The internal and external business environment changes, thus creating opportunities and challenges for the use of information technology. Researchers and practitioners observe, study, and write about these changes, thus expanding the body of knowledge about the management of information systems. Consequently, after only three years, we felt a need to revise the book.

We began by reviewing all the first-edition selections and discussing the important new developments in the field that deserved coverage in the second edition. We decided to keep some selections, drop some, and replace others if better articles were available. We also pinpointed specific topics that we wanted to cover if good alternatives were available. Against this background, we began to review academic, professional, and trade journals; conference proceedings; books; cases; and newsletters in search of the best materials. As in the first edition, to guide our search for readings, we established a set of principles for making selections. These guidelines included

- ◆ *Coverage of the domain of MoIS.* As we reviewed the existing literature, we found a wealth of outstanding material in several areas, such as the strategic use of information systems and artificial intelligence. Other areas, such as transaction processing systems, are being neglected. We made our selections in such a way as to cover the whole field, but generally limited ourselves to one article on any given topic.
- ◆ *Relevance to the domain of MoIS.* We found many worthy selections that deal with the technical details of information systems but do not cover their management. Such articles were not selected.
- ◆ *Emerging importance.* An advantage of a book of readings over other books is that it can be easily revised with each edition. This is particularly

important in the information systems field, where change is continual. We have aggressively tried to include selections that are at the cutting edge of what is taking place today and are likely to be important in the future. As a result, topics such as outsourcing, group support technology, and downsizing to smaller computing platforms are included.

- *Timeliness and timelessness.* Most of the selections have appeared recently. MoIS is a rapidly changing field, and we sought to present as contemporary a picture as possible. In making our selections, we looked for articles that would remain current over time because they deal with principles, rather than ones that deal with the ephemeral details of the moment. A few articles were selected because they are classics and continue to be the best available coverage of a particular topic.
- *Quality and interest.* It goes almost without saying that we used criteria of high quality and broad interest. We rejected some articles that discuss important topics but fail the quality test. We also avoided articles on topics that covered significant but narrow issues, for example, negotiating contracts for hardware.
- *Readability.* Given a choice between articles of nearly equal quality, we chose the one that was most easily understood by the nonspecialist reader and that avoided overdoses of jargon and abbreviations.
- *Generality.* We tended to limit our selections to articles that dealt with information systems for the firm as a whole. We chose not to focus on articles that dealt primarily with specific functional areas such as finance or manufacturing; to do so, we would have had to create a much larger book. Our generality criterion and our readability criterion also led us to avoid contributions that reported specific research results.

An important consideration in selecting articles was to provide a comprehensive coverage of the domain of MoIS: the set of topics that students of MoIS should understand. We present this domain in the first selection in the book (Reading 1.1).

Each editor evaluated the articles that we thought were good candidates for the book. After a series of meetings, we determined the final contents. We had to exclude many fine articles that met our guidelines in order to keep the book a manageable size. The bibliography lists many excellent articles not included. Of the 34 selections chosen, more than 75 percent of them are new or revised for this edition. This high percentage reflects our efforts to provide readers with the most up-to-date selections possible.

What Is in This Book

The 34 readings in the book are organized into six sections.

- Overview of MoIS
- Managing the Constellation of IS Applications
- Managing IS Technology
- Managing IS Application Development

- Managing the IS Function
- Managing IS Organizational Relationship

Each section is preceded by an overview that introduces the topic area and ties the selections together. Questions and exercises follow each section. A bibliography is included at the end of the book to help you dig more deeply into areas of special interest to you.

We have also been fortunate in including a foreword from Robert E. Woodley, executive consultant, formerly of IBM, that puts this book into context. The foreword should be read before reading the selections.

How You Can Use This Book

This book can be used either as the primary text or as a supplement for a course in MoIS. Instructors who stress the case method may want to use cases in conjunction with this book. Some instructors may find this book useful in an action-oriented course in which students visit firms and report on how the principles described in this book are being employed in industry. Additional ideas and details for using the book are provided in the instructor's manual.

Acknowledgments

This book, like most, depends not only upon its editors but upon many people. We would like to acknowledge first and foremost the authors of the articles included and the publishers who granted us permission to reprint copyrighted material.

We are particularly indebted to DeVilla Williams, our first editor at The Dryden Press, who brought us together and nurtured us through the process of creating this book, and to Richard Bonacci, our current Dryden acquisitions editor, who has continued to support and encourage our efforts.

The grants to our institutions from the International Business Machines Corporation sensitized each of us to the importance of MoIS and led us to recognize the void in textbooks on the subject. The IBM Corporation is also a sponsor of BITNET, the electronic mail system that facilitated our work.

We also would like to thank Bob Woodley for writing the foreword. While at IBM, Bob provided the leadership for the annual meeting between IBM and the grant schools.

Ranjit Tinaikar and Sandeep Rustagi, graduate students at the University of Pittsburgh, assisted in reading the page proofs.

Paul Gray
Claremont Graduate School

Ephraim R. McLean
Georgia State University

William R. King
University of Pittsburgh

Hugh J. Watson
University of Georgia

Foreword

Technology, through its rapid evolution and increasing complexity, continues to challenge managers seeking to harness its benefits. This structured compilation of articles provides insight into specific areas of concern, as well as guidance for decision making. Unfortunately, it does not contain ultimate solutions; the definitive article, "Ten Steps to Managing Information Systems," has yet to be written.

This book, like its previous edition, demonstrates the perceptiveness and timeliness of the 1985 investment made by the IBM Corporation to further graduate education and research into the management issues surrounding information systems. There had been considerable technically oriented research for many decades. However, prior to the IBM grant program, there was insufficient investigation into general management issues, as reflected in the sparseness of high quality articles and, more importantly, in the content of most business schools' curricula.

The 33 articles selected by the editors for the first edition of *MoIS* provided a noteworthy compendium of the materials that were then available. This edition expands on that base and incorporates writings and new topics. The editors, all principal investigators at award-winning graduate business schools during the IBM grant competition, are to be commended for their thoughtful selection of these current, topical articles for the benefit of practitioners, educators, and students.

Since the grants were awarded, it was my good fortune to act as chairman of the annual meeting of grant school representatives and IBM executives. Each year, at least one emerging trend found a prominent place on our agenda for which little, if any, research had been conducted on the related management issues.

Since the initial edition of *MoIS*, the dynamics associated with executive decision making in this field have spawned new concepts, opportunities, and fears. Peter Keen's contribution to the first edition noted that investing in information technology requires capital, technology, management, and time. An interesting and important development is that firms are now finding alternative ways to assemble these resources. A multibillion-dollar industry known as "outsourcing" has emerged. Service companies specializing in offering systems operations, network management, and application development now provide an alternative means of technology delivery at a negotiated, predictable cost and service level bound within a long-term contract. This solution allows the firms' managers to focus on their primary business and reduce their in-house technology skills to those of strategic utilization and deployment. In the current turbulent economic environment, outsourcing may also yield a short-term infusion of capital associated with the transfer of assets from previous information processing equipment.

The debate of centralization versus decentralization continues to rage in corporate corridors, fueled by the emergence of Local Area Networks (LAN), some at the direction of chief information officers, many designed and implemented by functional groups. Some firms are moving toward strategies aimed at off-loading large host processors with hopes of economic gain. Now, executives must not only determine the direction but whether to proceed with their in-house staff, supplement them with external business partners, or turn all or part of the execution phase over to a provider of outsourcing solutions.

Electronic Data Interchange (EDI) has become a competitive necessity in many industries and is becoming commonplace as firms link networks to each other to improve customer, supplier, and vendor relationships.

All three of these current trends—outsourcing, decentralization, and EDI—also raise the issue of data security to new heights and increase the need for adequate backup and recovery processes as information systems control an ever-growing percentage of mainstream business.

The globalization of industry, corporate quality initiatives spurred by the federal government's Baldrige Award competition, downsizing, restructuring, and other factors are causing an upheaval in the existing business processes of many firms. This translates into additional demand for software and increases the focus and urgency for tools and platforms to support process reengineering efforts, application development projects, and systems integration opportunities. The reduction of cycle time, elimination of errors for core business operations, and an extension of functional capabilities demand urgent attention in many companies if they are to continue as competitors in their industry.

As if these business-driven requirements were not enough to fill the calendars of those who manage information systems and telecommunications, technology itself continues to blossom and involves everyone. Each industry is finding new ways to incorporate computing capability. While back-room operations focus on increased connectivity and reduced costs, front-end operations are moving technology to the consumer. From automobiles to shopping carts, ATMs to emergency rooms, we are all involved with computers on a daily basis.

To some of us, it seems that the technical-capability challenges of this evolution are being met and often exceeded well in advance of the related management aspects by the manufacturers and technical entrepreneurs. To fully exploit this technology, however, will require a community of individuals well versed in the management of information systems. I believe this book of readings, combined with its predecessor, will enable this community to increase its base of knowledge and comprehension, thereby preparing it for the challenges ahead.

Robert E. Woodley
Executive consultant

Contents

MANAGEMENT
OF
INFORMATION
SYSTEMS

SECOND EDITION

SECTION 1

Overview of MoIS

In what some people might view as "the good old days," decisions about information technology could largely be left in the hands of "the high priests of computing"—the specialists who were trained, knowledgeable, and experienced in the technical nuances of computing. Part of the reason for this lack of concern was because most of the decisions about computers were not terribly important. Managers were, of course, concerned about how much was being spent and that operational systems were up and running, but information technology was not usually critical to whether the company succeeded or failed. This is clearly not the case today.

There are few aspects of organizational life and practices that have not been affected by computers. For example, from the lowest clerical worker to the chief executive officer, the computer serves as a critical resource for carrying out job responsibilities. Jobs are being redesigned to eliminate needless steps and to take advantage of computer capabilities. Efforts of work groups are increasingly supported by information technology. Organizations are establishing electronic links to customers and suppliers in order to operate faster, more economically, and more effectively. Firms are using information technology as a weapon to compete in the marketplace.

Information technology has become as important as production, marketing, and finance to most firms. As a consequence, information technology can no longer be left to the "high priests." It is so important and pervasive that its management becomes every manager's responsibility, including yours, either now or in the future.

The first section of this book sets the stage for learning about the management of information systems (MoIS). The two readings explore what needs to be managed, critical issues, and current developments in organizations. Hopefully, the readings will excite and add to your interest in MoIS, and make you want to learn more about this dynamic and challenging field.

1

Issues

MoIS: the domain, key issues, and future environment

The opening article was written by the editors especially for this book. It identifies what we consider the domain of MoIS. Five categories are explored: managing the constellation of IS applications, managing IS technology, managing IS application development, managing the IS function, and managing IS relationships within the firm. Some of the topics within the domain are very important today. Others are likely to become more important in the near future, and they are given special coverage.

Survey of information technology

The Economist, the highly regarded British business publication, published an excellent overview of the current use of information technology in organizations. This overview is the second reading selection in this section. Its wide-ranging coverage includes how information technology is affecting jobs, worker and organizational productivity, computer systems design, how firms compete, personal and organizational communications, and responsiveness to customer needs and market conditions. These and other topics are discussed, drawing from a wealth of real-world examples.

1.1
MoIS: The Domain, Key Issues, and Future Environment

Introduction

Business information systems have come a long way since their commercial introduction in the 1950s. The computer on your desk has more processing power than many of its room-sized predecessors. Computers have come out of the "glass houses" in which they were carefully kept and are now found throughout organizations. They are no longer the exclusive property of the "high priests of computing," with their highly specialized knowledge and seemingly mysterious ways. Computers can now be used by almost anyone. Applications range from automated clerical tasks to tasks that allow the organization to compete better in the marketplace. Companies such as banks and airlines, in which information systems are the "core technologies" of the business, cannot operate without the continuous efficient and effective employment of computer systems. Increasingly, industries that have not traditionally been "information intensive," such as manufacturers and some service providers, are finding that they too are dependent on, and can derive business advantage from, computer systems.

For people charged with managing organizational information resources, this is both good news and bad news. The good news is that the job has expanded and opened new career opportunities. Information systems is a functional area, just like finance, accounting, or manufacturing. The senior information systems (IS) manager may now carry the title Manager of IS, Vice President for Information Services, or Director of Information Resources. Many firms have created the position of Chief Information Officer (CIO). It is a position of responsibility associated with the organization's top management group.

The bad news is that managing organizational information resources has become more difficult. IS is unique in that it is both a business function and something that permeates all other business functions and all aspects of a business' activities. Rather than needing just technical computer skills, IS managers also

3

need personal, managerial, and business skills. Not all IS managers have handled this transition well. Some have found it difficult to grow beyond their technical interests, training, and experience. More than one organization has put a non-information-systems person in charge of managing its information systems.

IS is a rapidly changing field, and the need for more effective management of information systems (MoIS) is increasing, if only because information systems are becoming more critical in determining an organization's success or failure. IS managers face a multitude of issues in a dynamic environment. In this section we first explore these managerial issues and then describe the areas involved in effective management of information systems (MoIS). The articles on MoIS that follow were selected for their excellence. They emphasize the topics of greatest current interest. With the exception of a few classics, these articles were written within the last several years. Thus they reflect the issues that businesspeople and academicians are currently addressing. This does not imply that areas such as managing computer operations or transaction processing systems are unimportant, rather it underscores that these areas are reasonably well understood and hence need not be extensively discussed in the literature today.

Key Issues Facing IS Managers

A number of studies have investigated the key issues facing IS managers. The findings of these studies are important to practitioners and academicians for several reasons:

> Businesses make decisions about where to commit limited funds. Researchers make decisions about which issues to study. Academic institu-

TABLE 1   Key Issues Facing IS Managers

RANK	ISSUE
1.	Developing an information architecture
2.	Making effective use of the data resource
3.	Improving IS strategic planning
4.	Specifying, recruiting and developing human resources
5.	Facilitating organizational learning and use of IS technologies
6.	Building a responsive IT infrastructure
7.	Aligning the IS organization with that of the enterprise
8.	Using IS for competitive advantage
9.	Improving the quality of software development
10.	Planning and implementing a telecommunications system

SOURCE: "Key Issues Facing IS Managers" by F. Neiderman, James C. Brancheau, and James C. Wetherbe, from *MIS Quarterly* Vol. 15, Number 4, December 1991, pp. 475–50. Copyright 1991 by the Society for Information Management Systems Research Center at the University of Minnesota. Reprinted by special permission.

tions make decisions on the shape and direction of educational programs. Professional societies arrange conferences to deal with contemporary issues. For these reasons and more, an awareness of issues that leading professionals feel are of critical importance is very useful.[1]

Table 1 shows the top ten issues that IS executives identified in a recent study. Each of these issues is discussed below.

- *Developing an information architecture.* An information architecture is a high-level "map" of the information resources of an organization. It is a "blue-print" that can be used to guide the development and acquisition of data, technologies systems, and applications on a cost-effective basis. Often, an architecture includes the rules and policies that govern the deployment and use of information resources throughout the organization.
- *Making effective use of the data resource.* Information is now viewed as a "factor of production" along with labor and capital. However, making effective use of information without being overwhelmed by its sheer volume is a continuing concern of both IS managers and business managers.
- *Improving IS strategic planning.* IS strategic planning involves two major phases. First, it translates business objectives and strategies into IS terms so that appropriate systems, applications, data, and other information resources can be developed to support business plans. Second, the IS planning process must also deal with the assessment of IS resources so that they can be effectively used as elements of business strategy—that is, to seek competitive advantage. Although the first of these phases is better developed in many organizations, the second phase is of equal importance.
- *Specifying, recruiting, and developing human resources.* It is becoming increasingly apparent that effective IS personnel must possess a combination of personal, business, and technical skills. There are fewer jobs in IS for those who are merely technically proficient. The issues of how to acquire and/or develop people with such skills and the career paths that can be used to nurture them are of increasing concern, since in a dynamic field such as IS, there are few "traditional" answers.
- *Facilitating organizational learning and use of IS technologies.* There is a continuing need for individuals and organizations to learn how they can effectively employ the ever-changing array of IS technologies and applications to their business situations. The sharing of knowledge among individuals and departments of a firm, and between a firm and its suppliers and other "allies," is of great importance. This is because information resources have such great potential impact, and because there is already so high a cost associated with learning about the continuous stream of innovations that no one can afford to "reinvent the wheel" by repeatedly incurring excess learning costs.
- *Building a responsive IT infrastructure.* The fluctuating nature of business activities and of technology requires that an IT infrastructure be created that

---

[1]James C. Brancheau, and James C. Wetherbe, "Key Issues in Information Systems Management," *MIS Quarterly,* March 1987, p. 23.

can support the business in addressing its current needs and be sufficiently flexible to adapt to rapid change. For most firms, this involves the adaptation of an infrastructure of computers, software, and networks that was not originally implemented with the need for such flexibility in mind. So the IS manager must often begin with a relatively rigid infrastructure and adapt it to address new business conditions, new technologies, and new requirements for future adaptability.

◆ *Aligning the IS organization with that of the enterprise.* The issue of centralization versus decentralization of the IS function, which has been of concern to businesses since early in the computer era, is still of concern. However, technological advances have made this once simple choice vastly more complex. The IS function now serves many different roles, ranging from providing advice and help to end users to developing and maintaining large-scale systems. There is undoubtedly no overall "best" alignment that can be prescribed, since the dynamism of the firm's environment, its level of maturity in both business activities and IS functions, its existing systems, and many other factors influence the nature of the alignment that might be appropriate.

◆ *Using information systems for competitive advantage.* The idea that information systems could be used in modes other than in support of traditional business activities has been a prominent feature of IS thinking for more than a decade. Systems are employed to directly create competitive advantage in the marketplace by a wide variety of firms in industries as diverse as banking, transportation, and manufacturing. If the competitive advantage created is to be sustained, the information system must be an integral element of overall business strategy. This often means that such systems must be continually upgraded to provide additional services and benefits to customers or others to whom the systems are addressed.

◆ *Improving the quality of software development.* Software development has been more art than science for most of the computer era. As large-scale systems become more complex and more end users develop their own applications software, the problems of software development in the organization have become more complex. So despite the development of methodologies and computer-aided software engineering (CASE) tools, the quality and efficiency of software development is of continuing concern to IS managers.

◆ *Planning and implementing a telecommunication system.* Communications has always been a part of the overall information processing in an organization. Now that telecommunications systems and computer systems are interlinked, the domain of the IS manager has expanded explicitly to include the planning and implementation of an effective telecommunications system for his or her organization. This telecommunications system may involve the communication of data on basic transactions—for example, sales, inventory, and accounts records—as well as communications among individuals within the firm and between the firm and its suppliers and business allies.

The Future MoIS Environment

Recognizing the need for better trained IS managers, IBM created a multi-million dollar grant program for improving graduate education in the management of information systems. Thirteen universities were selected to receive grants on the basis of competitive proposals.[2]

The four editors of this book, each primarily responsible for his own institution becoming a grantee, have sought to identify and integrate some of the knowledge essential to the future of MoIS.

Each university that prepared an IBM grant proposal was asked to forecast the future MoIS environment. From the 13 schools that were awarded grants, a pattern emerges that reflects their thinking about current trends and what the future may hold. Three themes stand out:

1. End-user computing
2. The role of information in the organization
3. Systems and organizational integration

End-user computing

Managers and professionals increasingly rely on their own resources to perform most of the computing tasks formerly done by a central IS department.

End-user computing (EUC) resulted from quantum changes in:

- The capacity of computers (larger)

- The cost of hardware (lower)

- The availability of "user-friendly" software (greater)

- Data communications capabilities (greater)

These changes took place over several decades, but the pace of change has accelerated in the recent past. The advent of inexpensive personal computers; new classes of computers and systems, such as minicomputers, distributed systems, telecommunications networks, and office automation; and easy-to-use software all have occurred within the lifetime of most readers of this book.

These developments have resulted in enormous benefits. For the first time, computing knowledge and business task knowledge (both usually necessary to achieve maximum benefits) more frequently reside in the minds of the same individuals. The old, difficult, and sometimes ineffective process of finding ways for people who know the problem to communicate with people who know the computer has been eliminated. Businesses have been able to gain more of the benefits from computing.

---

[2]The schools receiving grants were Arizona, UCLA, Claremont Graduate School, Georgia, Georgia State, Illinois, Indiana, MIT, Minnesota, Pennsylvania, Pittsburgh, Rochester, and Texas.

For example, with EUC, the human resources staff, who had frequently been at the back of the line when IS services were allocated, can now develop a new personnel data base or a computer program for career path management.

Although the EUC revolution was facilitated by technological advances, EUC places new pressures on technology because it raises user expectations. Users are far less willing to tolerate "unfriendly" software or hardware. They recognize the value of networks that allow them to communicate freely with one another, wherever they may be geographically. They need access to the mainframe data bases that previously were the sole preserve of the IS professionals.

EUC also creates new organizational pressures. Sophisticated computer users are no longer willing to accept the word of the IS professionals as gospel. They require an entirely new kind of centralized organizational support. They no longer want computing performed for them, rather they want to be educated, trained, and on occasion helped to solve particularly difficult problems.

The new freedom does not come without a price. End users buying inexpensive PC-based systems and "going into the computing business" sometimes create problems (for example, hardware and software incompatibility, control, security, privacy, and data integrity) that can be solved only through organizational policies, policies that prescribe what may and may not be done and the rules that should be followed in "doing one's own thing."

As a result of end-user computing, IS professionals and managers have assumed new roles. Generally, the IS role has changed from provider of goods to provider of goods and services.

The role of information in the organization

Some banks and organizations, such as financial service firms, have long relied heavily on information systems as their core technology. However, many firms still use information systems only to replace operations, such as billing and ordering, previously done manually. These applications were justified by the cost savings from automation—fewer people, fewer file drawers, less space. Even if they did not realize all the expected savings, firms thought they had to use computers in these routine ways to be perceived as "modern."

Computers became important in the sense that organizations depended on them to do day-to-day tasks. If computers failed, just as if electrical power failed, the organization was stressed. In some cases, computer failure led to bankruptcy. However, except in failure mode, computers did not play an important role in business or in the lives of businesspeople.

The same forces that created EUC also led to the new role of information in the organization—a resource that is potentially as useful and as valuable as the financial, human, and physical resources. This change came gradually, over a long time, as knowledge workers came to have increasing importance relative to manual and clerical workers. Knowledge workers are those who have specialized expertise and who apply their expertise to decision making. Their "raw material" is information, and from it they produce choices or more valuable information. For example, financial analysts may obtain data on various companies, evaluate the companies for compatibility with the goals of their own firm, and either recommend that one be purchased or summarize the merits of each.

The combination of knowledge workers and EUC has created exciting new possibilities for the use of information creating organizational impacts hardly dreamed of previously. One of these impacts is the need for fewer levels of management. Many management jobs, indeed whole layers of management, once served primarily as relayers and interpreters of information from the operating level to management. The "restructuring," "downsizing," or "overhead reduction" in companies reflects this fundamental impact of information on organizations.

Knowledge workers also change the way organizations are managed. Knowledge workers are not faceless "factors of production" and cannot be treated as such. They respond little to "carrot and stick" management; they want to work on interesting problems, have potential for learning and growth, and enjoy the quality of their work life. Such people cannot be managed in the same way that most armies were managed. Yet, many of today's management practices come from those very roots and many need to be changed. Drucker tells us that typical American business firms 20 years from now will ". . . resemble organizations that neither the practicing manager nor the management scholar pays much attention to today: the hospital, the university, the symphony orchestra."[3]

These changes make it possible to use information and information technology directly to pursue an organization's basic strategy and objectives. For example, the computer-based reservation systems developed by United Airlines and American Airlines may appear at first glance merely to be services that support their basic business of carrying passengers. However, the way in which these airlines use these systems to achieve competitive goals is new.

First, both airlines strived to place reservation terminals into as many travel agent offices as they could. Their goal was to dominate the market by obtaining the lion's share of the agents' business. To further this goal, they programmed their systems to list their own flights first, because agents are more likely to select flights on the top of the list.

The reservation systems led to market dominance. Other carriers had to pay fees for reservations made for their flights through United's or American's system. When the advantage of first listing was lost due to competitor complaints and government pressure, the two airlines increased the fees that they charged their competitors. Furthermore, both airlines analyzed the reservations information to improve their scheduling, promotion, and pricing. In the case of American, their system has proved to be immensely profitable, providing 32 percent of their net profit in 1988 (while being only 6 percent of total revenues). Clearly, these computer systems have become much more than a back-room service system. They are an integral element of business strategy.

Many firms have, and are developing, such "strategic systems." They believe that these systems will profoundly change the role of information in organizations.

[3]Peter F. Drucker, "The Coming of the New Organization," *Harvard Business Review,* January–February, 1988, p. 45. (See 6.1.)

Systems and organizational integration

Information and information technology are organizational resources that must be managed in an integrated way if they are to perform effectively and efficiently. The era in which the telephone system and the computer were linked only through the telephone on the computer operator's desk is long past. IBM's entry into the telecommunications business and AT&T's into the computer business underscore the need for integration. It is a signal to all organizations to integrate their computer, telecommunications, and office systems. Failure to do so will make organizations relatively inefficient and not able to achieve results.

Organizational designs must be improved to integrate these new systems. This is a new idea. In the not-too-distant past, information systems were designed around the existing organization structure and processes. Today, information systems and organizational design are symbiotic. This is a radically new idea in any practical sense, and its implications are only now beginning to be realized. However, its manifestations have already begun to appear, as witnessed by the emergence of the chief information officer (CIO) function in the corporate hierarchy.

The MoIS Domain

As an area of study and in actual practice, MoIS has a management focus. It is concerned with the problems, issues, and activities associated with managing an organization's IS resources—the technologies, data, applications, and personnel. The primary management responsibility resides with IS, but it is increasingly being shared with line management as IS becomes more important and pervasive throughout organizations. For these and other reasons, a knowledge of MoIS is important to anyone with managerial aspirations.

What needs to be managed in regard to IS? In other words, what is the domain of MoIS? Our response is that there are five major areas:

- Managing the constellation of IS applications

- Managing the IS technology

- Managing IS application development

- Managing the IS function

- Managing IS–organizational relationships

Each area contains several topics, as shown in Figure 1. Most topics are covered in detail by articles in this book. The numbers in Figure 1 reference the articles. Topics without reading references are covered indirectly. For example, no article deals specifically with interorganizational systems, but the articles on the use of information and information technology for competitive advantage use these systems in their examples. Let's now briefly survey the domain.

FIGURE 1 The Domain of MoIS

2. Managing the Constellation of IS Applications

2.1 Decision Support Systems
2.2 Executive Information Systems
2.3 Expert Systems
2.4 Functional Area Systems
2.5 Transaction Processing Systems
2.6 Interorganizational Systems
2.7 International Systems
2.8 Applications of the Future

3. Managing IS Technology

3.1 Assimilating Technology Innovation
3.2 Managing Telecommunications
3.3 Groupware
3.4 Imaging
3.5 Selecting Computer Hardware

4. Managing IS Application Development

4.1 Development Methodologies
4.2 The Software Development Process
4.3 Software Productivity
4.4 Software Development Planning
4.5 System Implementation
4.6 Application Maintenance

5. Managing the IS Function

5.1 Strategic IS Planning
5.2 IS Functional Structure
5.3 Critical Success Factors
5.4 Managing IS Costs
5.5 Managing IS Personnel
5.6 Managing IS for Performance
5.7 Measuring IS Performance

6. Managing the IS-Organizational Relationship

6.1 The Information-Based Organization
6.2 Centralization and Decentralization
6.3 Planning for Competitive Advantage
6.4 Business Process Redesign
6.5 The Future of IS

Managing the constellation of IS applications

We begin with the spectrum of IS applications because it is through applications that IS ultimately creates value for the organization.

Applications can be viewed in several ways. One perspective is to focus on the activities supported. This view includes data processing, recording/tracking, problem solving/decision making, and communicating. Another perspective is to look at the areas inside and outside the organization served by IS applications. This view includes applications in the functional areas of business (for example, marketing, production, and finance) and applications that span company, inter-organizational, and even national boundaries. A third perspective, used here, distinguishes among applications based on their characteristics, who uses the applications, who develops the applications, how the applications are developed, the technology used by the applications, and so on. These distinguishing characteristics have led to the following widely used taxonomy.

- *Transaction processing systems (TPS).* These applications capture, process, and maintain the data associated with the day-to-day operations of the organization.
- *Management information systems (MIS).* These systems provide scheduled and demand reports and allow managers and other organizational personnel to access information contained in corporate data bases.
- *Office systems (OS).* These are a collection of computer and communications-based systems used to enhance the productivity of office workers.
- *Decision support systems (DSS).* These systems provide users easy access to data and models in support of poorly structured decision-making tasks.
- *Executive information systems (EIS).* These systems give top management on-line access to information about the firm's current activities.
- *Expert systems (ES).* These applications contain the decision-making expertise of well-trained and experienced managers and professionals.

These different IS applications and systems can be thought of as comprising a constellation of IS applications.

Managing IS technology

The information systems field is technology-intensive and constantly changing. The IS manager is expected to utilize the technology that is currently available and to keep abreast of what might be available in the future.

There are important and interesting technological developments currently taking place. In the communications area, local area networks (LANs) are tying mainframes, minicomputers, and microcomputers together. Data, voice, and image are being transmitted along the same communications channels. Direct communications links between suppliers and customers are being put into place. In the software area, products are emerging that facilitate group processes, such as idea generation, planning, problem finding, and decision making. This is just part of a larger trend of the increasing availability of end-user-oriented software.

The IS manager is responsible for integrating these new and existing technologies together. Just as an architect develops the plans for buildings based on the user's needs, available materials, and costs, the IS manager designs the computing architecture. In this case, the end product is the configuration of hardware, software, communications, and data.

Technology by itself does not provide organizational benefits. It is how this technology is used that is important, and for it to be used effectively, it must be assimilated. Our understanding of how to assimilate technology has grown over time, and this knowledge is important to IS managers, who are continually introducing new technology into their organizations.

Managing IS application development

Applications and systems do not magically appear in organizations. Rather, they are the end result of development efforts. Until recently, application development was the responsibility of IS professionals. Now end users are taking on more and more of this responsibility.

There are a number of application development approaches in use (for example, systems development life cycle, prototyping, and iterative design). Each has advantages and disadvantages, depending on the nature of the application. There are also advances in computer-assisted software engineering (CASE) tools and fourth-generation languages (4GLs) that are affecting and facilitating application development.

Computer applications "wear out," although not in the physical sense. They may no longer satisfy their intended purposes and consequently must be revised or replaced. In most organizations, 50 to 80 percent of all development work is expended on maintaining existing applications. At some point, applications may become prohibitively expensive to maintain (that is, the unstructured code is too difficult to revise) or to run (that is, long execution times) and will need to be replaced.

Application and system development can be an expensive and time-consuming process. Potential applications need to be evaluated individually and in terms of their contribution to the entire portfolio of applications. There are project management techniques (for example, PERT) that can be used to support the management of application development.

The introduction of a new system involves change. There are many technical considerations involved in the implementation of a system: systems programming, converting files, and testing code with live data. There are also important behavioral considerations: convincing people of the need for change, assuaging fears about the change, and training people to use the system. In many instances, insufficient attention is given to these behavioral aspects of implementing new systems.

Managing the IS function

IS is a "business within a business," and as such it is an organizational entity that must be managed. It includes physical resources, such as computers, disk drives, and communications controllers. Then there are the human resources—operators, systems programmers, systems analysts, and data-base specialists. Data must be managed and systems developed. It is a challenging management task, one that requires technical, business, and managerial skills.

We discussed earlier the importance of developing an IS plan that supports the strategic plan of the organization. From the strategic plan evolves the tactical and operational plans for IS.

It used to be that IS was composed of data entry, operations, and systems development groups. Now new organizational arrangements are necessary to accommodate new areas, such as telecommunications and end-user computing support. How IS is organized affects its ability to provide goods and, especially, services.

Management must ensure that IS operations run smoothly. Many organizations would go "belly up" if IS ceased functioning for more than a few days. System security is a concern. There have been many well-publicized computer-related crimes over the years.

Managing human resources is always challenging, but managing IS personnel has several unique dimensions. IS professionals tend to be young, bright, and well-educated, with high needs for professional growth. Unless these high needs are accommodated, they may take their skills to another organization; and the tight labor market for experienced IS personnel creates high job mobility.

Organizations are putting considerable resources into IS. A logical question to ask is, "What is the return on their investment?" It is difficult to assess the value of IS because many of the returns are not easily quantified. However, the question demands answers if good management practices are to prevail.

Managing IS—organizational relationships

As we have seen, IS is affecting the entire organization and relationships among organizations. It is influencing how a growing number of firms compete in the marketplace. The end-user computing phenomenon is dispersing computing activity throughout the organization. Organizations are changing their structure as a consequence of IS and to take advantage of IS. The chief information officer (CIO) position is emerging as IS is increasingly being recognized as a corporate asset that must be well managed, like the other major functional areas.

One way of looking at the emerging role of IS is by analogy to a highway system. Policy with regard to highways is set by state legislatures and transportation departments. Their decisions are influenced by the users of the highways. In a similar way, information policy is determined or influenced by senior management, IS management, and end users. The system of highways should be a planned architecture; so should the information provided to the organization. This is realized by having a comprehensive constellation of IS applications in place: TPS, MIS, OS, DSS, ES, and EIS. It is necessary to police highways in order to protect drivers from themselves and others. So too must IS have policies and rules that are in the best interests of the organization. And finally, service stations are necessary to support the users of highways. In a similar way, IS must support end users.

Conclusion

This is an exciting time for MoIS because of the many changes that are taking place. Developments such as using information and information technology for competitive advantage, executive information systems, and end-user computing are changing the nature and importance of applications, serving a new group of users, and creating an impact on how and by whom applications are developed. As we have seen, these changes are creating opportunities, pressures, and problems for today's IS managers. A positive way of viewing this is to suggest that IS has new and recognizable ways of adding value to organizations if the opportunities are recognized and fulfilled. Serving these opportunities requires a strong mix of technical, business, and managerial skills. The articles that follow will help you in these areas. They will enhance your understanding of IS technology, especially in regard to what is new and important. You will see how IS affects the functioning and effectiveness of organizations. Finally, you will learn how to manage IS resources better, whether you are an IS manager or a functional area manager.

Questions

1. It is sometimes said that "IS is technology driven." That is to say, what happens in regard to IS is as a consequence of technological advances. Review the top ten key issues facing IS managers and discuss to what extent and how they are driven by technology.

2. One of the major IS developments is the emergence of end-user computing. Is it possible that sometime in the future there will be no centralized IS group because all IS responsibilities are assumed by the functional areas? Discuss.

3. Assume that you are in a functional area such as production or finance. Why is it important for you to be an actively involved partner in MoIS? Give specific examples of why it is important.

4. The acronyms TPS, MIS, OS, DSS, ES and EIS are used on page 14. Despite the fact that it may encourage one to communicate in arcane jargon, it is important to understand these often-used acronyms. Make certain that you know what each means. If you don't, refer back to page 12 where they are discussed.

1.2

A Question of Communication*

A Survey of Information Technology

John Browning

The Ubiquitous Machine

It has been a momentous change. Information technology is no longer a business resource; it is the business environment. Most white-collar workers now have computers on their desks. By 1995, predicts the Institute for the Future, a Californian think-tank, 90% of American white-collar workers will have a screen. In a generation or two electronic mail, electronic databases and, no doubt, one or two computer tricks as yet unimagined, will be as ubiquitous, and as taken for granted, as the telephone, the mailbox and the book today. But getting from here to there promises to be a wild and wonderful ride.

Perhaps the hardest problem posed by information technology is that it is so flexible. Computers can be programmed to do all sorts of things. Already they are adding up payrolls, storing data on crop pests, helping design electronic circuits and advising motor mechanics on how to fix the latest model. As individual computers are increasingly linked together over communications lines, the machines both send messages and act as a sort of collective memory to record and analyse who said what to whom, when. Increasingly, the right question to ask about computers is not "What can the machines do?" but "What do we want them to do?"

*SOURCE: "A Survey of Information Technology" by John Browning, from *The Economist*, June 16, 1990. Copyright © 1990 The Economist Newspaper Group, Inc. Reprinted with permission.

So far, a generation of automation has evolved three broad answers to that question. Each presents its own opportunities and creates its own problems. They are:

- **Productivity.** By replacing people in routine jobs with machines doing the same work, companies can cut their wage bills. Unfortunately, planned-for productivity improvements have a nasty habit of failing to materialise.
- **Competitive advantage.** By building information technology into their products, companies can influence their customers. So American Airlines automated travel agents, and by so doing made it easiest for the agents to buy seats on its flights rather than its competitors'. American Hospital Supply put terminals on the desks of hospital administrators to help them purchase its potions. But companies are quickly learning how to blunt the competitive impact of rivals' information systems—often simply by joining with others in the industry to copy them.
- **Responsiveness.** Information technology enables many companies to deliver a more customised product faster than the old-fashioned way of doing things. McGraw Hill will this autumn offer professors the chance to create textbooks tailor-made to their courses by choosing individual chapters from a database of texts on topics like computer science and accounting. Information technology also enables firms to build up a company-wide encyclopedia of their customers' likes and dislikes. And that raises a vision of a sort of corporate utopia—the "learning organisation", which uses technology ceaselessly to refresh its knowledge of its customers' wants and to devise new ways of satisfying them. But while many have been inspired by this vision, none has yet worked out in detail how such perpetual-learning machines will overcome human inertia, sloth and bureaucracy.

Setting broad goals for the use of information technology has always been easier than reaching them. Part of the problem is that the technology itself keeps moving the goal posts. Some of the biggest recent goal-post movements have been brought about by huge declines in the price of technology.

Never mind how many supersonic Volkswagens could fit on the head of a pin if the price, size and performance of cars had changed as quickly as those of computers. The real consequence of cheaper computing is simply that the machines are no longer so expensive that humans must dance attendance on them. Machines are instead going to work alongside humans—typically in one of three roles. As **assistants,** computers do boring, routine work, like adding numbers, editing documents or preparing dossiers of information from databases. As **advisers,** the machines store and search huge quantities of information to provide facts and advice on everything from maintaining aircraft engines to plant diseases. And as **communicators,** they spread information across companies and countries.

It is as communicators that the effect of computers is likely to be felt most strongly over the next decade. Now that it is economic to put a terminal on every worker's desk, wiring those terminals together creates new communities of knowledge. If they want to, everybody can see everybody else's work as it is done. Though few will carry things to this extreme, easier access to information can have a revolutionary effect on organisations. Mr Paul Strassman, former head of data processing at Xerox and now a business academic, reckons that many organisations spend most of their time and energy on internal communications. Why should they continue to work so hard passing around buckets when they can now all dip straight into the same well?

Take two small examples of the sorts of things which the newly ubiquitous computers can do. A company marketing brand-name consumer goods now uses computers to help local managers react quickly to local market opportunities. If that manager wants to organise, say, a promotion, the computer shows him what inventories are available (from the warehouse computer) and helps him to co-ordinate delivery of product and promotional material (with the shipping computer). A container-shipping company, by contrast, uses its new system to put its salesmen a step ahead of the competition. Before a salesman calls on a prospective client he summons up on his laptop computer a briefing on the client's past shipments. The briefing also provides any news garnered from the grapevine about what discounts or other temptations competitors might be offering the client, plus advice from regional headquarters on how to fight back.

The Carnegie Group, a firm of consultants in Pittsburgh which is involved in state-of-the-art applications of information technology, uses the word "disintermediation" to describe the impact of many of its systems. Instead of Joe asking Sally to ask Fred to get a certain piece of information from George, Joe gets it straight from the computer, where George left it. At some companies cutting Sally and Fred out of the line of command also puts them out of a job. But at most firms something far more interesting and complex is happening.

When the agricultural revolution in the nineteenth century enabled a few men to produce what had previously required a nation, the western world was not converted *en masse* to lives of leisure. Instead it invented disposable income and new "necessities" to buy with it—like factory-made clothes, cars and television. So some information workers who find machines providing the answers will simply find new questions to ask. As one manufacturing executive complains, only half-jokingly: "We've automated our payroll clerks out of a job four times already—and now they are 'compensation consultants' earning 50% more than we paid them as clerks."

One of the side effects of installing information technology is that it gives information workers an unprecedented view of how their organisation works—and thus suggests new ways of working within it. As Miss Shoshana Zuboff of the Harvard Business School pointed out in her book, "In the Age of the Smart Machine", mechanisation makes it harder for employees to understand their work. Instead of a roomful of people, the industrial revolution put workers alongside machines with levers that clunked up and down. They could not ask the machines questions or look inside—and even if they could work out what the machine was doing there was little they could do to change it. Information technology, Miss Zuboff argues, has the opposite effect. Once a person gets over the initial shock of things happening intangibly behind the screen, it is easy to deduce the logic of a computerised process, and to use the technology as a window on the organisation as a whole.

One British insurance giant had this lesson brought home to it in an unexpected way. It installed a computer system to speed the processing of claims. Unfortunately, the system came to a near halt, deluged by a flood of claims. The problem, it turned out, was that clerks had quickly discovered that the system had rules built into it to weed out dubious claims—so asking it to decide on a dubious claim was much easier than asking a supervisor or fumbling through obscure rulebooks. This extra volume flooded the system. A relatively easy technical fix unclogged the computer. But managerial conundrums remain: if the computer can administer rules for checking claims, part of the existing staff is doing useless work. But which part—those writing the rulebook or those using it? And how should their jobs be reorganised?

Such surprises can give managers an unprecedented opportunity to create a new breed of "self-aware" corporations in which all work together to assess weaknesses and to create and teach the new skills needed to overcome them. They also wreak havoc with the best-laid plans of managers installing information technology. But from the confusion springs a wealth of opportunities.

Often the key to success is to sit back and ask the simplest of questions. "What would make our customers happiest?" "What would make our employees happiest?" Too few organisations do this. Instead they typically reason something like: "Computers are good; computers typically do such and such; therefore we will be better if we use computers to do such and such"—which is a recipe for expensive disaster. The encouraging realisation for many of those independent-minded enough to ask simple questions is that information technology can make many of their wishes come true. The snag, however, is that all involved must first agree on what they want, and how they are willing to change in order to get it. That is the challenge of the information revolution. To see how companies are coping, read on.

Now for Something Completely Different

Productivity, competitive advantage and responsiveness—all three visions of automation have created both successes and failures. But they are increasingly united by a common theme. To reap the benefits of new technology, companies must create new organisations, doing new things in new ways. That means questioning the day-to-day traditions of centuries of business.

Mr Michael Treacy, an information-technology consultant, tells an instructive tale about Ford's efforts to reduce the number of paper-shufflers. What seemed at first to be a mundane efficiency campaign became a challenge to Ford's long-established ways of doing business. Ford employed about 500 people to order components, receive the parts and pay suppliers. Mazda, a Japanese car-maker with which Ford has formed an alliance cemented by a 25% shareholding, did the same job with less than 100. An elaborate automated system cut Ford's order-shufflers only to about 400. So Ford's folk took a harder look at Mazda. Mazda, Ford discovered, had fewer computers than Ford. Its secret was that it did not wait for invoices from its suppliers. When goods arrive at the loading dock, a warehouseman waves a bar-code reader over each box. That single action enters the parts into inventory, updates production schedules (if necessary) and sends electronic payment to the supplier.

This seemed a bit like magic to some of Ford's managers. They had viewed invoices as a capitalist essential, like double-entry book-keeping. Once shown the trick, the possibilities for boosting efficiency by eliminating the complications of matching parts and invoices seem obvious. But tapping these efficiencies requires changes in the way people work: close relations with suppliers, a warehouse that can talk directly to the finance department and workers who adapt happily to new ways of doing things. Ford is working on all those, and it hopes within a few years to institute payment on receipt worldwide.

Creating such change is hard; creating it with information technology is harder still. Though computers have become catalysts of change for western companies, it is not a role to which they are completely suited. Information technology is expensive and complicated. It introduces new ways of getting things wrong. British banks, for example, first organised their automated systems by account number because that is how transactions are recorded. Now, however, they want to reorganise their systems to work by customer name to provide more sophisticated services and marketing. One bank, which prefers to remain nameless, calculates that reorganising all of its systems will require about five years and cost nearly £1 billion ($1.7 billion).

More daunting than the technical obstacles to successful automation, however, are the organisational ones. Information technology throws a searchlight on the most uncomfortable question any organisation can ask itself: what should be each worker's responsibilities? Worse, each successful application of the technology changes the answer.

Mr N. Venkatraman, who studied the impact of information technology on business as part of the "Management in the 1990s" project for the Sloan School of Management at the Massachusetts Institute of Technology, reckons that there are five stages to the exploitation of information technology. Each creates different opportunities.

- **Automating existing jobs.** Jobs within a company are automated, typically to boost productivity—eg, by installing a computerised accounting system. Little changes but the number of people and the capital costs of doing business.
- **Electronic infrastructure.** Islands of functional automation are linked together. Nothing has to change in order to create ways of sharing information between all of a firm's computers. But without change there is usually little economic incentive to overcome the inevitable technical incompatibilities and to battles over who does what. That incentive typically comes bundled up in one of three other sorts of change:
- **Business-process redesign.** Just as Ford found it could do away with invoices, computers enable things to be done in new and more efficient ways.
- **Business-network redesign.** Creating links with suppliers and customers not only creates new opportunities for changing business processes, it also changes the balance of competition.

- ◆ **Business-scope redesign.** As part of the process of self-improvement, information technology enables some companies to move into new businesses. Merrill Lynch's cash-management account, for example, put the firm into competition with banks by each day sweeping the cash balances of brokerage accounts into interest-bearing securities.

Each step changes jobs. Putting a design engineer on to a computer-aided design system (CAD) changes the way he works. His work changes again when that CAD system is linked to manufacturing. And yet again when the newly integrated computer system is linked with similar systems at its suppliers. Part of the change is personal. The engineer may miss the feel of drafting paper, or rejoice at an end to ink smudges. But many of the most confusing changes concern the engineer's relationships with his fellow workers—both inside his company and out.

As Mr Richard Walton of the Harvard Business School notes in a shrewd book, "Up and Running", the same basic technology can promote either centralisation or the opposite, decentralisation. Automating a process captures a pool of information—such as a record of sales or a history of inventory levels. Viewed from the top of the organisation, this information gives bosses an unprecedented ability to look over the shoulders of their subordinates, and to centralise decision-making. But giving the same information, packaged slightly differently, to front-line workers can act just as powerfully for decentralisation by giving them a bird's-eye view of their work previously available only to their superiors.

Fitting the style of automation to a particular company and task is one of the hardest challenges facing today's managers. For some companies the basic choice is straightforward, though challenges remain in the implementation. Fast-food restaurants—who employ inexperienced, uneducated workers to do routine jobs—have long traditions of centralised control. At McDonald's just about everything an employee does, from how he greets a customer to the order in which he puts the food into the bag, is laid down by company policy. Automated systems simply reinforce that central control. Investment banks, on the other hand, employ educated, responsible adults (well, mostly) and thus require a decentralising approach to automation.

Most companies fall somewhere in between. They often end up using automation to centralise control over some parts of an employee's job and decentralising others. Though often neither decided nor presented as such, each new computer system is in effect a statement of priorities. In apportioning work between man and machine, a company tells its workers which skills it values in its people. Identifying those core skills is hard. It is also sometimes painful for employees who suddenly discover that they are not loved for the reasons they thought they were. But setting priorities is only half the challenge of successful automation. Companies must also learn to build computer systems that can enable workers to do their redesigned jobs more comfortably.

Both challenges are hard. Take the example of Mrs Fields Cookies, which in 1989 sold $130m-worth of chocolate-chip cookies from shops around the world.

Mrs Debbi Fields, who founded the first cookie store in 1978, oversees the over 400 stores now in her empire from Park City, a ski resort in Utah, together with her husband, Mr Randy Fields. Over the past few years they have installed an elaborate automated system to manage the stores. The idea is that the system should take over many of the administrative, number- and policy-geared tasks, leaving store managers free to concentrate on people-oriented jobs like selling and creating a pleasant environment in the store. So the system monitors hourly sales and plans hourly production. It handles accounting and stocks, and it administers personnel tests for hiring. Through voice mail and electronic mail, store managers are also encouraged to talk direct to Mrs Fields and she to them.

Whether this system is controlling or enabling depends on each store manager's personality. Those that had enjoyed the administrative part of their work presumably felt crushed; those who preferred the people side, liberated. But even for those in tune with the basic thrust of the system, questions remain over whether or not the detailed division of labour between man and machine is viable. Is the presence of the system's supervising eye reassuring or intrusive? How about all those little messages from Mrs Fields? Can store managers really create the "right" environment with the system's strong, centralised influence on hiring? The jury is still out. Mrs Fields Cookies has not made much money recently, and a recent reorganisation, in which Mr and Mrs Fields stepped back from day-to-day operations, adds to the uncertainties.

In meeting the challenges of automation, each company must rely on three sets of skills: engineering the technology (getting the machines to work), managing the technology (getting machines to work with people) and managing the organisation (getting our people and machines to work more efficiently than their people and machines). Twenty years ago just getting computers to work was a challenge, and companies rightly stressed engineering over management. But the priorities are shifting. Look at each skill in turn.

Help Wanted

A sign said to hang in IBM's Tokyo office sums up the capabilities of computer technology. It reads:

    IBM: FAST, ACCURATE, STUPID
    MAN: SLOW, SLOVENLY, SMART

One of the most common mistakes about computers is the impression that a machine which can calculate pi to several thousand decimal points in the twinkling of an eye must somehow be cleverer than the average toaster. And the most common manifestations of that false impression are attempts to put computers in charge of people. Changes in technology and economics now allow men to put computers in their place.

Around 1970, when a computer cost several times the combined annual salaries of a typical accounting department in a medium-sized company, there was little choice but to organise work to make the most of this expensive asset. Now that similar computing power can be purchased for less than a clerk's holiday pay, there is no excuse for doing so. Computers make bad taskmasters, and researchers are creating technologies which enable them to be better assistants. That means building systems which are both flexible and easy to understand.

The history of attempts to automate computer programming shows the challenges and progress. In the late 1960s researchers were confident that computers could quickly be taught to program themselves, given a broad description of the task to be accomplished. (This was also the age of the "General Problem Solver," an artificial-intelligence program which hoped to solve any and all problems that could be posed in logical form.) By the early 1970s researchers had discovered their error. Many problems could not comfortably be stated logically. Programs which, like the General Problem Solver, tried to search methodically through all possible solutions to logical problems often required a few millennia of computing to find answers.

Some boffins decided that the way ahead lay in building assistants rather than gurus. Two young researchers at the Massachusetts Institute of Technology, Mr Charles Rich and Mr Richard Waters, decided to build such an assistant for computer programmers. Called the "Programmer's Apprentice," it would help programmers rather than replace them. Like an efficient secretary, the machine would suggest ways of coping with familiar problems, point out inconsistencies in the work and generally try to make itself useful. This new role, however, required a different approach to design. To work with people, the computer's ability to explain what it was doing became as important as its ability to do the job.

Messrs Rich and Waters have not always found it easy to give their creation the ability to explain itself. Two ideas have helped. One is that the system should be organised around a collection of "clichés." The phrase "quicksort" describes commonly-used procedures to programmers in much the same way that "sauté" works as a shorthand for chefs. Because it is part of the human programmer's vocabulary, a phrase should also be part of his mechanical assistant's. As well as sharing the human's language, it should also be able to share his thought processes. That means that it should at least be able to explain its workings in the sort of "if . . . then" rules that humans understand—even if its actual workings are more arcane.

Several developments make it easier for such ideas to be adopted in a variety of systems. One is simply that there are a lot more clichés around than there used to be. With each year that goes by, more technical problems in computing get solutions that an expert can refer to in shorthand, and take largely for granted. Many are also understood by the nontechnical. While X.400, the worldwide electronic-mail standard, might not be a phrase on everyone's lips, most people now understand what is meant by "word-processor," "spreadsheet" and "database." And they can use those tools as an *entrée* into more complicated systems.

Meanwhile, some of the more complicated systems are coming to meet humans halfway. Cheaper computers mean that more processing power can be devoted to making the machines easy to use. Increasingly, companies are organising their machines to do just that. Huge databases are stored on mainframes. Smaller databases reside on minicomputers, which also provide serious computing muscle for heavy jobs like running computer models of bridges or markets. But people gain access to such big machines through desktop personal computers which, helped by easy-to-use graphical interfaces, can hide the complication of composing a query for a database or of analysing the results of a computer simulation.

Better still, computer technology itself has become more predictable. Relational databases, commercialised in the 1980s, are much less fussy about how their data are organised. Such capabilities, had they been available when banks first automated in the 1960s, could have saved many pin-striped folk the pain of discovering that questions concerning individual customers could be excruciatingly hard to answer on databases organised by account number. But databases are not the only area where progress is being made. Experience with communications standards steadily make it easier to link computers across both local-area networks and telephone lines.

And new technologies are making computers both more capable and easier to understand. So-called expert systems can seem very familiar to humans. Their programs come in the form of "if then" rules: "If the engine won't start, then check the battery." Programs called "expert system shells"—like Inference's Corporation's ART and Teknowledge's KEE—then combine rules and data to deduce what can be learnt from the data.

Expert systems let computers do new jobs. The Carnegie Group, a firm of consultants in Pittsburgh which is expert in the real-world applications of artificial intelligence, has built a system for Reuters which automatically classifies news stories coming over the news wire—and so decides which stories should be sent over which specialised news services. Another expert system built by Carnegie Group for Emerson Motor, a builder of electric motors, translates into manufacturable plans and diagrams orders saying simply "just like the last one except we want it to work at 220 volts."

Nearly all of those now working with expert systems have also learnt a new way of working with the machines. No expert system is right all of the time. Most can handle only two-thirds of the work they encounter. That is useful. By taking over the routine bulk of people's work, they can free up humans for the really tricky questions. But this means that humans and machines must work side-by-side—each handing over to the other the parts of the job he or it can do best. That takes some getting used to. It also places a premium on the skills needed to build both reliable, flexible systems and comprehensible, flexible organisations.

Tools for the Trades

Systems development—particularly if it involves writing software—provides some of modern business's most lurid horror stories. Tales of projects only one-third finished but already costing double or triple their budgets are common. So are tales of systems which never work. Building systems is hard work, and sometimes things just go wrong. But companies often make things harder for themselves by throwing common sense out the window.

Take the following history, from a company which, for obvious reasons, wishes to remain nameless. It had planned to buy software off the shelf for $2m. Because the off-the-shelf product did not work exactly the same way the company did, it then planned to spend another $2m and two years adapting its business practices to the software. It bought the software for $2m. Then some bright spark convinced the company that it would be better if they converted the software to run on the same "operating system" as its existing software. That cost $8m. So long as it was adapting the software to a new operating system, the company decided to adapt the software to its business practices, too. That cost $10m. Eight years later, when the project was finished—five times over budget and four times over schedule—it had become irrelevant.

There are ways of doing better. One is to buy packaged software and use it as it was meant to be used. After all, companies do not feel compelled to rebuild their photocopiers or their computers; why should they feel the compulsion to do so with their software? With the rise of "open systems" based on the Unix operating system, it is becoming increasingly easy to buy a collection of software tools which can be linked together to do even the biggest jobs. Each tool does only a step of the job, and passes the result on to the next. So, by mixing and matching tools, a user can create exactly the system he wants. Microsoft's OS/2 operating system is developing similar capabilities. Mr Roger Pavitt, head of Price Waterhouse's British information-technology practice, says that his clients are becoming increasingly interested in open systems. Though neither Unix nor OS/2 applications can yet do everything that packages built for big mainframes can, such disadvantages can be outweighed by the ease with which changes can be made in systems built of a collection of small, interconnected pieces.

But taking advantage of open systems usually requires changes in the way information technology is managed. Having in the 1980s decentralised decisions about computers to take advantage of the opportunities created by personal computers, many companies are now re-centralising part of the job. The idea is that a small, central information-services group should lay down a corporate "architecture" to ensure that everybody's new automation project will work with everybody else's. But the work of systems design and implementation typically remains decentralised, to tap the enthusiasm and expertise of those doing the jobs with which the system is meant to help.

Creating flexibility also requires changes in the way individual systems are designed and built. The traditional way of looking at systems design, called the "waterfall model," held that, like a tangible machine, software evolved through several stages of design and implementation until, one day, it was "finished" (see Figure 1). Work done after that to fix, update, or improve the system was called "maintenance." Companies discovered that their information services were spending up to 80% of their time on maintenance, while the backlog for even the simplest new systems stretched out for years.

Part of the solution to this problem lies in admitting that systems evolve—and that software maintenance is not really, as the name implies, as simple as keeping your car running. Instead of the "waterfall model" of development, some are adopting the "spiral model" (see Figure 2). Implicit in this model is

▮FIGURE 1▮ Conventional Waterfall

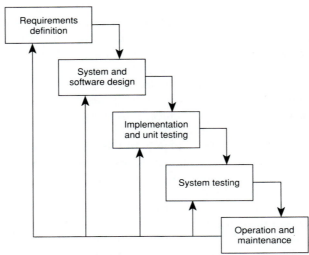

Source: Ian Sommerville "Software Engineering"

▮FIGURE 2▮ Virtuous Spiral

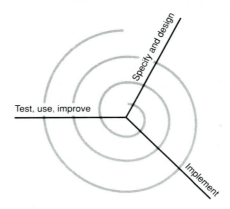

the idea that a system is never really finished; it merely passes though successive cycles of design, implementation, testing and improvement.

Experience has evolved several techniques to help make systems evolution more efficient. So-called "computer-aided software engineering" (CASE) tools automate part of the process of programming, and so speed changes. "Structured" and "object-oriented" design methods help designers to get a grip on the complexity of systems, and so make change more manageable. Together with "layered architectures," such design methodologies can, cleverly used, enable systems to be built in modules so that some functions can be ripped out and rewritten without changing anything else. But even the best design methods and technical expertise can help only with the question of how to change, not decide what changes to make.

One obvious idea here is to involve the users of the system in design, implementation and improvement. If anyone knows how to make a system better, it must be those that use it. Though this admonition appears constantly in textbooks and lectures, a recent study by the Kobler Unit at London's Imperial College found that only about half of the (British) firms in its sample actually did so. And many of those that do not are still surprised—and blame the computer—when users do not work well with new systems.

Electronic suggestion boxes would be a huge step forward for many firms. But some companies have already gone far beyond this. They are trying to use information technology to create new forms of organisation in which learning is part of the daily round of going about one's business.

A Curriculum for Change

Anyone who tells you that it is easy to change the way groups of people do things is either a liar, a management consultant or both. Change is hard for individuals; for groups it is next to impossible. That said, information technology is going to force most organisations to change over the next few years. Those who have some control over the process will find it less painful.

Mr Patrick Jeffries of McKinsey, a management consultancy which admits that change can be difficult even if you can afford its fees, argues that two simple questions should be the starting point for thinking about change. The first concerns commitment: why should the change be made? The second concerns skills: what is it that must be done to meet the new goals? Neither question is ever as simple as it sounds.

For change created by information technology, the question "why change" should first be answered by explaining how the new computer system supports a company's overall strategy. The sad truth is that many managers are not terribly clear on this point. There is often an unbridgable gap between general managers and their colleagues in information services. One group lives in a world of return on equity, JIT, TQC and LIBOR; the other talks of bits, bytes, CASE and COBOL. Worse, companies give them no incentive to work together to thrash out a common language. The two groups often have different performance standards and career paths.

Some companies, however, are striving at least to bridge the gap—if not close it completely. Safeway has given its information-services employees the same two goals as the rest of the business: improve margins and increase market share. Their projects and performances are judged on these, just like the marketing department. IBM, like many Japanese companies, rotates general managers through information-services assignments. The present head of information services, Mr Larry Ford, had marketing and general-management experience with IBM before he took over IBM's internal automators.

For its big information-technology projects, Ford Motor Company has devised a three-tier system of management which forces information services and general managers to work side-by-side on committees at several levels. At the top, divisional vice-presidents set broad goals: the system's strategic purpose and its links to overall, corporate information systems. One level down, middle managers thrash out more detailed plans covering the sorts of information that will go into the system, how it will change responsibilities between departments and so on. Finally, the users-to-be of the system sit down with systems analysts to sort out what they would like to see on the screen and other exact details of how the system will work.

Unfortunately, the "what change" questions raised by automation can often make the "whys" seem easy. The problem is that automation changes many things at once. Even with the best motivation, learning how to do your old job in a new way, with a machine, is hard enough. Learning how to do a new job with new technology is even harder. Yet that is exactly what automation often forces people to do.

Morgan Stanley, for example, experimented with centralising responsibilities when it set up a state-of-the-art trading-room to try to find new opportunities in computerised stock arbitrage. Though on-the-spot decision-making is required in much share-trading, experienced equity traders lacked discipline in executing arbitrage opportunities identified by the computer. They could not resist second-guessing the machines. Though the machines were indeed often wrong, the lack of consistency made it impossible to carry out computer-guided arbitrage, or even to judge new arbitrage ideas. So the firm hired book-keepers to execute trades—and set experienced share traders and theoreticians the task of serving them, particularly by trying to make sure that the recommendations which came up on their screens would be profitable.

Frito-Lay, an American snack-food producer, moved decisions in the opposite direction. It had traditionally run a centralised system of sales and distribution, but wanted to decentralise to enable local promotions, and to allow local distributors greater flexibility in dealing with customers ranging from mom-and-pop stores to giant supermarket chains. Attempts to do this without computers flopped. The key to success, points out Miss Lynda Applegate of the Harvard Business School, turned out to be a little handheld computer terminals on which each delivery and sale could be logged. Not only did this free up distributors' time and improve efficiency, it also created a pool of timely sales information that could be doled out as and where it could be used most effectively.

The simple lesson, well drawn by Mr Paul Strassman in his book "The Information Payoff," is that training costs—both to learn the new technology and the new ways of doing things—are likely to be the most expensive and time-consuming parts of automation. But training is only part of the answer. Harvard's Miss Applegate reckons that many companies have muffed the opportunities offered by information technology to change the ways in which they make decisions. Instead of simply automating the status quo, companies today have a unique opportunity to re-assess where and how decisions should be taken. Only a few have even begun to grasp it.

So far, even those furthest advanced in this endeavour are still struggling with parts of the puzzle—nobody has yet worked out the big picture. But interesting experiments include:

- **Knowledge management.** Companies are building up curricula of the skills and knowledge which their employees need, and are devising ways, both formal and informal, of teaching them. Management consultants at Arthur Andersen are, as part of their normal career progression, expected to spend some time teaching their peers. Computer programmers at Microsoft are building a vast database of software know-how. Its software-developing customers can electronically query the database, and the answers to their questions add to the overall body of knowledge. Similarly management consultants at McKinsey are building a database which will help consultants with a problem get in touch with a colleague whose specialised knowledge might help solve it.
- **Planning.** Xerox uses computers to help executives co-operate in planning the future. The machine combines individual forecasts and budgets so that each individual can see how his plans affect the group and vice versa. Royal Dutch/Shell is experimenting with a yet more ambitious technique. It is involving executives in planning as a sort of do-it-yourself computer game. Instead of "scenarios"—thick books which detail what might happen to Shell if oil prices do this and interest rates do that—Shell is trying to bring scenarios to life inside the computer. Ideally, however, it would like executives to create their own models of how Shell might react to various events, and play them out on the computer to test and improve their ideas.
- **Groupware.** Lotus Development, a company famous for the 1-2-3 spreadsheet, has developed a product to help people work together in groups. It monitors electronic mail and work in progress, handles ad-hoc correspondence and maintains informal databases. If a client calls a salesman working with Lotus's "Notes," he can immediately call up all his colleagues' contacts with the client, check the status of his order on the manufacturing computer and leave a note recording his conversation with the client for whoever contacts him next. Other firms have worked out other forms of computerised social lubricants. One common trick is to use computers to keep track of the various versions of a plan or drawing as engineers modify it.
- **Responding to customers.** Computers allow tailor-made products where previously only off-the-shelf had been economic. Rocky Mountain Log Homes, a builder of pre-fabricated housing, now lets its customers play architect on-screen. Previously customers had had to content themselves with one of a few pre-designed homes. Now the computer can feed the customer's own design straight to the factory. British Telecom, among others, is building systems to improve the handling of customers' queries. By bringing all relevant information to screen while the customer is on the telephone, it hopes to resolve queries with less cost and frustration.

But huge challenges face those who would use information technology to improve their ability to learn. One problem that crops up time and again in western companies' experiences with computers is the failure to communicate. Learning, as any teacher will tell you, is a moving target. Curricula have to be revised continually to reflect advances in knowledge or changes in students' abilities. That requires several sorts of dialogue. Companies are often fairly good at measuring employees' performance against a fixed standard. Sometimes they can help teach workers the skills they need to do better. And some firms can use feedback from workers to modify what the standard or performance can be. But only a handful can put all these skills together to create the sort of dialogue that keeps a good university faculty evolving in step with its discipline.

On the contrary, an anecdote from General Motors exemplifies the current state of affairs. In GM's Hamtramck Cadillac factory, all the welding robots are linked to a computer which prints out their performance daily for maintenance engineers. Unfortunately, maintenance engineers could not understand the stream of numbers which emerged from the machines. Their work suffered while they had to wade through reams of print-outs to try to decipher which machines needed to be tuned. Eventually, some bright spark noticed that charting the data made it possible to tell at a glance which machines were in trouble. But the problem should never have arisen in the first place. As the western world's experience with computers has shown, however, it is depressingly common. Look at progress towards the three goals of automation: productivity, competitive advantage and responsiveness.

Working Harder, Doing Less

Productivity is the *raison d'être* of automation. Even those companies who admit to other uses for information technology often justify their investments by productivity-generated savings. Some companies can boast. IBM (which has no excuse for not making a success of automation) reckons that it averages a $4 return on each $1 invested in information technology. But plenty of IBM's customers must be very disappointed. Using statistics from America's Commerce Department, Mr Stephen Roach, an economist at Morgan Stanley, calculates that the average output of an American information worker has not budged since the early 1960s—despite huge growth in both the number of information workers and the average technology investment sitting on each one's desk.

Mr Roach's studies make sobering reading. They indicate that computers have so far failed to boost productivity even on the most generous measure, output per worker. Including capital costs, as any truly accurate measure should, would make the picture look even worse.

Part of the problem is simply that so many Americans joined the managerial ranks in the 1980s. Between 1978 and 1986 annual growth in white-collar employment was almost five times that of production workers. In manufacturing, employment of production workers declined while that of white-collar workers grew unabated. Much was invested in these decision-makers. Analysts at DRI, a firm of economic forecasters, estimate that the share of office equipment in American's stocks of fixed capital (excluding property) has climbed from 3% in 1980 to 18% in 1990. All to no avail.

Though separating the contributions of white-collar and blue-collar workers is not easy, Mr Roach calculates that by 1986 the average white-collar worker's output had declined to nearly 7% below his average level in the 1970s (back to the average of the early 1960s, before the high-tech investment boom began). Financiers performed particularly badly, with a 10% drop in average output. Production workers, by contrast, boosted output by nearly 17% from the 1970s to 1986.

There are three sorts of reaction to this depressing picture. One far too common group holds that the answer to white-collar productivity problems lies in "an action committee to re-prioritise the managerial matrix and its links to corporate culture" (or some similar nonsense) . . . in other words, that the cure for too many unproductive managers is more managers. Leaving aside these members of the cult of management—who seem more part of the problem than its solution—the world divides into optimists, who believe that information-technology investments have already planted the seeds for future productivity growth, and pessimists, who reckon that a cure requires full-scale managerial revolution.

One point for the optimists is that Mr Roach's national averages hide some smaller successes. Studies of the effects of information technology on individual bits of the economy paint a rosier picture of productivity. Mr Paul Osterman, of MIT, analysed forty American industries, mostly in manufacturing. He found that from 1972 to 1978, on average, each 10% growth in computer-processing

FIGURE 3   A Very Comfortable Pace: U.S. Productivity

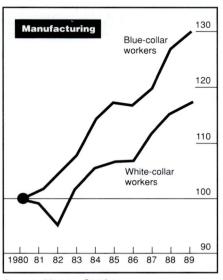

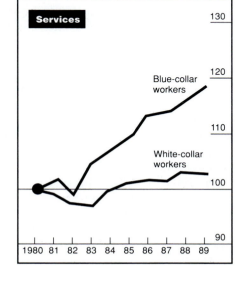

Source: Morgan Stanley

power translated into a 1% reduction in the number of managers employed and a 2% reduction in clerks.

Mr Thomas Steiner, a consultant who studies banking for McKinsey, reckons that productivity-boosting forces are now making themselves felt in banking. In his book, "Technology in Banking"—which is one of the best studies of the effects of information technology yet written—Mr Steiner argues that employment in American banking peaked in 1986, and will decline steadily in the 1990s.

Though bank spending on information technology has been climbing steadily since the 1960s, two factors delayed its effect on productivity. One was that banks have for many years run paper systems alongside automated ones, lest a computer glitch wipe out the business. As experience with computers and computer security grows, those paper systems are being dismantled. More fundamentally, however, it also took time for the banks to discover how information technology—and, in many countries, deregulation—would change their ability to add value and profit to their activities.

Take funds transfer, the movement of large sums of money from one bank to another. At the beginning of the 1980s, New York's eight biggest banks made about $1 billion a year from funds transfer, a third of their total profits. Internally, funds transfer was pretty well automated. So efficiency was high. But inertia and ignorance meant that the banks could still charge many customers pre-automation prices for pre-automation service. No longer. Customers now know that transfers will reliably go through in a day—so they will no longer allow the banks to rack up four or five days' worth of interest on their money. Similarly, many customers now initiate transfers from terminals in their own offices. So they will not pay the banks a fee for doing that. This year, New York's eight biggest banks will make less than $100m on funds transfer, and the pressure on back-office employment is increasing.

This is only the beginning of change for the banks. The real efficiency-boosting potential, as Mr Steiner points out, lies in eliminating more of the 50 billion cheques which American homes and businesses write each year. Banks have a strong incentive to do this. Each cheque costs nearly $1 to process. They have made a start with automated cash dispensers, and they hope to go further by installing the machinery for direct-debit cards at supermarkets, petrol stations and convenience stores (which between them account for about two-thirds of America's 60 billion retail transactions a year).

Unfortunately for the banks, progress with direct-debit cards, automated cash dispensers and other innovations like home-banking has been consistently slower than they had hoped. People simply do not like to change. Nor do they have much incentive to do so. Price, the traditional capitalist incentive, is only slowly being brought to bear because the banks know that it would be competitive suicide to try to pass on to the customer the full cost of cheque-handling. In many other industries, there is even less hope of achieving efficiency-boosting changes because companies do not know how much their products and services really cost to provide—let alone how they should price them.

Herein lies the nub of the pessimists' argument that a managerial revolution will be needed to tap the productivity gains offered by information technology.

Many of the productivity gains of the early twentieth century, they note, were achieved with the help of new ways of defining and costing work, notably Frederick Jackson Taylor's "time and motion" studies. Taylorism is viewed with some horror by most modern managers—who quite rightly point out that choreographing a worker's movements, limb-by-limb, minute-by-minute is oppressive, alienating and usually counterproductive. But without some renewed job discipline, some of today's "enlightened" management structures are in danger of collapsing under their own weight.

One part of this task is simply getting a handle on costs in increasingly capital-intensive industries. As Mr Thomas Johnson of Pacific Lutheran University and Mr Robert Kaplan of the Harvard Business School point out in their damning analysis of management accounting, "Relevance Lost", many, if not most, companies get misleading information from their cost accountants. The problem is "overheads," general costs incurred by the business as a whole rather than by any specific product—like many information systems and almost all general management.

As businesses become more service-minded and more capital-intensive, overheads' share of total costs increases. In banks Mr Steiner reckons the fixed cost of computers is now 50–60% of the cost of providing some products. Messrs Johnson and Kaplan cite a "typical" cost-breakdown for a manufactured product in which overheads are 60% of total cost, materials 29% and direct labour 11%. Apportioning overheads thus becomes crucial to product costing. Unfortunately many companies, following the prevailing wisdom of accounting textbooks, apportion overheads according to direct labour costs. This vastly exaggerates the benefits to managers of further reducing what is already the smallest component of their costs, direct labour. In some cases it can even make cost increases look like reductions. "Outsourcing" of components, for example, raises the overhead cost of administering contracts and quality while it reduces direct labour. But because the overheads are shared across a range of products, it is difficult to compare costs and benefits—nor do individual product managers have any incentive to do so.

Messrs Johnson and Kaplan offer no easy solution to this problem. They simply urge each company to try to work out for itself what drives the cost of its products, and how to measure and control them. Some progress is being made. Information technology, which conquers the complexity of building customised measurement and control systems, helps greatly. But many managers, particularly in service industries, face an even more basic problem than working out the costs of their products: they have to work out exactly what their products are in the first place.

Information technology changes the things which banks and other service industries sell as well as the cost of creating them. A favourite example of business-school textbooks is Merrill Lynch's cash-management account, which, by each day sweeping the cash balances of its brokerage accounts into interest-bearing securities, brought brokerages into competition with banks—and helped to set in train forces which forced banks, in turn, to offer interest on chequeing accounts. It is only human, after all. Rather like the executive who wanders down the corridor to poke into other people's business while his personal computer cranks out his latest sales report, some companies have taken advantage of the resources freed—and new capabilities created—by information technology to poke into other companies' businesses. From their innovations have come some of the most startling success stories of the past 20 years.

Magic Circles

What Mr Marshall McLuhan called "the global village" modern businessmen may prefer to see as "the global office suite." Information technology's ability to overcome distance enables companies to work more closely together in a variety of ways. One of the neatest tricks is for a company to put its computer system on a customer's desk—so that the first name he sees when it is time to make a purchase is . . . you guessed it.

American business-school professors call this sort of thing "using information technology to gain competitive advantage." Strictly, that seems a misnomer—every use of information technology should be aimed at gaining competitive advantage. But the phrase often proves a useful shorthand for describing the ways in which a company can use its information-technology capabilities to alter the behaviour of those around it. Some influence customers by building information technology into new products, like banks' cash dispensers or Merrill Lynch's cash-management account. Others are building electronic links to suppliers to create relationships which are at once more flexible, more efficient and more exclusive.

It is an ironic testimony to the power of corporate inertia that, in using information technology, companies have often had better initial results from trying to change the behaviour of others than from improving themselves. Airlines, banks, air conditioners, drugs, linen and a host of other industries provide examples of products that have succeeded in large part because the vendors' information technology has made their wares the most productive for customers to buy. These systems provide the initials which dot textbooks on information technology. The question, however, is how many companies today can duplicate successes like:

- ◆ SABRE. American Airlines' seat-reservation system helped revolutionise the airline business. By making it easiest for travel agents to buy seats on American, it boosted the airline's market share. It provided the information on customers needed to create innovative and complex fare structures aimed at filling every seat. In 1984 11 rival airlines paid American the compliment of bringing an antitrust suit against it on the grounds that SABRE had become an "essential facility" to which they were unfairly denied equal access. More recently American has been trying to run SABRE as a general travel-reservations service—with equal access for all willing to pay its fees. As such, SABRE has in some years made more money than the airline which spawned it.

- OTISLINE. Otis Elevators decided in the early 1980s that one of the things that would give its customers most satisfaction is the prompt service of ailing lifts. So it built an automated system to dispatch repairmen. When something starts going wrong with Otis's newer lifts, they automatically call in their complaints to the computer—without human intervention. Otis's rivals suddenly had to compete on quality of service as well as on the price and quality of lifts themselves.
- Thomson Holidays. Thomson was one of the first firms to let British travel agents reserve package holidays from a computer screen—which was usually much quicker and cheaper than telephoning the tour operator. Thomson still has the easiest-to-use system, offering the broadest range of packages. Travel agents often turn to Thomson first.
- Federal Express. To grow huge in parcel-delivery Federal Express backed up its skills in moving packages about with a computer system that can tell a customer exactly where his shipments are at any given moment. This ability has won new kinds of business. Federal Express now manages much of IBM's spare-parts inventory. Its system also creates a barrier to competition.
- ASAP. American Hospital Supply provided quicker, cheaper delivery of medical odds and ends by encouraging customers to tap their orders directly into its computer system. Market share grew dramatically.

Inspiring as these examples may be to young executives, they are dicey role models. The opportunities for computer-powered success are more limited today. Companies have already built many of the obvious ideas for systems which could change consumer preferences at a stroke—including many which looked like obvious winners but in practice fell flat. One such was the system built by ICI agrichemicals to provide farmers with the latest research on plant diseases while they placed electronic orders for pesticide: farmers, it seems, would rather talk to the neighbours about bugs.

Worse, competitors have learnt to blunt the impact of systems that do provide something the customers want. The trick is simply to copy them. Most effective of all is when companies band together to copy a successful system because each then gets its capabilities for a fraction of the price paid by an innovator. So New York retail banks joined together to build a network of cash dispensers to compete with the lead that Citicorp, New York's biggest retail bank, had gained in the size and convenience of its cash-dispenser network. America's smaller insurance companies have joined together through a trade association to build a network that can eliminate much of the paperwork which independent agents must wade through in filing a policy or a claim. Their collective system counters much of the advantage garnered by the proprietary networks built by industry giants like Aetna.

Some of the most resourceful, and luckiest, innovators may find new ways to make money out of their systems. Baxter Health Care is offering to use the ASAP system built by its American Hospital Supply subsidiary to provide hospitals with a complete supplies-management service. Baxter says that it will order whatever brand of supplies the hospitals want. With its expertise in inventory management and automation, Baxter reckons it can make a big saving for the hospital and still have profit left for itself. Similarly, McKesson, which earned its automating credentials with the "Economost" system to supply drug stores (chemists, in English English), is offering to use the system to provide pharmacists with direct reimbursement for drugs covered by health insurance. The pharmacist can offer his customer the convenience of not having to reclaim drug costs on his own, and the health insurers, McKesson hopes, will welcome a chance to get more direct control of their drug costs.

But some industries do not enjoy even the slimmest of chances of creating instant success with automation. They are simply too complex. No single system could matter that much to a customer. And here the process of change is a painful groping indeed. Look, for example, at motor cars.

A Game Everyone Can Play

Information technology promises to help solve two of the most crucial problems facing western carmakers. One is product-delivery time. Walk into a showroom and order a car that is not already on the lot, and you will probably have to wait six weeks for delivery—yet it takes only about 36 hours to build a car, and no more than a week to deliver it to most places. The second, bigger problem tackled by carmakers' computers is the time it takes to create a new product. Western companies take six or seven years from drawing board to product launch; the Japanese take half that. For both problems, the solution lies in improving the flow of information. Carmakers' efforts to use information technology to make those improvements are transforming their industry.

The interesting part of this process of change is that the carmakers cannot automate just on their own. Ford, for example, buys in from outside suppliers about two-thirds of a car's parts. Those suppliers, too, must be brought into the carmakers' electronic networks. In a generation or so, those networks will be ubiquitous. Using them will confer no more competitive advantage than posting a letter today. But in the transition, suppliers will rise and fall not just on the price and quality of their parts, but also on their ability to deliver them using the new techniques.

At Nissan's British factory in Sunderland, for example, the plant computer each morning calls up the computer of its seat-supplier, Akeda Hoover, to schedule Hoover's daily production. Seats of each colour and style are scheduled so that they can roll straight out of Hoover's door and into a car waiting on Nissan's assembly line. Similarly, Ford reckons that it now does daily production-scheduling with about half of the 1,000 European suppliers with electronic links to it.

As Ford changes the way in which deliveries are scheduled, it also changes the way in which it pays for them. Instead of trading several bits of paper—each of which must be matched with physical parts or payment—the goal is a simple, two-step process which Ford calls "push-button receiving." Ford's computer sends an order to its supplier, and payment is sent electronically as soon as that order appears at the receiving dock.

Achieving this wondrous simplicity requires some complicated changes in the relationship between supplier and customer. At the least, customers must be able to take quality for granted. But a super-efficient link between buyer and seller also highlights the inefficiencies of each. Ford, though efficient by the standards of western carmakers, could not deliver to its own customers as quickly as it is asking its suppliers to do. Some of the problems lie in the size of the necessary information systems. Building a system just to keep track of which parts Ford engineers use around the world—so that the company can begin to rationalise its parts purchasing—took several years and nearly $100m. The finished system handles over 500,000 queries daily from 20,000 users, and tracks over 1m parts.

But the technology is only part of the problem. Part of the delay in delivering a Ford car is caused by the need to draw up and reconcile two production schedules. The marketing department does one production schedule, which concentrates on sharing out best-selling cars in short supply. Then production does a second schedule which concentrates on sharing out production facilities in short supply. Doing one schedule would, Ford admits, be simpler and quicker. Someday, soonish, it will. But building an organisation that knows about both demand and production—and can balance the two—takes time.

Suppliers face similar problems, at all sorts of levels. One problem is simply how much to invest in information technology. At a recent meeting of the Index Interchange—a group of European information-services directors organised by consultants at the Index Group to promote discussion of mutual problems—many said they saw little point in replacing paper with electronic systems to swap data and orders without making other changes. Just going "paperless" does not provide a big enough payoff. Yet many of the changes companies would most like to make require the ability to swap orders and data electronically.

Ford and other big customers have already broken the deadlock for some suppliers. Ford suppliers have been told to adopt its electronic ordering and payment systems. Some suppliers of key parts have been told exactly which computer-aided design system to buy so that Ford engineers can load new designs straight into suppliers' computers (which in turn will automatically instruct the appropriate machine tools). But even those who have decisions made for them must now decide what to do with their own suppliers, and so on.

As they automate, companies must also learn to manage the new trading relationships which information technology creates. Ford, like many others, is dramatically reducing the number of suppliers it deals with. And it measures those it does keep by different criteria. Simple price becomes less important than quality and the ability to evolve new products in harmony with Ford's own evolution. The new emphasis on flexibility and design skills often highlights new weaknesses.

Mr Ramchandran Jaikumar of the Harvard Business School studied American metal-working companies with advanced "flexible manufacturing systems" capable of switching quickly from the production of one type of part to another.

Compared with their Japanese counterparts, the westerners barely used the capability of their technology. The average "flexible" American plant turned out ten parts, with an average production volume of 1,727 of each. The average Japanese plant turned out 93 parts with an average production volume of 258. Worst of all, the Japanese introduced 22 new parts for every one introduced in America.

It is tempting to diagnose such findings as another failure of communication. Having set up automated systems, many in the West then seem to want to forget them, to let them chug away at the same jobs people have always done, rather than discussing with those around them ways in which all might change to take most advantage of the technology. This can make automation downright self-destructive. There are few things more wasteful than the expense and complication of automating business as usual—and few firms more vulnerable than a giant company which has expensively replaced its paper-shufflers with print-out-shufflers.

School, Inc.

No wonder western managers are growing disenchanted with information technology. It promises wonderful things. But when companies work those wonders for their customers, they are quickly copied. Those that innovate up the supply chain typically find that each bottleneck eliminated simply shows up a new blockage elsewhere. True, automation creates islands of efficiency. True, islands of automation are gradually linking up to form archipelagos. But with each "success" companies seem to find themselves running harder just to stay in the same place.

Some businessmen, however, have eased their disappointment simply by taking it to its logical conclusion. Instead of looking to information technology to provide answers to competitive problems, they are using it to ask better questions—like "what do our customers really want?" Instead of the "best" way of doing things, they are looking for better ways of changing in harmony with their customers' changing needs.

Some see a military analogy. One of the first uses for computers on the battlefield was to shoot down aircraft. Computer brains extrapolated the course of a moving aeroplane, and helped guide anti-aircraft guns along that track. Wonderful theories and technologies were created to build such systems. But much of the work was wasted. Aeroplanes changed course in the seconds between the time a shell left the gun and when it arrived at its target. So weapons designers changed tack. They built a "shell" that could change course, too—called the Sidewinder missile. Instead of the vast electronic brain which guided the gun, they imbued it with a wonderfully simple control system. The missile simply identified a target, and then kept turning towards it.

Some companies are similarly shifting the emphasis of their automation strategies towards responsiveness. It is not easy. At the least, the change requires the humility to listen to customers—no matter how bright your own people are.

Achieving responsiveness also often requires handing some routine decisions over to the computer to make sure they are done quickly and predictably. Mr John Thompson—head of the European part of the Computer Sciences Corporation, a firm of consultants on information technology—argues that some firms will have to be run more like the spreadsheets on which their results are modelled: change one number and others dependent on it adjust automatically.

So far, most of those who have successfully made this transition have simply had no other choice. Take Digital Equipment (DEC), a computer-maker. In the early 1980s DEC decided to let its customers choose for themselves which options they wanted with their computers. Combined with the technical advances of DEC's VAX range of computers, so-called *à la carte* computers proved wonderfully popular. This popularity nearly killed DEC. DEC's staff simply found it impossible to keep abreast of the possible permutations of components. Computers arrived without crucial bits of cable, or with parts that did not fit together. As DEC did not collect payment until the computer worked, the mounting piles of mis-specified machines were as expensive for DEC as they were irksome for its customers.

With great effort, DEC automated the process by which orders from the sales-force were translated into schedules for the factory and lists of parts to be delivered to the customer. Unfortunately, this did not solve the problem. Some of the orders were simply wrong to start with. Salesmen had not read technical changes to the product line, or had not understood the original technical specifications. So DEC went back to the drawing board. It came up with a collection of automated systems to manage the whole process of ordering, configuring and building computers—from product catalogue to shop floor.

Because DEC's product catalogue is kept on-line, it can be updated at a stroke—so salesmen do not specify out-of-date equipment. The computer maintains the rules by which computers are configured: "if you have a whizzo-wonder super-attachment, you will need a whizzo-wonder cable". An "expert system" called XCON automatically applies those rules to the task of making up orders. Other, related expert systems schedule production, help take orders from salesmen and so on.

DEC calls this sort of automation "knowledge-based systems." The key is that the computer helps with the whole business process—both organising data (like a product catalogue) and administering some of the simpler decisions taken from the data (eg, applying rules about how computers are made up). By so doing, the machines enable people to overcome complexity in order to respond quickly to new challenges.

Inevitably, DEC is now selling its expertise in building knowledge-based systems. Mr Themis Pappageorge, head of the marketing effort, reckons that some of the most successful customers have been those faced with challenges as severe as DEC's configuration problem. However good their intentions, those taking a rational approach cannot as readily break down the barriers to the new ways of doing business.

One company whose experience supports Mr Pappageorge's observation is Phillips 66, the product-marketing arm of Phillips Petroleum. After fending off two attacks by corporate raiders, Phillips was deep in debt and deep in trouble. To help revive its fortunes, it reorganised the way in which it sold refined-oil products. Instead of setting petrol prices over three broad regions (defined by which of Phillips's three big pipelines fed them), it started setting prices in 240 smaller regions, defined more rationally according to market. Prices were changed daily, if need be. Both local managers, who set regional prices, and national managers, who coordinated the regions, got information on inventories and sales just as fast. Competitors, who were still working largely according to the old timescales and the old geography, were flummoxed.

Some of the most ambitious, and best articulated, plans to use information technology to build a more responsive company come from the mother ship of computing, IBM. IBM reckons that it will be increasingly hard to maintain a competitive edge in the technical brilliance of its computers and software. There are simply too many bright, innovative companies out there. By its sheer size and scope, however, IBM may well be able to get ahead in the amount and quality of its information about what customers really want. IBM is now building information systems to gather that information and to deliver it to the people who should respond to it.

IBM's internal information strategy was the subject of its annual conference of top executives last year. The conference compared IBM's information systems with those of its customers and its competitors and found room for improvement. What IBM did was excellent, but too often irrelevant. So IBM's chairman, Mr John Akers, and his colleagues decided to shift the focus of IBM's internal information services. Instead of being charged with providing information-processing—as measured by lines of program code delivered, capacity of networks and the millions or billions of instructions which its computers can execute each second—IBM is now asking its information services to provide the company with information itself.

To begin the task of providing food for his colleagues' thoughts, Mr Larry Ford, head of IBM's internal information services, came away from the meeting with his colleagues' backing for three broad initiatives:

- Create competitive advantage from information about customers and markets. In practical terms, this means building up huge "warehouses" of that information, which can be got at by any part of the company, anywhere.
- Define internal information needs and fill them. One result of this has been a proliferation of "executive information systems" designed to give each IBM executive access to up-to-the second information on results and performance from around the world. So far, says Mr Ford, the question of who gets what information has proved relatively uncontroversial. But the discussions could grow more interesting as IBM tries to shift the emphasis of both business and systems from internal functions (eg, manufacturing or marketing) to market segments (eg, American computer-aided design or European personal computers).
- Create new measures of performance for information services. Instead of rewarding information services for technical excellence, IBM is trying to

link their rewards to business goals. In practice, this often means creating new goals for each project. Measurements which would track changes in customer satisfaction in computer-aided design markets—to judge the performance of the builders of an IBM system designed to do that—would have little relevance to the satisfaction of personal-computer customers, for example.

Mr Ford's 27,000 employees (7% of IBM's total workforce) are generally enthusiastic about the new initiatives, and confident. They mostly find it more satisfying, he reports, when they can try to make sure that their systems are used to their full potential to benefit the business—not just to the limits of the technology. Besides, the systems staff get more varied work. As part of the deal, IBM is encouraging its systems people to spend a bit of their time doing consulting work for outside clients, both to make money and to learn how others do things.

To help in their new endeavours, Mr Ford is training his folk with a variety of new skills. Some of the most important are tricks for understanding how organisations work and how they can be helped to change. The same lesson, in a different form, will be brought home to many managers—and indeed to whole corporations. Information is slippery stuff. As men and machines work more closely to take advantage of it, the world will, at a minimum, become a faster-changing place. To cope with that change, managers may have to rewrite the curricula of skills needed to prosper in the capitalist world, and to keep rewriting it.

The Search for Knowledge

If time is money, then so must information be. Both fit into the equations with which every business-school student is taught to value an investment. Value, say the textbooks, is the expected payoff discounted by the time an investor has to wait for his money back and the risk that that money will not come back. Information, say other textbooks, is data that reduce uncertainty, and thus risk. But information technology may subtly change the role played by information in the business world.

One of the ironies of the "information revolution" is that so few of those involved can give any definition of what information is. Starting point for most who would try to do that is still the theory of information published in 1948 by Mr Claude Shannon in the *Bell Systems Technical Journal*. Information, argued Mr Shannon, reduces uncertainty. If a piece of data convinces you of something you had previously thought very unlikely, then there is a great deal of information in it. If it merely tells you what you know, then there is no information in it.

Mr Shannon built from this insight a detailed mathematical definition of information. Though his intent was to quantify the information-carrying capacity of telephone lines, his theory can also describe most uses of computers. Most of what computers do is to reduce uncertainty in one way or another. As number-crunchers they can distill answers from data about sales or inventory levels; as databases they store complete libraries of information; enhanced with the technology of expert systems they can dispense scarce human expertise to whoever needs it; and as communicators they can send the information they hold across the world.

This does not mean that computers—however advanced they may be—can work with information in anything like the way people do. The distinction between people's information-handling skills and those of machines will largely determine which of today's human activities are duplicated by computers—and thus devalued. A big part of it is computers' sheer predictability.

Given the same inputs a thousand times, a computer will produce the same outputs a thousand times. It will not get bored, make mistakes, or have a flash of inspiration that enables it to see the problem in a new light. That predictability is what makes computers so useful. It is also their greatest weakness.

Given any well-defined question, information technology is making it increasingly easy to get answers. "What were our sales last month?" "What does it mean when the engine goes 'chunk-a-lunk thump thump'?" The machines cannot, however, do much to help provide questions in the first place. But if answers are easier to come by, good questions become all the more valuable.

People seldom seem to have any shortage of questions. Individuals move from job to job, learning new skills and ways of looking at the world at each step. Groups, by contrast, get stuck. Many is the company which churns out similar products or services year after year, doing the same business in the same way. Information technology will make such firms increasingly easy to copy—when copying is worthwhile. But it may also make it easier for groups to learn new tricks.

The technology can show all workers the same overview of the company—so that they can see why this year the emphasis should be on, say, speeding delivery while last year it was on quality in manufacturing. The technology can show each worker, day-to-day, month-to-month how his actions affect the group. And it can broadcast his bright ideas to the company as a whole.

Building such learning organisations is a vast challenge. It requires new skills, clever people and capable machines. It requires both high standards and a commitment to keep learning. Many, particularly in the West, do not want to learn.

At Toyota's factories, one of the main measures of performance looked at by management is the number of suggestions for improvements submitted each day by workers. Compare that with the history of automation in the West where time and again managers have taken great trouble and expense to install information technology whose purpose is to enable workers to do their jobs more effectively—without bothering to consult the workers or to ask them whether or not the machines really help. Workers are no better. Britain is particularly full of examples of workers clinging to too dangerous, boring and low-paid jobs despite all efforts at convincing them to change their ways.

Information technology will not sweep away the legacy of years of suspicion or inertia overnight. But it will expose to increasing competition those firms not adept at change and self-improvement. The developing world is full of cheap and willing workers. Sit still long enough, and some competitor will piece-by-piece duplicate, with computers' help, much of your information-gathering and decision-making. The ability to learn as a group will become increasingly important for firms looking to avoid being dragged down by hordes of copycat competitors. Learning from and with fellow workers helps to keep a step ahead of the competition. Helping customers to learn can inspire them to keep buying your product. Learning from customers helps to pay attention to their changing needs. Learning is still something that humans do best, and being more human is the best way for men to work with machines.

Questions

1. Some studies have found that the use of information technology has not resulted in productivity gains. If true, why might this be the case? Is there anything in the way productivity is measured that might explain the study findings?

2. It is clear that organizations are having to respond more quickly to changing conditions than in the past. How can information technology help in this area?

3. Computers and communications technology are being used to link companies together. Choose an example like electronic data interchange and describe how it affects workers' jobs.

4. It is becoming increasingly important for people to "work smarter." How can information technology support this objective? Give specific examples.

SECTION 2

Managing the Constellation of IS Applications

As indicated in Section 1, the range or "constellation" of IS applications can be characterized in a number of ways. One is to focus on the type of activity being supported (for example, capturing data or telecommunications). Another is to look at the functional areas of the business (for example, marketing or finance or accounting) and see what systems have been created to meet their specialized needs. A third approach, the one used in this section, is to examine the generic characteristics of applications such as decision support systems, expert systems, and team support systems. By using this approach, the articles chosen are less likely to become dated as technology and specific applications change.

Issues

A framework for decision support systems

The first article, written by Ralph Sprague, is a classic. Written over 10 years ago, it is still the basic conceptual framework for thinking about decision support systems (DSS). The systems, which Sprague characterizes as *"interactive computer-based systems which help decision makers utilize data and models* to solve *unstructured* problems," involve three levels of technology: a specific DSS, DSS generators, and DSS tools. Linked to each of these levels are the roles played by the user, the builder, and the "toolsmith." Taken together, these three actors provide a comprehensive view of what DSSs are and where they are going.

A practical example of DSS

In the next article, George Houdeshel and Hugh Watson describe a specific "management information and decision support system" in use at Lockheed-Georgia. This system, a blend of off-the-shelf hardware and in-house developed software, supports a wide variety of information needs within the company. The key factors to its success were top management's commitment; an evolutionary team approach to development; and careful attention to the hardware, software, systems, and information requirements of the final system. Initially built in the 1980s, the system was upgraded to take into account the business and technological changes of the 1990s. In a special section at the end of this article, prepared specifically for this book, the authors describe the upgrades and the upgrade process.

Expert support systems

To many people, expert systems, which are a branch of artificial intelligence, appear to be a logical extension of decision support systems. Meadow and Mahler show how two companies, Digital Equipment Corporation and DuPont, introduced and disseminated such systems in their firms. The process used matched the nature of the companies. Digital Equipment, with a small number of expensive products of the same type, used a centralized approach, whereas DuPont, with a multiplicity of diverse products, used a "bottoms up" approach. Both companies use expert systems to help their people solve difficult problems well.

Supporting the marketing function

Information systems are being used by every business function to accomplish tasks. Many systems simply replicate the previous business process, saving labor and providing better service. Others create entirely new products and new organizational forms. Still others enhance operations in ways that change their fundamental character. John D. C. Little describes an example of the latter that is taking place behind the scenes in the consumer packaged-goods industry. The data being generated by bar code scanners at grocery stores is creating volumes of data never previously available and thereby making it possible to increase marketing effectiveness by delivering many differentiated products to a large number of differentiated markets.

Transaction processing systems

With widespread computer sophistication and user-friendly interfaces between computer and user, it is now possible to transfer a considerable portion of the data entry and service delivery functions for individual computer transactions directly to the customer. Jerry Kanter, Stephen Shiffman, and J. Faye Horn describe the growth of these self-service transaction systems. Whether it is an automatic teller at the bank, automated checkout at the supermarket, or computer information and shopping services, these systems are taking hold and shaping the way services are being provided.

Electronic data interchange

Information flows not only within a firm but also among firms. Whether it is correspondence, orders, invoices, bills of lading, or payments, every firm must communicate with both its suppliers and its customers. Much of the information flow among trading partners is routine, following standard forms or formats. As James Senn points out, to speed the flow and reduce the cost of exchanging routine information, large firms and small have turned to Electronic Data Interchange (EDI) to "exchange business data in structured formats that can be processed by computer applications software." To gain the strategic and tactical advantages EDI offers, businesses will restructure their fundamental activities.

International systems

Carefully crafted investments in global information technology offer firms an opportunity to increase control and enhance coordination, while opening access to new global markets and businesses. Blake Ives and Sirkka Jarvenpaa describe the numerous challenges that these global opportunities present to management. They sketch four common approaches for managing global information technology. To succeed globally, firms will need to integrate their internal processing systems and build interorganizational information bridges.

Thinking about future applications

We are certainly a long way from having thought about all the possible ways in which information systems can be applied. The future promises to bring many innovations which will change all our lives. Richard Kurzweil, an inventor and entrepreneur, presents a series of scenarios that describe potential future applications. A scenario must meet three criteria: it must be

1. possible,
2. plausible, and
3. internally consistent.

"Possible" requires that a scenario does not violate known physical and economic constraints. "Plausible" implies that the reader agrees with the author that such an outcome could occur within the specified time frame. "Internally consistent" implies that there are no contradictions within the scenario. As you read through these scenarios, test them against these three criteria. The future that Kurzweil envisions is a bright one. Only time will tell if it comes to pass.

2.1

*A Framework for the Development of Decision Support Systems**

Ralph H. Sprague, Jr.

Introduction

We seem to be on the verge of another "era" in the relentless advancement of computer based information systems in organizations. Designated by the term Decision Support Systems (DSS), these systems are receiving reactions ranging from "a major breakthrough" to "just another 'buzz word.' "

One view is that the natural evolutionary advancement of information technology and its use in the organizational context has led from EDP to MIS to the current DSS thrust. In this view, the DSS picks up where MIS leaves off. A contrary view portrays DSS as an important subset of what MIS has been and will continue to be. Still another view recognizes a type of system that has been developing for several years and "now we have a name for it." Meanwhile, the skeptics suspect that DSS is just another "buzz word" to justify the next round of visits from the vendors.

The purpose of this article is to briefly examine these alternative views of DSS, and present a framework that proves valuable in reconciling them. The framework articulates and integrates major concerns of several "stakeholders" in

*SOURCE: "A Framework for the Development of Decision Support Systems" by Ralph Sprague, from *MIS Quarterly*, Vol. 4, Number 4, December 1980. Copyright 1980 by the Society for Information Management Systems Research Center at the University of Minnesota. Reprinted by special permission.

the development of DSS: executives and professionals who use them, the MIS managers who manage the process of developing and installing them, the information specialists who build and develop them, the system designers who create and assemble the technology on which they are based, and the researchers who study the DSS subject and process.

Definition, Examples, Characteristics

The concepts involved in DSS were first articulated in the early '70's by Michael S. Scott Morton under the term "management decision systems" [32]. A few firms and scholars began to develop and research DSS, which became characterized as *interactive* computer based systems, which *help* decision makers utilize *data* and *models* to solve *unstructured* problems. The unique contribution of DSS resulted from these key words. That definition proved restrictive enough that few actual systems completely satisfied it. Some authors recently extended the definition of DSS to include any system that makes some contribution to decision making; in this way the term can be applied to all but transaction processing. A serious definitional problem is that the words have a certain "intuitive validity"; any system that supports a decision, in any way, is a "Decision Support System."

Unfortunately, neither the restrictive nor the broad definition helps much, because they do not provide guidance for understanding the value, the technical requirements, or the approach for developing a DSS. A complicating factor is that people from different backgrounds and contexts view a DSS quite differently. A manager and computer scientist seldom see things in the same way.

Another way to get a feeling for a complex subject like a DSS is to consider examples. Several specific examples were discussed in The Society for Management Information Systems (SMIS) Workshop on DSS in 1979 [35]. Alter examined 56 systems which might have some claim to the DSS label, and used this sample to develop a set of abstractions describing their characteristics [1, 2]. More recently, Keen has designated about 30 examples of what he feels are DSS and compares their characteristics [26].

The "characteristics" approach seems to hold more promise than either definitions or collections of examples in understanding a DSS and its potential. More specifically, a DSS may be defined by its capabilities in several critical areas—capabilities which are required to accomplish the objectives which are pursued by the development and use of a DSS. Observed characteristics of a DSS which have evolved from the work of Alter, Keen, and others include:

- ◆ They tend to be aimed at the less well structured, underspecified problems that upper level managers typically face.

- ◆ They attempt to combine the use of models or analytic techniques with traditional data access and retrieval functions.

◆ They specifically focus on features which make them easy to use by non-computer people in an interactive mode.

◆ They emphasize flexibility and adaptability to accommodate changes in the environment and the decision making approach of the user.

A serious question remains. Are the definitions, examples, and characteristics of a DSS sufficiently different to justify the use of a new term and the inference of a new era in information systems for organizations, or are the skeptics right? Is it just another "buzz word" to replace the fading appeal of MIS?

DSS Versus MIS

Much of the difficulty and controversy with terms like "DSS" and "MIS" can be traced to the difference between an academic or theoretical definition and "connotational" definition. The former is carefully articulated by people who write textbooks and articles in journals. The latter evolves from what actually is developed and used in practice, and is heavily influenced by the personal experiences that the user of the term has had with the subject. It is this connotational definition of EDP/MIS/DSS that is used in justifying the assertion that a DSS is an evolutionary advancement beyond MIS.

This view can be expressed using Figure 1, a simple organizational chart, as a model of an organization. EDP was first applied to the lower operational levels of the organization to automate the paperwork. Its basic characteristics include:

◆ A focus on data, storage, processing, and flows at the operational level

◆ Efficient transaction processing

◼FIGURE 1◼ The Connotational View

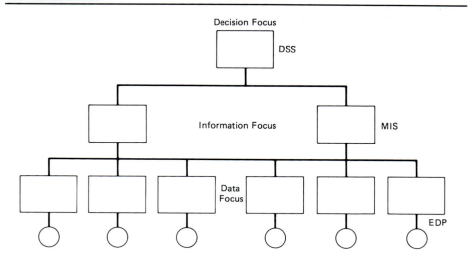

- Scheduled and optimized computer runs

- Integrated files for related jobs

- Summary reports for management

In recent years, the EDP level of activity in many firms has become a well-oiled and efficient production facility for transactions processing.

The MIS approach elevated the focus of information systems activities, with additional emphasis on integration and planning of the information systems function. In *practice*, the characteristics of MIS include:

- An information focus, aimed at the middle managers

- Structured information flow

- An integration of EDP jobs by business function, such as production MIS, marketing MIS, personnel MIS, etc.

- Inquiry and report generation, usually with a database

The MIS era contributed a new level of information to serve management needs, but was still very much oriented to, and built upon, information flows and data files.

According to this connotational view, a DSS is focused still higher in the organization with an emphasis on the following characteristics:

- Decision focused, aimed at the top managers and executive decision makers

- Emphasis on flexibility, adaptability, and quick response

- User initiated and controlled

- Support for the personal decision making styles of individual managers

This connotational and evolutionary view has some credence because it roughly corresponds to developments in practice over time. A recent study found MIS managers able to distinguish the level of advancement of their application systems using criteria similar to those above [27]. Many installations with MIS type applications planned to develop applications with DSS type characteristics. However, the "connotational" view has some serious deficiencies, and is definitely misleading in the further development of a DSS.

- It implies that *decision support* is needed only at the top levels. In fact, *decision support* is required at all levels of management in the organization.

- The decision making which occurs at several levels frequently must be coordinated. Therefore, an important dimension of *decision support* is the communication and coordination between decision makers across organizational levels, as well as at the same level.

- It implies that *decision support* is the only thing top managers need from the information system. In fact, decision making is only one of the activities of managers that benefits from information systems support.

There is also the problem that many information systems professionals, especially those in SMIS, are not willing to accept the narrow connotational view of the term "MIS." To us, MIS refers to the entire set of systems and activities required to manage, process, and use information as a resource in the organization.

The Theoretical View

To consider the appropriate role of a DSS in this overall context of information systems, the broad charter and objectives of the information systems function in the organization is characterized:

Dedicated to improving the performance of knowledge workers in organizations through the application of information technology.

- ◆ Improving the performance is the ultimate objective of information systems—not the storage of data, the production of reports, or even "getting the right information to the right person at the right time." The ultimate objective must be viewed in terms of the ability of information systems to support the improved performance of people in organizations.

- ◆ Knowledge workers are the clientele. This group includes managers, professionals, staff analysts, and clerical workers whose primary job responsibility is the handling of information in some form.

- ◆ Organizations are the context. The focus is on information handling in goal seeking organizations of all kinds.

- ◆ The application of information technology is the challenge and opportunity facing the information systems professional for the purposes and in the contexts given above.

A triangle was used by Robert Head in the late '60's as a visual model to characterize MIS in this broad comprehensive sense [22]. It has become a classic way to view the dimensions of an information system. The vertical dimension represented the levels of management, and the horizontal dimension represented the main functional areas of the business organization. Later authors added transactional processing as a base on which the entire system rested. The result was a two dimensional model of an MIS in the broad sense—the total activities which comprise the information system in an organization. Figure 2 is a further extension of the basic triangle to help describe the concept of the potential role of a DSS. The depth dimension shows the major technology "subsystems" which provide support for the activities of knowledge workers.

Three major thrusts are shown here, but there could be more. The structured reporting system includes the reports required for the management and control of the organization, and for satisfying the information needs of external parties. It has been evolving from efforts in EDP and MIS, in the narrow sense, for several years. Systems to support the communication needs of the organization

FIGURE 2   The Complete View

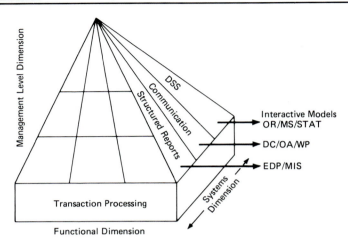

are evolving rapidly from advances in telecommunications with a strong impetus from office automation and word processing. DSS seems to be evolving from the coalescence of information technology and operations research/management science approaches in the form of interactive modeling.

To summarize this introductory section, a DSS is not merely an evolutionary advancement of EDP and MIS, and it will certainly not replace either. Nor is it merely a type of information system aimed exclusively at top management, where other information systems seem to have failed. A DSS is a class of information system that draws on transaction processing systems and interacts with the other parts of the overall information system to support the decision making activities of managers and other knowledge workers in the organizations. However, there are some subtle but significant differences between a DSS and traditional EDP or so-called MIS approaches. Moreover, these systems require a new combination of information systems technology to satisfy a set of heretofore unmet needs. It is not yet clear exactly how these technologies fit together, or which important problems need to be solved. Indeed, that is a large part of the purpose of this article. It is apparent, however, that a DSS has the potential to become another powerful weapon in the arsenal of the information systems professional to help improve the effectiveness of the people in organizations.

The Framework

The remainder of this article is devoted to an exploration of the nature of this "thrust" in information systems called "DSS." The mechanism for this exploration is another of the often maligned but repeatedly used "frameworks."

A framework, in the absence of theory, is helpful in organizing a complex subject, identifying the relationships between the parts, and revealing the areas in which further developments will be required. The framework presented here has evolved over the past two years in discussions with many different groups of people. It is organized in two major parts. The first part considers: (a) three levels of technology, all of which have been designated as a DSS, with considerable confusion; (b) the developmental approach that is evolving for the creation of a DSS; and (c) the roles of several key types of people in the building and use of a DSS. The second part of the framework develops a descriptive model to assess the performance objectives and the capabilities of a DSS as viewed by three of the major stakeholders in their continued development and use.

Three technology levels

It is helpful to identify three levels of hardware/software which have been included in the label "DSS." They are used by people with different levels of technical capability, and vary in the nature and scope of task to which they can be applied.

Specific DSS

The system which actually accomplishes the work might be called the *Specific DSS*. It is an information systems "application," but with characteristics that make it significantly different from a typical data processing application. It is the hardware/software that allows a specific decision maker or group of decision makers to deal with a specific set of related problems. An early example is the portfolio management system [20] also described in the first major DSS book by Keen and Scott Morton [23]. Another example is the police beat allocation system used on an experimental basis by the City of San Jose, California [9]. The latter system allowed a police officer to display a map outline and call up data by geographical zone, showing police calls for service, activity levels, service time, etc. The interactive graphic capability of the system enabled the officer to manipulate the maps, zones, and data to try a variety of police beat alternatives quickly and easily. In effect, the system provided tools to *amplify* a manager's judgment. Incidentally, a later experiment attempted to apply a traditional linear programming model to the problem. The solution was less satisfactory than the one designed by the police officer.

DSS Generator

The second technology level might be called a *DSS Generator*. This is a "package" of related hardware and software which provides a set of capabilities to quickly and easily build a Specific DSS. For example, the police beat system described above was built from the Geodata Analysis and Display System (GADS), an experimental system developed at the IBM Research Laboratory in San Jose [8]. By loading different maps, data, menu choices, and procedures or command strings, GADS was later used to build a Specific DSS to support the routing of

IBM copier repairmen [42]. The development of this new "application" required less than one month.

Another example of a *DSS Generator* is the Executive Information System (EIS) marketed by Boeing Computer Services [6]. EIS is an integrated set of capabilities which includes report preparation, inquiry capability, a modeling language, graphic display commands, and a set of financial and statistical analysis subroutines. These capabilities have all been available individually for some time. The unique contribution of EIS is that these capabilities are available through a common command language which acts on a common set of data. The result is that EIS can be used as a DSS Generator, especially for a Specific DSS to help in financial decision making situations.

Evolutionary growth toward DSS Generators has come from special purpose languages. In fact, most of the software systems that might be used as Generators are evolving from enhanced planning languages or modeling languages, perhaps with report preparation and graphic display capabilities added. The Interactive Financial Planning System (IFPS) marketed by Execucom Systems of Austin, Texas [18], and EXPRESS available from TYMSHARE [44], are good examples.

DSS Tools

The third and most fundamental level of technology applied to the development of a DSS might be called *DSS Tools*. These are hardware or software elements which facilitate the development of a Specific DSS *or* a DSS Generator. This category of technology has seen the greatest amount of recent development, including new special purpose languages, improvements in operating systems to support conversational approaches, color graphics hardware and supporting

FIGURE 3   Three Levels of DSS Technology

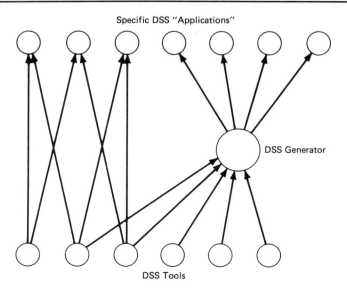

Specific DSS "Applications"

DSS Generator

DSS Tools

software, etc. For example, the GADS system described above was written in FORTRAN using an experimental graphics subroutine package as the primary dialogue handling software, a laboratory enhanced rasterscan color monitor, and a powerful interactive data extraction/database management system.

Relationships

The relationships between these three levels of technology and types of DSS are illustrated by Figure 3. The DSS Tools can be used to develop a Specific DSS application directly as shown on the left half of the diagram. This is the same approach used to develop most traditional applications with tools such as a general purpose language, data access software, subroutine packages, etc. The difficulty with this approach for developing DSS applications is the constant change and flexibility which characterize them. A DSS changes character not only in response to changes in the environment, but to changes in the way managers want to approach the problem. Therefore, a serious complicating factor in the use of basic tools is the need to involve the user directly in the change and modification of the Specific DSS.

APL was heavily used in the development of Specific DSS because it proved to be cheap and easy for APL programmers, especially the APL enthusiasts, to produce "throw-away" code which could be easily revised or discarded as the nature of the application changed. However, except for the few users who became members of the APL fan club, that language *did not* help capture the involvement of users in the building and modification of the DSS. The development and use of DSS Generators promises to create a "platform" or staging area from which Specific DSS can be constantly developed and modified with the cooperation of the user, and without heavy consumption of time and effort.

Evolving roles in DSS

All three levels of technology will probably be used over time in the development and operation of a DSS. Some interesting developments are occurring, however, in the roles that managers and technicians will play.

Figure 4 repeats part of the earlier diagram with a spectrum of five roles spread across the three levels.

- The *manager* or *user* is the person faced with the problem or decision—the one that must take action and be responsible for the consequences.

- The *intermediary* is the person who helps the user, perhaps merely as a clerical assistant to push the buttons of the terminal, or perhaps as a more substantial "staff assistant" to interact and make suggestions.

- The *DSS builder* or facilitator assembles the necessary capabilities from the DSS Generator to "configure" the specific DSS with which the user/intermediary interacts directly. This person must have some familiarity with the problem area and also be comfortable with the information system technology components and capabilities.

FIGURE 4 Three Levels of DSS with Five Associated Roles for Managers and Technicians

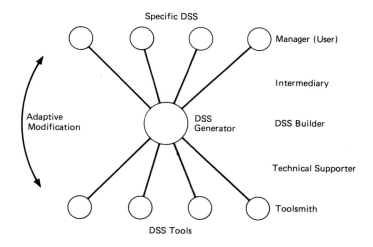

The *technical supporter* develops additional information system capabilities or components when they are needed as part of the Generator. New databases, new analysis models, and additional data display formats will be developed by the person filling this role. It requires a strong familiarity with technology, and a minor acquaintance with the problem or application area.

◆ The *toolsmith* develops new technology, new languages, new hardware and software, improves the efficiency of linkages between subsystems, etc.

Two observations about this spectrum of roles are appropriate. First, it is clear that they do not necessarily align with individuals on a one-to-one basis. One person may assume several roles, or more than one person may be required to fill a role. The appropriate role assignment will generally depend on:

◆ The nature of the problem, particularly how narrow or broad

◆ The nature of the person, particularly how comfortable the individual is with the computer equipment, language, and concepts

◆ The strength of the technology, particularly how user oriented it is

Some managers do not need or want an intermediary. There are even a few chief executives who take the terminal home on weekends to write programs, thereby assuming the upper three or four roles. In fact, a recent survey of the users of IFPS shows that more than one third of them are middle and top level managers [45]. Decisions which require group consensus or systems design (builder) teams are examples of multiple persons per role.

Secondly, these roles appear similar to those present in traditional systems development, but there are subtle differences. The top two are familiar even in name for the development of many interactive or online systems. It is common

practice in some systems to combine them into one "virtual" user for convenience. The user of the DSS, however, will play a much more active and controlling role in the design and development of the system than has been true in
the past. The builder/technical supporter dichotomy is relatively close to the
information specialist/system designer dichotomy discussed in the ACM curriculum recommendations [3]. Increasingly, however, the DSS builder resides in the
functional area and not in the MIS department. The toolsmith is similar to a
systems programmer, software designer, or computer scientist, but is increasingly
employed by a hardware or software vendor, and not by the user's organization.
The net result is less direct involvement in the DSS process by the information
systems professional in the EDP/MIS department. (Some implications of this
trend are discussed later.) Moreover, the interplay between these roles is evolving into a unique development approach for a DSS.

The development approach for DSS

The very nature of a DSS requires a different design technique from traditional batch, or online, transaction processing systems. The traditional approaches for analysis and design have proven inadequate because there is no
single comprehensive theory of decision making, and because of the rapidity of
change in the conditions which decision makers face. Designers literally "cannot
get to first base" because no one, least of all the decision maker or user, can
define in advance what the functional requirements of the system should be. A
DSS needs to be built with short, rapid feedback from users to ensure that development is proceeding correctly. It must be developed to permit change quickly
and easily.

Iterative Design

The result is that the most important four steps in the typical systems development process—analysis, design, construction, implementation—are combined
into a single step which is iteratively repeated. Several names are evolving to
describe this process including breadboarding [31], L'Approache Evolutive [14],
and "middle out" [30]. The essence of the approach is that the manager and
builder agree on a small but significant subproblem, then design and develop an
initial system to support the decision making which it requires. After a short
period of use, for instance, a few weeks, the system is evaluated, modified, and
incrementally expanded. This cycle is repeated three to six times over the course
of a few months until a *relatively* stable system is evolved which supports decision
making for a cluster of tasks. The word "relatively" is important, because although the frequency and extent of change will decrease, it will never be stable.
The system will always be changing, not as a necessary evil in response to imposed environmental changes, but as a conscious strategy on the part of the user
and builder.

In terms of the three level model presented earlier, this process can be viewed
as the iterative cycling between the DSS Generator and the Specific DSS as
shown in Figure 4. With each cycle, capabilities are added to, or deleted from,

the Specific DSS from those available in the DSS Generator. Keen depicts the expansion and growth of the system in terms of adding verbs which represent actions managers require [24]. Carlson adds more dimension by focusing on representations, operations, control, and memories as the elements of expansion and modification [11]. In another paper, Keen deals substantively with the interaction between the user, the builder, and the technology in this iterative, adaptive design process [25].

Note that this approach requires an unusual level of management involvement or management participation in the design. The manager is actually the iterative designer of the system; the systems analyst is merely the catalyst between the manager and the system, implementing the required changes and modifications.

Note also that this is different from the concept of "prototyping"; the initial system is real, live, and usable, not just a pilot test. The iterative process does not *merely* lead to a good understanding of the systems performance requirements, which are then frozen. The iterative changeability is actually *built into* the DSS as it is used over time. In fact, the development approach *becomes the system*. Rather than developing a system which is then "run" as a traditional EDP system, the DSS development approach results in the installation of an adaptive process in which a decision maker and a set of information system "capabilities" interact to confront problems while responding to changes from a variety of sources.

The Adaptive System

In the broad sense, the DSS is an adaptive system which consists of all three levels of technology in place and operating with the participants (roles), and the technology adapting to changes over time. Thus, the development of a DSS is actually the development and installation of this adaptive system. Simon describes such a system as one that adapts to changes of several kinds over three time horizons [34]. In the short run, the system allows a *search* for answers within a relatively narrow scope. In the intermediate time horizon, the system *learns* by modifying its capabilities and activities, i.e., the scope or domain changes. In the long run, the system evolves to accommodate much different behavior styles and capabilities.

The three level model of a DSS is analogous to Simon's adaptive system. The Specific DSS gives the manager the capabilities and flexibility to *search*, explore, and experiment with the problem area, within certain boundaries. Over time, as changes occur in a task, the environment, and the user's behavior, the Specific DSS must *learn* to accommodate these changes through the reconfiguration of the elements in the DSS generator, with the aid of the DSS builder. Over a longer period of time, the basic tools evolve to provide the technology for changing the capabilities of the Generators out of which the Specific DSS is constructed, through the efforts of the toolsmith.

The ideas expressed above are not particularly new. Rapid feedback between the systems analyst and the client has been pursued for years. In the long run, most computer systems *are* adaptive systems. They are changed and modified during the normal system life cycle, and they evolve through major enhancements and extensions as the life cycle is repeated. However, when the length of that life cycle is shortened from 3 to 5 years to 3 to 5 months, or even weeks, there are significant implications. The resulting changes in the development approach and the traditional view of the systems life cycle promises to be one of the important impacts of the growing use of a DSS.

Performance Objectives and Capabilities

Most of the foregoing discussion has dealt with some aspects of the technological and organizational contexts within which a DSS will be built and operated. The second part of the framework deals with what a DSS must accomplish, and what capabilities or characteristics it must have. The three levels of hardware/software technology and the corresponding three major "stakeholders" or interested parties in the development and use of a DSS can be used to identify the characteristics and attributes of a DSS.

At the top level are the *managers* or *users* who are primarily concerned with what the Specific DSS can do for them. Their focus is the problem solving or decision making task they face, and the organizational environment in which they operate. They will assess a DSS in terms of the assistance they receive in pursuing these tasks. At the level of the DSS Generator, the *builders* or designers must use the capabilities of the generator to configure a Specific DSS to meet the manager's needs. They will be concerned with the capabilities the Generator offers, and how these capabilities can be assembled to create the Specific DSS. At the DSS tool level, the *"toolsmiths"* are concerned with the development of basic technology components, and how they can be integrated to form a DSS Generator which has the necessary capabilities.

The attributes and characteristics of a DSS as viewed from each level must be examined. From the manager's view, six general performance objectives for the Specific DSS can be identified. They are not the only six that could be identified, but as a group they represent the overall performance of a DSS that seems to be expected and desirable from a managerial viewpoint. The characteristics of the DSS Generator from the viewpoint of the builder are described by a conceptual model which identifies performance characteristics in three categories: dialogue handling or the man-machine interface, database and database management capability, and modeling and analytic capability. The same three part model is used to depict the viewpoint of the "toolsmith," but from the aspect of the technology, tactics, and architecture required to produce those capabilities required by the builders.

Manager's view: performance objectives

The following performance requirements are phrased using the normative word "should." It is likely that no Specific DSS will be required to satisfy all six of the performance requirements given here. In fact, it is important to recall that the performance criteria for any Specific DSS will depend entirely on the task, the organizational environment, and the decision maker(s) involved. Nevertheless, the following objectives collectively represent a set of capabilities which characterize the full value of the DSS concept from the manager/user point of view. The first three pertain to the type of decision making task which managers and professionals face. The latter three relate to the type of support which is needed.

1. *A DSS should provide support for decision making, but with emphasis on semi-structured and unstructured decisions.* These are the types of decisions that have had little or no support from EDP, MIS, or management science/operations research (MS/OR) in the past. It might be better to refer to "hard" or underspecified problems, because the concept of "structure" in decision making is heavily dependent on the cognitive style and approach to problem solving of the decision maker. It is clear from their expressed concerns, however, that managers need additional support for certain kinds of problems.
2. *A DSS should provide decision making support for managers at all levels, assisting in integration between the levels whenever appropriate.* This requirement evolves from the realization that managers at *all* organizational levels face "tough" problems as described in the first objective above. Moreover, a major need articulated by managers is the integration and coordination of decision making by several managers dealing with related parts of a larger problem.
3. *A DSS should support decisions which are interdependent as well as those that are independent.* Much of the early DSS work inferred that a decision maker would sit at a terminal, use a system, and develop a decision *alone*. DSS development experience has shown that a DSS must accommodate decisions which are made by groups or made in part by several people in sequence. Keen and Hackathorn [24] explore three decision types as:
   ◆ *Independent.* A decision maker has full responsibility and authority to make a complete implementable decision.
   ◆ *Sequential Interdependent.* A decision maker makes part of a decision which is passed on to someone else.
   ◆ *Pooled Interdependent.* The decision must result from negotiation and interaction among decision makers. Different capabilities will be required to support each type of decision—personal support, organizational support, and group support respectively.
4. *A DSS should support all phases of the decision making process.* A popular model of the decision making process is given in the work of Herbert Simon [33]. He characterized three main steps in the process as follows:
   ◆ *Intelligence.* Searching the environment for conditions calling for decisions. Raw data is obtained, processed, and examined for clues that may identify problems.
   ◆ *Design.* Inventing, developing, and analyzing possible courses of action. This involves processes to understand the problem, generate solutions, and test solutions for feasibility.
   ◆ *Choice.* Selecting a particular course of action from those available. A choice is made and implemented.

Although the third phase includes implementation, many authors feel that it is significant enough to be shown separately. It has been added to Figure 5 to show the relationships between the steps. Simon's model also illustrates the contribution of MIS/EDP and MS/OR to decision making. From the definition of the three stages given above, it is clear that EDP and MIS, in the narrow sense, have made major contributions to the intelligence phase, while MS/OR has been primarily useful at the choice phase. There has been no substantial support for the design phase, which seems to be one of the primary potential contributions of a DSS. There also has been very little support from traditional systems for the implementation phase, but some early experience has shown that a DSS can make a major contribution here also [42].

5. *A DSS should support a variety of decision making processes, but not be dependent on any one.* Simon's model, though widely accepted, is only one model of how decisions are actually made. In fact, there is no universally accepted model of the decision making process, and there is no promise of such a general theory in the foreseeable future. There are too many variables, too many different types of decisions, and too much variety in the characteristics of decision makers. Consequently, a very important characteristic of a DSS is that it provide the decision maker with a set of capabilities to apply in a sequence and form that fits each individual cognitive style. In short, a DSS should be process independent, and user driven or controlled.

FIGURE 5   Phases of Decision Making

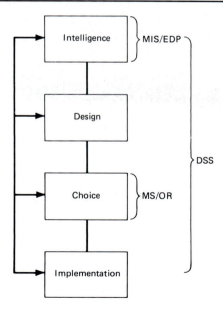

6. *Finally, a DSS should be easy to use.* A variety of terms have been used to describe this characteristic, including flexibility, user-friendly, nonthreatening, etc. The importance of this characteristic is underscored by the discretionary latitude of a DSS's clientele. Although some systems which require heavy organizational support or group support may limit the discretion somewhat, the user of a DSS has much more latitude to ignore or circumvent the system than the user of a more traditional transaction system or required reporting system. Therefore, a DSS must "earn" its users' allegiance by being valuable and convenient.

The builder's view: technical capabilities

The DSS Builder has the responsibility of drawing on computer based tools and techniques to provide the decision support required by the manager. DSS Tools can be used directly, but it is generally more efficient and effective to use a DSS Generator for this task. The Generator must have a set of capabilities which facilitate the quick and easy configuration of a Specific DSS and modifi-

FIGURE 6   **Components of the DSS**

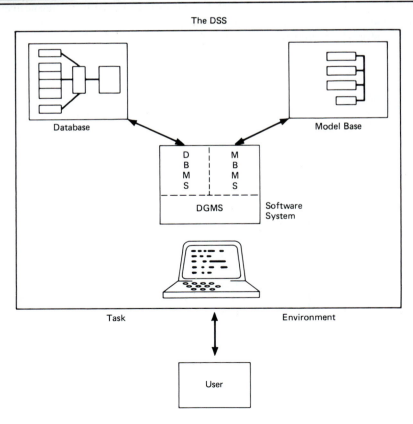

The DSS

Database

Model Base

D
B
M
S

M
B
M
S

DGMS

Software System

Task

Environment

User

cation in response to changes in the manager's requirements, environment, tasks, and thinking approaches. A conceptual model can be used to organize these capabilities, both for the builders and for the "toolsmith" who will develop the technology to provide these capabilities.

The old "black box" approach is helpful here, starting with the view of the system as a black box, successively "opening" the boxes to understand the subsystems and how they are interconnected. Although the DSS is treated as the black box here, it is important to recall that the overall system is the decision *making* system, consisting of a manager/user who uses a DSS to confront a task in an organizational environment.

Opening the large DSS box reveals a database, a model base, and a complex software system for linking the user to each of them as shown in Figure 6. Opening each of these boxes reveals that the database and model base have some interrelated components, and that the software system is comprised of three sets of capabilities: database management software (DBMS), model base management software (MBMS), and the software for managing the interface between the user and the system, which might be called the dialogue generation and management software (DGMS). These three major subsystems provide a convenient scheme for identifying the technical capability which a DSS must have. The key aspects in each category that are critical to a DSS from the Builder's point of view, and a list of capabilities which will be required in each category, must now be considered.

The data subsystem

The data subsystem is thought to be a well understood set of capabilities because of the rapidly maturing technology related to databases and their management. The typical advantages of the database approach, and the powerful functions of the DBMS, are also important to the development and use of a DSS. There are, however, some significant differences between the Database/Data Communication approach for traditional systems, and those applicable for a DSS. Opening the Database box summarizes these key characteristics as shown in Figure 7.

First is the importance of a much richer set of data sources than are usually found in typical non-DSS applications. Data must come from external as well as internal sources, since decision making, especially in the upper management levels, is heavily dependent on external data sources. In addition, the typical accounting oriented transaction data must be supplemented with non-transactional, non-accounting data, some of which has not been computerized in the past.

Another significant difference is the importance of the data capture and extraction process from this wider set of data sources. The nature of a DSS requires that the extraction process, and the DBMS which manages it, be flexible enough to allow rapid additions and changes in response to unanticipated user requests. Finally, most successful DSS's have found it necessary to create a DSS database which is logically separate from other operational databases. A partial set of capabilities required in the database area can be summarized by the following:

FIGURE 7   The Data Subsystem

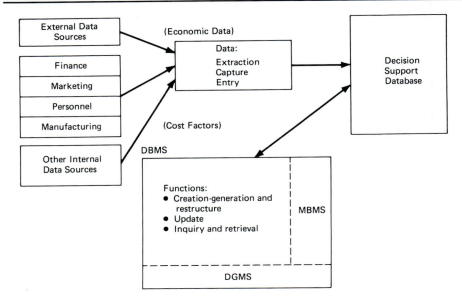

◆ The ability to combine a variety of data sources through a data capture and extraction process

◆ The ability to add and delete data sources quickly and easily

◆ The ability to portray logical data structures in user terms so the user understands what is available and can specify needed additions and deletions

◆ The ability to handle personal and unofficial data so the user can experiment with alternatives based on personal judgment

◆ The ability to manage this wide variety of data with a full range of data management functions

The model subsystem

A very promising aspect of a DSS is its ability to integrate data access and decision models. It does so by imbedding the decision models in an information system which uses the database as the integration and communication mechanism between models. This characteristic unifies the strength of data retrieval and reporting from the EDP field and the significant developments in management science in a way the manager can use and trust.

The misuse and disuse of models have been widely discussed [21, 28, 36, 39]. One major problem has been that model builders were frequently preoccupied with the structure of the model. The existence of the correct input data and the proper delivery of the output to the user was assumed. In addition to these heroic assumptions, models tended to suffer from inadequacy because of

the difficulty of developing an integrated model to handle a realistic set of interrelated decisions. The solution was a collection of separate models, each of
which dealt with a distinct part of the problem. Communication between
these related models was left to the decision maker as a manual and intellectual
process.

A more enlightened view of models suggests that they be imbedded in an
information system with the database as the integration and communication
mechanism between them. Figure 8 summarizes the components of the model
base "box." The model creation process must be flexible, with a strong modeling language and a set of building blocks, much like subroutines, which can be
assembled to assist the modeling process. In fact, there are a set of model management functions, very much analogous to data management functions. The
key capabilities for a DSS in the model subsystems include:

- The ability to create new models quickly and easily

- The ability to catalog and maintain a wide range of models, supporting all
  levels of management

FIGURE 8   **The Models Subsystem**

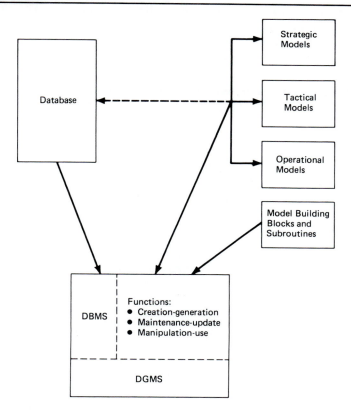

- The ability to interrelate these models with appropriate linkages through the database

- The ability to access and integrate model "building blocks"

- The ability to manage the model base with management functions analogous to database management (e.g., mechanisms for storing, cataloging, linking, and accessing models)

For a more detailed discussion of the model base and its management see [37, 38, 46].

The User System Interface

Much of the power, flexibility, and usability characteristics of a DSS are derived from capabilities in the user system interface. Bennett identifies the user, terminal, and software system as the components of the interface subsystem [5]. He then divides the dialogue, or interface experience itself, into three parts as shown in Figure 9:

1. *The action language*—what the user can do in communicating with the system. It includes such options as the availability of a regular keyboard, function keys, touch panels, joy stick, voice command, *etc.*
2. *The display or presentation language*—what the user sees. The display language includes options such as character or line printer, display screen, graphics, color, plotters, audio output, *etc.*
3. *The knowledge base*—what the user *must know*. The knowledge base consists

FIGURE 9 The User System Interface

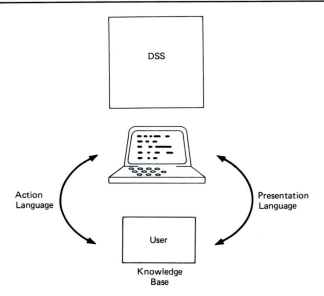

of what the user needs to bring to the session with the system in order to effectively use it. The knowledge may be in the user's head, on a reference card or instruction sheet, in a user's manual, in a series of "help" commands available upon request, *etc.*

The "richness" of the interface will depend on the strength of capabilities in each of these areas.

Another dimension of the user system interface is the concept of "dialogue style." Examples include the questions/answer approach, command languages, menus, and "fill in the blanks." Each style has pro's and con's depending on the type of user, task, and decision situation. For a more detailed discussion of dialogue styles see [13].

Although this just scratches the surface in this important area, a partial set of desirable capabilities for a DSS generator to support the user/system interface includes:

◆ the ability to handle a variety of dialogue styles, perhaps with the ability to shift among them at the user's choice;

◆ the ability to accommodate user actions in a variety of media;

◆ the ability to present data in a variety of formats and media; and

◆ the ability to provide the flexible support for the users' knowledge base.

The toolsmith view: the underlying technology

The toolsmith is concerned with the science involved in creating the information technology to support a DSS, and the architecture of combining the basic tools into a coherent system. The same three part model can be used to describe the toolsmith's concerns because the tools must be designed and combined to provide the three sets of capabilities.

Each of the three areas—dialogue, data handling, and model handling—has received a fair amount of attention from toolsmiths in the past. The topic of DSS and the requirements it imposes has put these efforts in a new perspective, revealing how they can be interrelated to increase their collective effectiveness. Moreover, the DSS requirements have revealed some missing elements in existing efforts, indicating valuable potential areas for development.

Dialogue Management

There has been a great deal of theoretical and some empirical work on systems requirements for good man/machine interface. Many of these studies are based on watching users' behavior in using terminals, or surveying users or programmers to ascertain what they want in interactive systems [10, 16]. A recent study examines a series of interactive applications, many of which are DSS's, to assess the *type* of software capabilities required by the applications [43]. This study led directly to some creative work on the software architecture for dialogue generation and management systems (DGMS) as characterized in the model of the previous section [12]. This research uses a relation as the data structure for storing each picture or "frame" used in the system, and a decision table for storing the control mechanism for representing the potential users' option in branching from one frame to another.

Data Management

Most of the significant work in the database management area during the past several years is aimed at transaction processing against large databases. Large DBMS's generally have inquiry/retrieval and flexible report preparation capabilities, but their largest contribution has been in the reduction of program maintenance costs through the separation of application programs and data definitions. On the other hand, DBMS work has generally had a rather naive view of the user and the user's requirements. A DSS user will not be satisfied merely with the capability to issue a set of retrieval commands which select items from the database, or even to display those selected items in a report with the flexible definition of format and headings. A DSS user needs to interact repeatedly and creatively with a relatively small set of data. The user may only need 40–100 data variables, but they must be the *right ones;* and what is right may change from day to day and week to week. Required data will probably include time series data which are not handled comprehensively by typical DBMS's. Better ways are needed to handle and coordinate time series data as well as mechanisms for capturing, processing, and tagging judgmental and probabilistic data. Better ways are also needed for extracting data from existing files and capturing data from previously non-computerized sources. The critical area of data extraction with fast response, which allows additions and deletions to the DSS database from the large transaction database, was a major contribution of the GADS work [8, 29]. In short, the significant development in database technology needs to be focused and extended in some key areas in order to directly serve the needs of a DSS.

Model Management

The area of model creation and handling may have the greatest potential contribution to a DSS. So far, the analytic capability provided by systems has evolved from statistical or financial analysis subroutines which can be called from a common command language. More recently, modeling languages provide a way of formulating interrelationships between variables in a way that permits the creation of simulation or "what if" models. As we noted earlier, many of the currently viable DSS Generators have evolved from these efforts. Early forms of "model management" seem to be evolving from enhancements to some modeling languages, which permit a model of this type to be used for sensitivity testing or goal seeking by specifying target and flexibility variables.

The model management area also has the potential for bringing some of the contributions of artificial intelligence (AI) to bear on a DSS. MYCIN, a system to support medical diagnosis, is based on "production rules," in the AI sense, which play the role of models in performing analytic and decision guidance functions [15]. A more general characterization of "knowledge management" as a way of handling models and data has also been tentatively explored [7]. More recent work proposes the use of a version of semantic networks for model representation [17]. Though this latter work is promising, AI research has shown the semantic network approach to be relatively inefficient with today's technology. Usable capabilities in model management in the near future are more likely to evolve from modeling languages, expanded subroutine approaches, and, in some cases, AI production rules.

Issues for the Future

At this stage in the development of the DSS area, issues, problems, and fruitful directions for further research/development are plentiful. At a "task force" meeting this summer, 30 researchers from 12 countries gathered to discuss the nature of DSS's and to identify issues for the future. Their list, developed in group discussions over several days, was quite long [19]. The issues given here, phrased as difficult questions, seem to be the ones that must be dealt with quickly, lest the promise and potential benefits of DSS's be diluted or seriously delayed.

What's a DSS?

Earlier it was noted that some skeptics regard DSS as "just another buzz word." This article has shown that there is a significant amount of content behind the label. The danger remains, however, that the bandwagon effect will outrun our ability to define and develop potential contributions of a DSS. The market imperatives of the multibillion dollar information systems industry tend to generate pressures to create simple labels for intuitively good ideas. It happened in many cases, but not all, of course, with MIS. Some companies are still trying to live down the aftereffects of the over-promise/under-undelivery/disenchantment sequence from the MIS bandwagon of the late '60's. Eventually, a set of minimal capabilities or characteristics which characterize a DSS should evolve. In the short range, a partial solution is education—supplying managers with intellectual ammunition they can use in dealing with vendors. Managers should and must ask sharp, critical questions about the capabilities of any purported DSS, matching them against what is really needed.

What is really needed?

After nearly two decades of advancements in information technology, the real needs of managers from an information system are not well understood. The issue is further complicated by the realization that managers' needs and the needs of other "knowledge workers" with which they interact are heavily interdependent. The DSS philosophy and approach has already shed some light on this issue by emphasizing "capabilities"—the ability for a manager to do things with an information system—rather than just "information needs" which too often infer data items and totals on a report.

Nevertheless, it is tempting to call for a hesitation in the development of DSS's until decision making and related managerial activities are fully understood. Though logically appealing, such a strategy is not practical. Neither the managers who face increasingly complex tasks, nor the information systems industry which has increasingly strong technology to offer, will be denied. They point out that a truly comprehensive theory of decision making has been pursued for years with minimum success.

A potential resolution of this problem is to develop and use a DSS in a way that reveals what managers can and should receive from an information system. For example, one of Scott Morton's early suggestions was that the system be designed to capture and track the steps taken by managers in the process of making key decisions, both as an aid to the analysis of the process, and as a potential training device for new managers.

The counterpart of the "needs" issue is the extent to which the system meets those needs, and the value of the performance increase that results. Evaluation of a DSS will be just as difficult, and important, as the evaluation of MIS has been. The direct and constant involvement of users, the ones in the best position to evaluate the systems, provides a glimmer of hope on this tough problem. Pursuit of these two tasks together may yield progress on both fronts with the kind of synergistic effect often sought from systems efforts. The iterative design approach and the three levels of technology afford the opportunity, if such a strategy is developed from the beginning.

Who will do it?

A series of organizational issues will revolve around the roles and organizational placement of the people who will take the principle responsibility for the development of DSS's. Initiative and guidance for DSS development efforts frequently come from the user area, not from the EDP/MIS area. Yet current technology still requires technical support from the information systems professional. The DSS builder may work for the vice president of finance, but the technical support role is still played by someone in the MIS department. To some extent, the demand for a DSS supports the more general trend to distribute systems development efforts out of the MIS department into the user department. The difference is that many DSS software systems, or generators, specifically attempt to directly reach the end user without involvement of the MIS group. The enlightened MIS administrator considers this a healthy trend, and willingly supplies the required technical support and coordination. Less enlightened DP administrators often see it as a threat. Some companies have set up a group specifically charged with developing DSS type applications. This strategy creates a team of "DSS Builders" who can develop the necessary skills in dealing with users, become familiar with the available technology, and define the steps in the developmental approach for DSS's.

How should it be done?

One of the pillars on which the success of DSS rests is the iterative development or adaptive design approach. The traditional five to seven stage system development process and the system life cycle concept have been the backbone of systems analysis for years. Most project management systems and approaches are based on it. The adaptive design approach, because it combines all the stages into one quick step which is repeated, will require a redefinition of system development milestones and a major modification of project management mechanisms. Since many traditional systems will not be susceptible to the iterative approach, a way is also needed for deciding when an application should be developed in the new way instead of the traditional way. The outline of the approach described earlier is conceptually straightforward for applications that require only personal support. It becomes more complicated for group or organizational support when there are multiple users. In short, DSS builders will need to develop a set of milestones, checkpoints, documentation strategies, and project management procedures for DSS applications, and recognize when they should be used.

How much can be done?

The final issue is a caveat dealing with the limitations of technical solutions to the complexity faced by managers and decision makers. As information systems professionals, we must be careful not to feel, or even allow others to feel, that we can develop or devise a technological solution to all the problems of management. Managers will always "deal with complexity in a state of perplexity"—it is the nature of the job. Information technology can, and is, making a major contribution to improving the effectiveness of people in this situation, but the solution will never be total. With traditional systems, we continually narrow the scope and definition of the system until we know it will do the job it is required to do. If the specification/design/construction/implementation process is done right, the system is a success, measured against its original objectives. With a DSS, the user and his systems capabilities are constantly pursuing the problem, but the underspecified nature of the problem insures that there will never be a complete solution. Systems analysts have always had a little trouble with humility, but the DSS process requires a healthy dose of modesty with respect to the ability of technology to solve all the problems of managers in organizations.

Conclusion

The "Framework for Development" described above attempts to show the dimensions and scope of DSS in a way that will promote the further *development* of this highly promising type of information system.

1. The relationships between EDP, MIS, and DSS show that DSS is only one of several important technology subsystems for improving organizational performance, and that DSS development efforts must carefully integrate with these other systems.
2. The three levels of technology and the interrelationships between people that use them provide a context for organizing the development effort.
3. The iterative design approach shows that the ultimate goal of the DSS development effort is the installation of an *adaptive system* consisting of all three levels of technology and their users operating and adapting to changes over time.
4. The performance objectives show the types of decision making to be served by, and the types of support which should be built into, a DSS as it is developed.
5. The three technical capabilities illustrate that development efforts must provide the DSS with capabilities in dialogue management, data management, and model management.
6. The issues discussed at the end of the article identify some potential roadblocks that must be recognized and confronted to permit the continued development of DSS.

In closing, it should now be clear that DSS is more than just a "buzz word," but caution must be used in announcing a new "era" in information systems. Perhaps the best term is a "DSS Movement" as user organizations, information systems vendors, and researchers become aware of the field, its potential, and the many unanswered questions. Events and mechanisms in the DSS Movement include systems development experience in organizations, hardware/software developments by vendors, publishing activities to report experience and research, and conferences to provide a forum for the exchange of ideas among interested parties.

It is clear that the momentum of the DSS Movement is building. With appropriate care and reasonable restraint, the coordinated efforts of managers, builders, toolsmiths, and researchers can converge in the development of a significant set of information systems to help improve the effectiveness of organizations and the people who work in them.

Questions

1. How are decision support systems different from the more traditional management information systems? How are they alike?

2. Distinguish between DSS generators and DSS tools and describe how both support Specific DSSs.

3. According to the article, how should decision support systems be developed? Do you think that this approach is still appropriate?

References

1. Alter, S. "A Taxonomy of Decision Support Systems," *Sloan Management Review*, vol. 19, no. 1, Fall 1977, pp. 39–56.
2. Alter, S. *Decision Support Systems: Current Practice and Continuing Challenges*, Reading, Mass.: Addison-Wesley, 1980.
3. Ashenhurst, R. L. "Curriculum Recommendations for Graduate Professional Programs in Information Systems," *ACM Communications*, vol. 15, no. 5, May 1972, pp. 363–398.
4. Barbosa, L. C., and Hirko, R. G. "Integration of Algorithmic Aids into Decision Support Systems," *MIS Quarterly*, vol. 4, no. 1, March 1980, pp. 1–12.
5. Bennett, J. "User-Oriented Graphics, Systems for Decision Support in Unstructured Tasks," in *User-Oriented Design of Interactive Graphics Systems*, S. Treu (ed.), New York: Association for Computing Machinery, 1977, pp. 3–11.
6. Boeing Computer Services, c/o Mr. Park Thoreson, P. O. Box 24346, Seattle, Wash. 98124.
7. Bonezek, H., Hosapple, C. W., and Whinston, A. "Evolving Roles of Models in Decision Support Systems," *Decision Sciences*, vol. 11, no. 2, April 1980, pp. 337–356.
8. Carlson, E. D., Bennett, J., Giddings, G., and Mantey, P. "The Design and Evaluation of an Interactive Geo-Data Analysis and Display System," *Information Processing-74*, Amsterdam, Holland: North Holland, 1974.
9. Carlson, E. D., and Sutton, J. A. "A Case Study of Non-Programmer Interactive Problem Solving," *IBM Research Report RJ1382*, San Jose, Calif., 1974.
10. Carlson, E. D., Grace, B. F., and Sutton, J. A. "Case Studies of End User Requirements for Interactive Problem-Solving Systems," *MIS Quarterly*, vol. 1, no. 1, March 1977, pp. 51–63.
11. Carlson, E. D. "An Approach for Designing Decision Support Systems," *Proceedings*, 11th Hawaii International Conference on Systems Sciences, North Hollywood, Calif.: Western Periodicals, 1978, pp. 76–96.
12. Carlson, E. D., and Metz, W. "Integrating Dialog Management and Data Management," *IBM Research Report RJ2738*, February 1, 1980, San Jose, Calif.
13. Carlson, E. D. "The User-Interface for Decision Support Systems," unpublished working paper, IBM Research Laboratory, San Jose, Calif.
14. Courbon, J., Drageof, J., and Jose, T. "L'Approache Evolutive," *Information et Gestion No. 103*, Grenoble, France: Institute d'Administration des Enterprises, January–February 1979, pp. 51–59.
15. Davis, R. "A DSS for Diagnosis and Therapy," *Data Base*, vol. 8, no. 3, Winter 1977, pp. 58–72.
16. Dzida, W., Herda, S., and Itzfeldt, W. D. "User-Perceived Quality of Software Interactive Systems," *Proceedings*, Third Annual Conference on Engineering (IEEE) Computer Society, Long Beach, Calif., 1978, pp. 188–195.
17. Elam, J., Henderson, J., and Miller, L. "Model Management Systems: An Approach to Decision Support in Complex Organizations," *Proceedings*, Conference on Information Systems, The Society for Management Information Systems, Philadelphia, Penn., December 1980.
18. Execucom Systems Corporation, P.O. Box 9758, Austin, Tex. 78766.
19. Fick, G., and Sprague, R. H., Jr. (eds). *Decision Support Systems: Issues and Challenges*, Oxford, England: Pergamon, 1981.
20. Gerrity, T. P., Jr. "Design of Man-Machine Decision Systems: An Application to Portfolio Management," *Sloan Management Review 12*, vol. 12, no. 2, Winter 1971, pp. 59–75.
21. Hayes, R. H., and Noland, R. L. "What Kind of Corporate Modeling Functions Best?" *Harvard Business Review*, vol. 52, May–June 1974, pp. 102–112.
22. Head, R. "Management Information Systems: A Critical Appraisal," *Datamation*, vol. 13, no. 5, May 1967, pp. 22–28.

23. Keen, P. G. W., and Scott Morton, M. S. *Decision Support Systems: An Organizational Perspective*, Reading, Mass.: Addison-Wesley, 1978.

24. Keen, P. G. W., and Hackathorn, R. D. "Decision Support Systems and Personal Computing," Department of Decision Sciences, The Wharton School, The University of Pennsylvania, Working Paper 79-01-03, Philadelphia, Penn., April 3, 1979.

25. Keen, P. G. W. "Adaptive Design for DSS," *Database*, vol. 12, no. 1 and 2, Fall 1980, pp. 15–25.

26. Keen, P. G. W. "Decision Support Systems: A Research Perspective," in *Decision Support Systems: Issues and Challenges*, Oxford, England: Pergamon, 1981.

27. Kroeber, H. W., Watson, H. J., and Sprague, R. H., Jr. "An Empirical Investigation and Analysis of the Current State of Information Systems Evolution," *Journal of Information and Management*, vol. 3, no. 1, February 1980, pp. 35–43.

28. Little, J. D. C. "Models and Managers: The Concept of a Decision Calculus," *Management Science*, vol. 16, no. 8, April 1970, pp. B466–485.

29. Mantey, P. E., and Carlson, E. D. "Integrated Geographic Data Bases: The GADS Experience," IBM Research Division, *IBM Research Report RJ2702*, San Jose, Calif., December 3, 1979.

30. Ness, D. N. "Decision Support Systems: Theories of Design," presented at the Wharton Office of Naval Research Conference on Decision Support Systems, Philadelphia, Penn., November 4–7, 1975.

31. Scott, J. H. "The Management Science Opportunity: A Systems Development Management Viewpoint," *MIS Quarterly*, vol. 2, no. 4, December 1978, pp. 59–61.

32. Scott Morton, M. S. *Management Decision Systems: Computer Based Support for Decision Making*, Cambridge, Mass.: Division of Research, Harvard University, 1971.

33. Simon, H. *The New Science of Management Decision*, New York: Harper & Row, 1960.

34. Simon, H. "Cognitive Science: The Newest Science of the Artificial," *Cognitive Science*, vol. 4, 1980, pp. 33–46.

35. Society for Management Information Systems, *Proceedings of the Eleventh Annual Conference*, Chicago, Ill., September 10–13, 1979, pp. 45–56.

36. Sprague, R. H., and Watson, H. J. "MIS Concepts Part I," *Journal of Systems Management*, vol. 26, no. 1, January 1975, pp. 34–37.

37. Sprague, R. H., and Watson, H. J. "Model Management in MIS," *Proceedings, 7th National AIDS*, Cincinnati, Ohio, November 5, 1975, pp. 213–215.

38. Sprague, R. H., and Watson, H. "A Decision Support System for Banks," *Omega— The International Journal of Management Science*, vol. 4, no. 6, 1976, pp. 657–671.

39. Sprague, R. H., and Watson, H. J. "Bit by Bit: Toward Decision Support Systems," *California Management Review*, vol. XXII, no. 1, Fall 1979, pp. 60–68.

40. Sprague, R. H. "Decision Support Systems—Implications for the Systems Analysts," *Systems Analysis and Design: A Foundation for the 1980's*, New York: Elsevier-North Holland, 1980.

41. Sprague, R. H., "A Framework for Research on Decision Support Systems," in *Decision Support Systems: Issues and Challenges*, G. Fick and R. H. Sprague (eds.), Oxford, England: Pergamon, 1981.

42. Sutton, J. "Evaluation of a Decision Support System: A Case Study with the Office Products Division of IBM," *IBM Research Report FJ2214*, San Jose, Calif., 1978.

43. Sutton, J. A., and Sprague, R. H. "A Study of Display Generation and Management in Interactive Business Applications," *IBM Research Report RJ2392*, IBM Research Division, San Jose, Calif., November 9, 1978.

44. TYMSHARE. 20705 Valley Green Driver, Cupertino, Calif., 95014.

45. Wagner, G. R. "DSS: Hypotheses and Inferences," Internal Report, EX-ECUCOM Systems Corporation, Austin, Tex., 1980.

46. Will, Hart J. "Model Management Systems," in *Information Systems and Organizational Structure*, E. Grochla and H. Szyperski (eds.), New York: Walter de Gruyter, 1975, pp. 467–483.

2.2

*The Management Information and Decision Support (MIDS) System at Lockheed-Georgia**

George Houdeshel and Hugh J. Watson

Introduction

Senior executives at Lockheed-Georgia are hands-on users of the management information and decision support system (MIDS). It clearly illustrates that a carefully designed system can be an important source of information for top management. Consider a few examples of how the system is used.

- The president is concerned about employee morale which for him is a critical success factor. He calls up a display which shows employee contributions to company-sponsored programs such as blood drives, United Way, and savings plans. These are surrogate measures of morale, and because they have declined, he becomes more sensitive to a potential morale problem.

- The vice president of manufacturing is interested in the production status of a C-5B aircraft being manufactured for the U.S. Air Force. He calls up a

*SOURCE: "The Management Information and Decision Support (MIDS) System at Lockheed-Georgia," by George Houdeshel and Hugh J. Watson, from *MIS Quarterly*, Vol. 11, Number 1, March 1987. Copyright 1987 by the Society for Information Systems Research Center at the University of Minnesota. Reprinted by special permission. Revised in May 1992 to describe the ongoing evolution of the MIDS system.

display which pictorially presents the location and assembly status of the plane and information about its progress relative to schedule. He concludes that the aircraft is on schedule for delivery.

♦ The vice president of finance wants to determine whether actual cash flow corresponds with the amount forecasted. He is initially concerned when a $10 million unfavorable variance is indicated, but an explanatory note indicates that the funds are en route from Saudi Arabia. To verify the status of the payment, he calls the source of the information using the name and telephone number shown on the display and learns that the money should be in a Lockheed account by the end of the day.

♦ The vice president of human resources returns from an out-of-town trip and wants to review the major developments which took place while he was gone. While paging through the displays for the human resources area, he notices that labor grievances rose substantially. To learn more about the situation so that appropriate action can be taken, he calls the supervisor of the department where most of the grievances occurred.

These are not isolated incidents; other important uses of MIDS occur many times a day. They demonstrate that computerized systems can have a significant impact on the day-to-day functioning of senior executives.

The purpose of this article is to describe aspects of MIDS which are important to executives, information systems managers, and information systems professionals who are the potential participants in the approval design, development, operation, and use of systems similar to MIDS. As a starting point, we want to discuss MIDS in the context of various types of information systems (i.e., MIS, DSS, and EIS), because its positioning is important to understanding its hands-on use by senior Lockheed-Georgia executives. We will describe how it was justified and developed, because these are the keys to its success. While online systems are best seen in person to be fully appreciated, we will try to describe what an executive experiences when using MIDS and the kinds of information that are available. Any computer system is made possible by the hardware, software, personnel, and data used and these will be described. Then we will discuss the benefits of MIDS. An organization considering the development of a system like MIDS needs to focus on key factors of success, and we will describe those factors that were most important to MIDS' success. As a closing point of interest, future plans for the evolution of MIDS will be discussed.

MIDS in Context

Management information systems (MIS) were the first attempt by information systems professionals to provide managers and other organizational personnel with the information needed to perform their jobs effectively and efficiently. While originators of the MIS concept initially had high hopes and expectations for MIS, in practice MIS largely came to represent an expanded set of structured reports and has had only a minimal impact on upper management levels [11].

Decision support systems (DSS) were the next attempt to help management with its decision-making responsibilities. They have been successful to some extent, especially in regard to helping middle managers and functional area specialists such as financial planners and marketing researchers. However, their usefulness to top management has been primarily indirect. Middle managers and staff specialists may use a DSS to provide information for top management, but despite frequent claims of ease-of-use, top managers are seldom hands-on users of a DSS [4, 5].

With hindsight it is understandable why DSSs have not been used directly by senior executives. Many of the reasons are those typically given when discussing why managers do not use computers: poor keyboard skills, lack of training and experience in using computers, concerns about status, and a belief that hands-on computer use is not part of their job. Another set of reasons revolves around the tradeoff between simplicity and flexibility of use. Simpler systems tend to be less flexible while more flexible systems are usually more complex. Because DSSs are typically used to support poorly structured decision-making tasks, the flexibility required to analyze these decisions comes at the cost of greater complexity. Unless the senior executive is a "techie" at heart, or uses the system enough to master its capabilities, it is unlikely that the executive will feel comfortable using the system directly. Consequently, hands-on use of the DSS is typically delegated to a subordinate who performs the desired analysis.

Executive information systems (EIS), or executive support systems as they are sometimes called, are the least computerized attempt to help satisfy top management's information needs. These systems tend to have the following characteristics which differentiate them from MIS and DSS:

- They are used directly by top managers without the assistance of intermediaries.

- They provide easy online access to current information about the status of the organization.

- They are designed with management's critical success factors (CSF) in mind.

- They use state-of-the-art graphics, communications, and data storage and retrieval methods.

The limited reportings of EIS suggest that these types of systems can make top managers hands-on users of computer-based systems [2, 10, 12]. While a number of factors contribute to their success, one of the most important is ease-of-use. Because an EIS provides little analysis capabilities, it normally requires only a few, easy to enter keystrokes. Consequently, keyboard skills, previous training and experience in using computers, concerns about loss of status, and perceptions of how one should carry out job responsibilities are less likely to hinder system use.

MIDS is an example of an EIS. It is used directly by top Lockheed-Georgia managers to access online information about the current status of the firm. Great care, time, and effort goes into providing information that meets the special needs of its users. The system is graphics-oriented and draws heavily upon communications technology.

The Evolution of MIDS

Lockheed-Georgia, a subsidiary of the Lockheed Corporation, is a major producer of cargo aircraft. Over 19,000 employees work at their Marietta, Georgia plant. Their current major activities are production of the C-5B transport aircraft for the U.S. Air Force, Hercules aircraft for worldwide markets, and numerous modification and research programs.

In 1975, Robert B. Ormsby, then President of Lockheed-Georgia, first expressed an interest in the creation of an online status reporting system to provide information which was concise, timely, complete, easy to access, relevant to management's needs, and could be shared by organizational personnel. Though Lockheed's existing systems provided voluminous quantities of data and information, Ormsby thought them to be unsatisfactory for several reasons. It was difficult to quickly locate specific information to apply to a given problem. Reports often were not sufficiently current, leading to organizational units basing decisions on information which should have been the same but actually was not. This is often the case when different reports or the same report with different release dates are used. Little action was taken for several years as Ormsby and information services personnel waited for hardware and software to emerge which would be suitable for the desired type of system. In the fall of 1978, development of the MIDS system began.

The justification for MIDS was informal. No attempt was made to cost-justify its initial development. Ormsby felt that he and other Lockheed-Georgia executives needed the system and mandated its development. Over time, as different versions of MIDS were judged successful, authorization was given to develop enhanced versions. This approach is consistent with current thinking and research on systems to support decision making. It corresponds closely with the recommendation to view the initial system as a research and development project and to evolve later versions if the system proves to be successful [7]. It also is in keeping with findings that accurate, timely, and new kinds of information, an organizational champion, and managerial mandate are the factors which motivate systems development [6].

A number of key decisions were made early in the design of the system. First, an evolutionary design approach would be used. Only a limited number of displays would be created initially. Over time they would be modified or possibly deleted if they did not meet an information need. Additional screens would be added as needed and as MIDS was made available to a larger group of Lockheed-Georgia managers. Ease-of-use was considered to be of critical importance because of the nature of the user group. Most of the Lockheed-Georgia executives had all of the normal apprehensions about personally using terminals. In order to encourage hands-on use, it was decided to place a terminal in each user's office, to require a minimum number of keystrokes in order to call up any screen, and to make training largely unnecessary. Response time was to be fast and features were to be included to assist executives in locating needed information.

Bob Pittman was responsible for the system's development and he, in turn, reported to the vice president of finance. Pittman initially had a staff consisting of two people from finance and two from information services. The finance personnel were used because of their experience in preparing company reports and presentations to the corporate headquarters, customers, and government agencies. Their responsibility was to determine the system's content, screen designs, and operational requirements. The information services personnel were responsible for hardware selection and acquisition and software development.

Pittman and his group began by exploring the information requirements of Ormsby and his staff. This included determining what information was needed, in what form, at what level of detail, and when it had to be updated. Several approaches were used in making these determinations. Interviews were held with Ormsby and his staff. Their secretaries were asked about information requested of them by their superiors. The use of existing reports was studied. From these analyses emerged an initial understanding of the information requirements.

The next step was to locate the best data sources for the MIDS system. Two considerations guided this process. The first was to use data sources with greater detail than what would be included in the MIDS displays. Only by using data which had not already been filtered and processed could information be generated which the MIDS team felt would satisfy the information requirements. The second was to use data sources which had a perspective compatible with that of Ormsby and his staff. Multiple organizational units may have data seemingly appropriate for satisfying an information need, but choosing the best source or combination of sources requires care in order that the information provided is not distorted by the perspective of the organizational unit in which it originates.

The initial version of MIDS took 6 months to develop and allowed Ormsby to call up 31 displays. Over the past 8 years, MIDS has evolved to where it now offers over 700 displays for 30 top executives and 40 operating managers. It has continued to be successful through many changes in the senior executive ranks, including the position of president. MIDS subsystems are currently being developed for middle managers in the various functional areas and MIDS-like systems are being implemented in several other Lockheed companies.

MIDS from the User's Perspective

An executive typically has little interest in the hardware or software used in a system. Rather, the dialog between the executive and the system is what matters. The dialog can be thought of as consisting of the command language by which the user directs the actions of the system, the presentation language through which the system provides the response, and the knowledge that the user must have in order to effectively use the system [1]. From a user's perspective, the dialog *is* the system, and consequently, careful attention was given to the design of the dialog components in MIDS.

An executive gains access to MIDS through the IBM PC/XT on his or her desk. Entering a password is the only sign-on requirement, and every user has a unique password which allows access to an authorized set of displays. After the password is accepted, the executive is informed of any scheduled downtime for system maintenance. The user is then given a number of options. He can enter a maximum of four keystrokes and call up any of the screens that he is authorized to view, obtain a listing of all screens that have been updated, press the "RETURN/ENTER" key to view the major menu, access the on-line keyword index, or obtain a listing of all persons having access to the system.

The main menu and keyword index are designed to help the executive find needed information quickly. Figure 1 shows the main menu. Each subject area listed in the main menu is further broken down into additional menus. Information is available in a variety of subject areas, including by functional area, organizational level, and project. The user can also enter the first three letters of any keywords which are descriptive of the information needed. The system checks these words against the keyword index and lists all of the displays which are related to the user's request.

Information for a particular subject area is organized in a top down fashion. This organization is used within a single display or in a series of displays. A summary graph is presented at the top of a screen or first in a series of displays, followed by supporting graphs, and then by tables and text. This approach allows executives to quickly gain an overall perspective while providing backup detail when needed. An interesting finding has been that executives prefer as much information as possible on a single display, even if it appears "busy," rather than having the same information spread over several displays.

Executives tend to use MIDS differently. At one extreme are those who browse through displays. An important feature for them is the ability to stop the generation of a display with a single keystroke when it is not of further interest. At the other extreme are executives who regularly view a particular sequence of displays. To accommodate this type of system use, sequence files can be employed which allow executives to page through a series of displays whose sequence is defined in advance. Sequence files can either be created by the user, requested by the user and prepared by the MIDS staff, or offered by MIDS personnel after observing the user's viewing habits.

All displays contain a screen number, title, when it was last updated, the source(s) of the information presented, and a telephone number for the source(s). It also indicates the MIDS staff member who is responsible for maintaining the display. Every display has a backup person who is responsible for it when the primary person is on leave, sick, or unavailable for any reason. Knowing the information source and the identity of the responsible MIDS staff member is important when an executive has a question about a display.

Standards exist across the displays for the terms used, color codes, and graphic designs. These standards help eliminate possible misinterpretations of the information provided. Standard definitions have also improved communications in the company.

FIGURE 1 The MIDS Main Menu

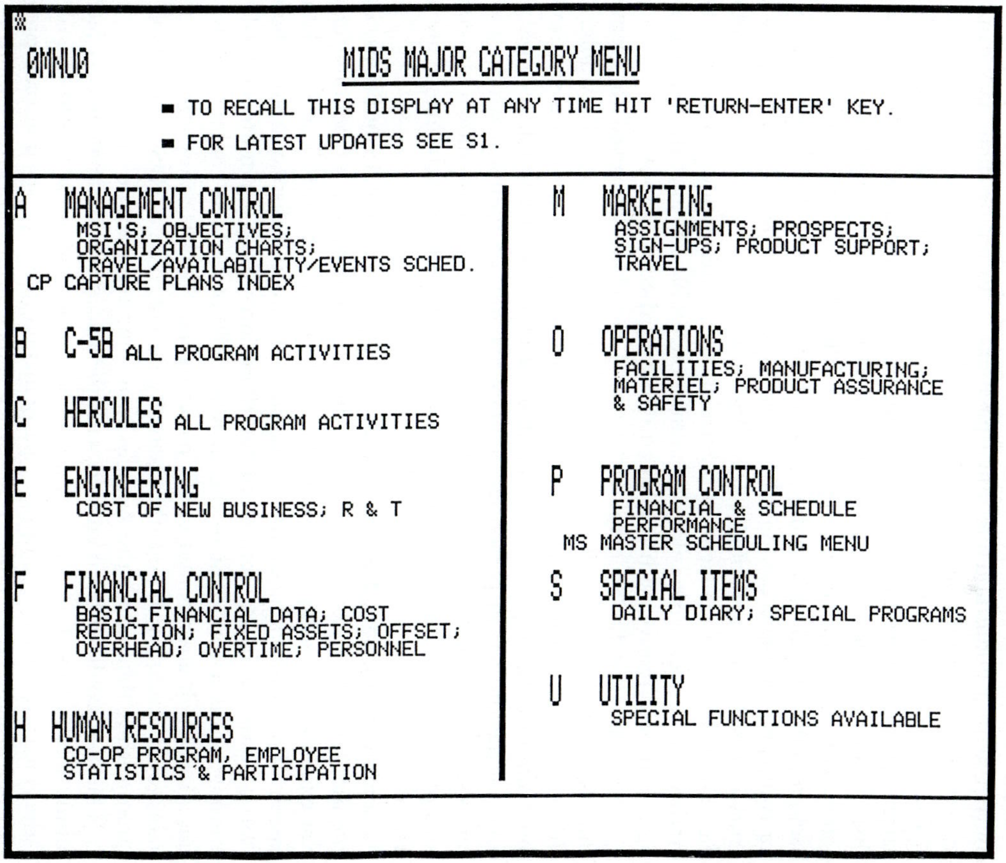

```
OMNU0          MIDS MAJOR CATEGORY MENU

               ■ TO RECALL THIS DISPLAY AT ANY TIME HIT 'RETURN-ENTER' KEY.
               ■ FOR LATEST UPDATES SEE S1.


A  MANAGEMENT CONTROL                       M  MARKETING
   MSI'S; OBJECTIVES;                           ASSIGNMENTS; PROSPECTS;
   ORGANIZATION CHARTS;                          SIGN-UPS; PRODUCT SUPPORT;
   TRAVEL/AVAILABILITY/EVENTS SCHED.             TRAVEL
CP CAPTURE PLANS INDEX

B  C-5B ALL PROGRAM ACTIVITIES              O  OPERATIONS
                                               FACILITIES; MANUFACTURING;
                                               MATERIEL; PRODUCT ASSURANCE
                                               & SAFETY
C  HERCULES ALL PROGRAM ACTIVITIES

                                            P  PROGRAM CONTROL
E  ENGINEERING                                 FINANCIAL & SCHEDULE
   COST OF NEW BUSINESS; R & T                  PERFORMANCE
                                            MS MASTER SCHEDULING MENU

F  FINANCIAL CONTROL                        S  SPECIAL ITEMS
   BASIC FINANCIAL DATA; COST                   DAILY DIARY; SPECIAL PROGRAMS
   REDUCTION; FIXED ASSETS; OFFSET;
   OVERHEAD; OVERTIME; PERSONNEL
                                            U  UTILITY
                                               SPECIAL FUNCTIONS AVAILABLE
H  HUMAN RESOURCES
   CO-OP PROGRAM; EMPLOYEE
   STATISTICS & PARTICIPATION
```

83

The importance of standard definitions can be illustrated by the use of the word "signup." In general, the term refers to a customer's agreement to buy an aircraft. However, prior to the establishment of a standard definition, it tended to be used differently by various organizational units. To marketing people, a signup was when a letter of intent to buy was received. Legal services considered it to be when a contract was received. Finance interpreted it as when a down payment was made. The standard definition of a signup now used is "a signed contract with a nonrefundable down payment." An online dictionary can be accessed if there is any question about how a term is defined.

Color is used in a standard way across all of the screens. The traffic light pattern is used for status: green is good; yellow is marginal; and red is unfavorable. Under budget or ahead of schedule is in green; on budget or on schedule is in yellow; over budget and behind schedule is in red. Bar graphs have a black background and yellow bars depict actual performance, cyan (light blue) is used for company goals and commitments to the corporate office, and magenta represents internal goals and objectives. Organization charts use different colors for the various levels of management. Special color combinations are used to accommodate executives with color differentiation problems, and all displays are designed to be effective with black and white hard copy output.

Standards exist for all graphic designs. Line charts are used for trends, bar charts for comparisons, and pie or stacked bar charts for parts of a whole. On all charts, vertical wording is avoided and abbreviations and acronyms are limited to those on an authorized list. All bar charts are zero at the origin to avoid distortions, scales are set in prescribed increments and are identical within a subject series, and bars that exceed the scale have numeric values shown. In comparisons of actual with predicted performance, bars for actual performance are always wider.

Comments are added to the displays to explain abnormal conditions, explain graphic depictions, reference related displays, and inform of pending changes. For example, a display may show that signups for May are three less than forecasted. The staff member who is responsible for the display knows, however, that a down payment from Peru for three aircrafts is en route and adds this information as a comment to the display. Without added comments, situations can arise which are referred to as "paper tigers," because they appear to require managerial attention though they actually do not. The MIDS staff believes that "transmitting data is not the same as conveying information" [8].

The displays have been created with the executives' critical success factors in mind. Some of the CSF measures, such as profits and aircrafts sold, are obvious. Other measures, such as employee participation in company-sponsored programs, are less obvious and reflect the MIDS staff's efforts to fully understand and accommodate the executives' information needs.

To illustrate a typical MIDS display, Figure 2 shows Lockheed-Georgia sales as of November 1986. It was accessed by entering F.3. The sources of the information and their Lockheed-Georgia telephone numbers are in the upper right-hand corner. The top graphs provide past history, current, and forecasted sales. The wider bars (in yellow) represent actual sales while budgeted sales are depicted by the narrower, (cyan) bars. Detailed, tabular information is provided

FIGURE 2 The Status of a Sale

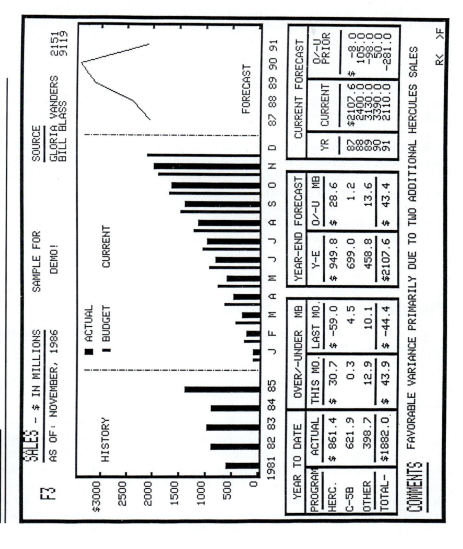

under the graphs. An explanatory comment is given at the bottom of the display. The R and F in the bottom right-hand corner indicate that related displays can be found by paging in a reverse or forward direction.

Executives are taught to use MIDS in a 15 minute tutorial. For several reasons, no written instructions for the use of the system have ever been prepared. An objective for MIDS has been to make the system easy enough to use so that written instructions are unnecessary. Features such as menus and the keyword index make this possible. Another reason is that senior executives are seldom willing to take the time to read instructions. And most importantly, if an executive has a problem in using the system, the MIDS staff prefers to learn about the problem and to handle it personally.

The IBM PC/XT on the executive's desk is useful for applications other than accessing MIDS displays. It can be used offline with any appropriate PC software. It is also the mechanism for tying the user through MIDS to other computer systems. For example, some senior executives and even more middle managers want access to outside reference services or internal systems with specific databases. Electronic messaging is the most common use of the IBM PC/XT's for other than MIDS displays. The executive need only request PROFS from within MIDS and the system automatically translates the user's MIDS password to a PROFS password and transfers the user from the DEC 780 VAX host to the IBM mainframe with PROFS. After using PROFS' electronic mail capabilities, the transfer back to MIDS is a simple two keystroke process.

The Components of MIDS

A number of component parts are essential to the functioning of MIDS: hardware, software, MIDS personnel, and data sources.

Hardware

A microcomputer from Intelligent Systems Corporation was used for the initial version of MIDS. Each day MIDS personnel updated the floppy disks which stored the displays. As more executives were given access to MIDS, it became impractical to update each executive's displays separately, and the decision was made to store them centrally on a DEC 11/34 where they could be accessed by all users. Executives currently interact with MIDS through IBM PC/XT's tied to a DEC 780 VAX. Next year MIDS will be migrated to an IBM 3081 as part of Lockheed's plan to standardize around IBM equipment. Because an objective of MIDS was to reduce the amount of paper, the generation of hard copy output has always been minimized. The only printers are in the MIDS office and include four Printronix 300 (black and white, dot matrix) and Xerox 6500 (color copier, laser unit, with paper and transparencies) printers.

Software

At the time that work on MIDS began, appropriate software was not commercially available. Consequently, the decision was made to develop the software in-house. Even though commercial EIS software such as Command Center and Metaphor are now available, none of it has justified a switch from what has been developed by the MIDS staff.

The software is used for three important tasks: creating and updating the displays; providing information about the system's use and status; and maintaining system security.

Creating and updating the displays

Each display has an edit program tailored to fit its needs. Special edit routines have been developed for graph drawing, color changes, scale changes, roll-offs, calculations, or drawing special characters such as airplanes. These edit functions are then combined to create a unique edit program for each display. This approach allows MIDS personnel to quickly update the displays and differs from off-the-shelf software which requires the user to answer questions for all routines, regardless of whether they are needed.

The edit software has other attractive features. There are computer-generated messages to the information analyst advising of other displays which could be affected by changes to the one currently being revised. Color changes are automatically made to display when conditions become unfavorable. When the most recent period data is entered, the oldest period data is automatically rolled off of all graphs. The edit software has error checks for unlikely or impossible conditions.

Providing information about the system's use and status

Daily reports are generated at night and are available the next morning for the MIDS staff to review. A daily log of system activity shows who requested what, when, and how. The log indicates everything but "why," and sometimes the staff even asks that question in order to better understand management's information needs. The log allows MIDS personnel to analyze system loads, user inquiry patterns, methods used to locate displays, utilization of special features, and any system and/or communication problems. Another report indicates the status of all displays, including the last time each display was updated, when the next update is scheduled, and who is responsible for the update. Yet another report lists all displays which have been added, deleted, or changed.

Weekly reports are generated on Sunday night and are available Monday morning for the MIDS staff. One report lists the previous week's users and the number of displays viewed by each executive. Another report lists the number of displays with the frequency of viewing by the president and his staff and others.

A number of reports are available on demand. They include an authorization matrix of users and terminals; a count of displays by major category and subsystem; a list of users by name, type of terminal, and system line number to the host computer; a list of displays in sequence; a list of display titles with their number organized by subject area; and a keyword exception report of available displays not referenced in the keyword file.

Maintaining system security

Careful thought goes into deciding who has access to which displays. Information is made available unless there are compelling reasons why it should be denied. For example, middle managers might not be allowed to view strategic plans for the company. System access is controlled through a double security system. Users can call up only displays which they are authorized to view and then only from certain terminals. This security system helps protect against unauthorized users gaining access to the system and the unintentional sharing of restricted information. As an example of the latter situation, a senior executive might be allowed to view sensitive information in his office, but be denied access to the information in a conference room or the office of lower management.

Personnel

The MIDS staff has grown from five to its current size of nine. Six of the staff members are classified as information analysts, two are computer analysts, and there is the manager of the MIDS group. The information analysts are responsible for determining the system's content, designing the screens, and keeping the system operational. Each information analyst is responsible for about 100 displays. Approximately 170 displays are updated daily by the MIDS staff. The computer analysts are responsible for hardware selection and acquisition and software development. While the two groups have different job responsibilities, they work together and make suggestions to each other for improving the system.

It is imperative that the information analysts understand the information that they enter into the system. Several actions are taken to ensure that this is the case. Most of the information analysts have work experience and/or training in the areas for which they supply information. They are encouraged to take courses which provide a better understanding of the users' areas. And they frequently attend functional area meetings, often serving as an important information resource.

Data

In order to provide the information needed, a variety of internal and external data sources must be used. The internal sources include transaction processing systems, financial applications, and human sources. Some of the data can be transferred directly to MIDS from other computerized systems, while others must be rekeyed or entered for the first time. Access to computerized data is provided by in-house software and commercial software such as DATATRIEVE. External sources are very important and include data from external databases, customers, other Lockheed companies, and Lockheed's Washington, D.C. office.

MIDS relies on both hard and soft data. Hard data comes from sources such as transaction processing systems and provides "the facts." Soft data often comes from human sources and results in information which could not be obtained in any other way; it provides meaning, context, and insight to hard data.

Benefits of MIDS

A variety of benefits are provided by MIDS: better information; improved communications; an evolving understanding of information requirements; a test-bed for system evolution; and cost reductions.

The information provided by MIDS has characteristics which are important to management. It supports decision making by identifying areas which require attention, providing answers to questions, and giving knowledge about related areas. It provides relevant information. Problem areas are highlighted and pertinent comments are included. The information is timely because displays are updated as important events occur. It is accurate because of the efforts of the MIDS staff, since all information is verified before it is made available.

MIDS has also improved communications in several ways. It is sometimes used to share information with vendors, customers, legislators, and others. MIDS users are able to quickly view the same information in the same format with the most current update. In the past, there were often disagreements, especially over the telephone, because executives were operating with different information. PROFS provides electronic mail. The daily diary announces major events as they occur.

Initially identifying a complete set of information requirements is difficult or impossible for systems which support decision making. The evolutionary nature of MIDS' development has allowed users to better understand and evolve their information requirements. Having seen a given set of information in a given format, an executive is often prompted to identify additional information or variations of formats that provide still better decision support.

The current system provides a test-bed for identifying and testing possible system changes. New state-of-the-art hardware and software can be compared with the current system in order to provide information for the evolution of MIDS. For example, a mouse-based system currently is being tested.

MIDS is responsible for cost savings in several areas. Many reports and graphs which were formerly produced manually are now printed from MIDS and distributed to non-MIDS users. Some requirements for special reports and presentation materials are obtained at less cost by modifying standard MIDS displays. Reports that are produced by other systems are summarized in MIDS and are no longer printed and distributed to MIDS users.

The Success of MIDS

Computer-based systems can be evaluated on the basis of cost/benefit, frequency of use, and user satisfaction considerations. Systems which support decision making, such as MIDS, normally do not lend themselves to a quantified assessment of their benefits. They do provide intangible benefits, however, as can be seen in the following example.

Lockheed-Georgia markets its aircrafts worldwide. In response to these efforts, it is common for a prospective buyer to call a company executive to discuss a proposed deal. Upon receipt of a phone call, the executive can call up a display which provides the following information: the aircraft's model and quantity; the dollar value of the offer; the aircraft's availability for delivery; previous purchases by the prospect; the sales representative's name and exact location for the week; and a description of the status of the possible sale. Such a display is shown in Figure 3. All of this information is available without putting the prospective customer on hold, transferring the call to someone else, or awaiting the retrieval of information from a file.

When a user can choose whether or not to use a system, frequency of use can be employed as a measure of success. Table 1 presents data on how the number of users and displays and the mean number of displays viewed per day by each executive has changed over time. The overall picture is one of increased usage; currently an average of 5.5 screens are viewed each day by the 70 executives who have access to MIDS. Unlike some systems which are initially successful but quickly fade away, the success of MIDS has increased over time.

Frequency of use can be a very imperfect measure of success. The MIDS group recognizes that a single display which has a significant impact on decision making is much more valuable than many screens which are paged through with passing interest. Consequently, frequency of use is used as only one indicator of success.

MIDS personnel have felt no need to conduct formal studies of user satisfaction. The data on system usage and daily contact with MIDS users provide ample information on how satisfied users are with MIDS. User satisfaction can be illustrated by the experience of Paul Frech who was Vice President of operations in 1979. When MIDS was offered to him, he had little interest in the system because he had well-established channels for the flow of information to support his job responsibilities. Shortly afterwards, Frech was promoted to the corporate headquarters staff in California. When he was again promoted to become the President of Lockheed-Georgia, MIDS had become a standard for executive information and he was reintroduced to the system. He has stated:

> I assumed the presidency of the Lockheed-Georgia Company in June 1984, and the MIDS system had been in operation for some time prior to that. The MIDS system enabled me to more quickly evaluate the current conditions of each of our operational areas and, although I had not been an advocate of executive computer systems, the ease and effectiveness of MIDS made it an essential part of my informational sources.

FIGURE 3 Lockheed-Georgia Sales

```
※    PERU
M5   ——————
     REP: DICK SIGLER                    SOURCE   BUD LAWLER    5431
                                                  JIM CERTAIN   2265

              MON   TUE   WED   THR   FRI   SAT   SUN
REP LOCATION  ---   ---   ---   ---   ---   ---   ---
IF AWAY                         CARACAS, VENEZUELA----------

FORECAST - THREE L-100-30s                       PREV.HERC.BUY----8

NEXT EVENT---               AS OF TODAY:  MEETINGS CONTINUE AMONG POTENTIAL
   FINALIZE FINANCING       LENDING INSTITUTIONS, INSURERS, AND GELAC'S INTER-
                            NATIONAL MARKETING/FINANCE/LEGAL TEAM TO DISCUSS
                            REQUIREMENTS AND CONDITIONS FOR FINANCING.  GELAC
KEY PERSON---CERTAIN        REPRESENTATIVES WILL BE IN LIMA MONDAY TO LAY GROUND-
                            WORK FOR FINAL NEGOTIATIONS.  NO PROBLEMS EXPECTED.
SIGN-UP-----NEXT MONTH

PROBABILITY--GOOD

ROM VALUE---$60M

A/C DELIVERY: 4th QTR
```

91

TABLE 1   MIDS Users, Displays and Displays Viewed

Year	Number of Users	Number of Displays	Mean Number of Displays Viewed, Per User Per Day
1979	12	69	*
1980	24	231	*
1981	27	327	*
1982	31	397	3
1983	31	441	4
1984	49	620	4.2
1985	70	710	5.5

* Figures not available

Because Frech and other senior executives have come to rely on MIDS, middle managers at Lockheed-Georgia and executives at other Lockheed companies want their own versions of MIDS. Within Lockheed-Georgia there is the feeling that "if the boss likes it, I need it." Currently, MIDS personnel are helping middle functional area managers develop subsystems of MIDS and are assisting other Lockheed companies with the development of similar systems.

Keys to the Success of MIDS

Descriptions of successful systems are useful to people responsible for conceptualizing, approving, and developing similar systems. Perhaps even more important are insights about what makes a system a success. We will identify the keys to MIDS' success here, but it should be remembered that differences exist among executive information systems, organizations, and possibly the factors that lead to success.

1. *A committed senior executive sponsor.* Ormsby served as the organizational champion for MIDS. He wanted a system like MIDS, committed the necessary resources, participated in its creation, and encouraged its use by others.
2. *Carefully defined system requirements.* Several considerations governed the design of the system. It had to be custom-tailored to meet the information needs of its users. Ease-of-use, an absolutely essential item to executives who were wary of computers, was critical. Response time had to be fast. The displays had to be updated quickly and easily as conditions changed.
3. *Carefully defined information requirements.* There has been a continuing effort to understand management's information requirements. Displays have been added, modified, and deleted over time. Providing information relevant to managements' CSFs has been of paramount importance.

4. *A team approach to systems development.* The staff that developed, operates, and evolves MIDS combines information systems skills and functional area knowledge. The computer analysts are responsible for the technical aspects of the system while the information analysts are responsible for providing the information needed by management. This latter responsibility demands that the information analysts know the business and maintain close contact with information sources and users.

5. *An evolutionary development approach.* The initial version of MIDS successfully addressed the most critical information needs of the company president and strengthened his support for the system. There is little doubt that developing a fully integrated system for a full complement of users would have resulted in substantial delays and less enthusiasm for the system. Over the years, MIDS has expanded and evolved as more users have been provided access to MIDS, management's information requirements have changed, better ways to analyze and present information have been discovered, and improved computer technology has become integrated into the system.

6. *Careful computer hardware and software selection.* The decision to proceed with the development of MIDS was made when good color terminals at reasonable prices became available. At that time graphics software was very limited and it was necessary to develop the software for MIDS in-house. The development of MIDS could have been postponed until hardware and software with improved performance at reduced cost appeared, but this decision would have delayed providing management with the information needed. Also affecting the hardware selection was the existing hardware within the organization and the need to integrate MIDS into the overall computing architecture. While it is believed that excellent hardware and software decisions have been made for MIDS, different circumstances at other firms may lead to different hardware and software configurations.

MIDS II: The Ongoing Story

In 1990, after 12 years of successful MIDS operations, it became necessary to update the hardware technology used with Lockheed's executive information system. This change was required because the Intelligent Systems Company (ISC) graphics computers that were used by the MIDS support staff to design and update the screens were no longer in production, and replacement parts were becoming increasingly difficult to find. The MIDS staff faced the real possibility of not being able to maintain the system because of a lack of hardware. Faced with this situation, it was decided to undertake a comprehensive review of the hardware and software options that were available for EIS.

After a review of the software alternatives, it was decided that it was more economical to purchase commercial EIS software than to develop another system in-house. Several commercial products were evaluated and Comshare's Commander EIS was ultimately chosen. This best-selling product offers a large

TABLE 2   Capabilities of Commander EIS

- Support for multiple user interfaces
- Online, context-dependent help screens
- Command files
- Multiple methods for locating information
- Access to external databases (for example, Dow Jones News Retrieval)
- Interfaces to other software (for example, Profs, Lotus 1-2-3)
- Integrated decision support (for example, System W, IFPS)
- Easy screen design and maintenance
- Screen design templates
- Application shells
- Data extraction from existing organizational databases
- Graphical, tabular, and textual information on the same screen
- Integration of data from different sources
- Security for data, screens, and systems
- Support for rapid prototyping
- Support for multiple computing platforms
- Support for hard-copy output (for example, paper, overhead transparencies, 35 mm slides)

number of capabilities that facilitate the development and maintenance of an EIS (see Table 2). Two important changes to the Comshare software were requested, however, before a contract was signed. The changes retained capabilities that were in MIDS but not in Commander EIS. It was deemed important to the MIDS staff that the changes be made to the basic Comshare product and not to just a special version for Lockheed in order to ensure compatibility with later releases of the Comshare software.

The two changes permitted users to operate the system through a keyboard (in addition to a mouse or touch screen) and provided for monitoring the use of the system. Lockheed executives had enjoyed the MIDS system advantage of going from one screen to any other screen without retracing a path or returning to a predetermined point. This capability was retained by allowing executives to enter the number of the desired screen. Monitoring of system usage had always been performed by the MIDS system management and it had become invaluable in keeping the MIDS system up-to-date. With these changes, Commander EIS became the development environment for MIDS II.

Even though commercial EIS software was selected for MIDS II, the original screen designs were retained. In fact, when Lockheed asked vendors to prepare demonstration prototypes, they requested screens that looked like those currently in use. Considerable thought and experimentation had gone into screen design over the years. Lockheed's executives were familiar with them, and MIDS II was to continue the look and feel of the original system.

In addition to new software, hardware improvements were made to take advantage of state-of-the-art technology and to position MIDS II in Lockheed's long-range computing plans. The Comshare software helped make this possible because of its ability to run on a mixed platform of IBM PS/2s and Apple Macintoshes. The executives use PS/2s and screens are developed and maintained on Macintoshes by the support staff. A Novell local area network was installed to improve the system's response time and reliability.

MIDS II was developed and rolled out to users in 1992 and is expected to provide a variety of benefits over the original system: faster response time, easier navigation through the system (drilldown to related, more detailed information), better links to other resources (internal and external databases), reduced maintenance costs (automatic update of some screens), shared EIS techniques with other Commander EIS users, and a state-of-the-art technology platform that permits future improvements and growth within information systems long-range plans. The original MIDS system has served Lockheed very well since 1978, and MIDS II is designed to carry this tradition into the future.

Questions

1. Is the distinction made by the authors between decision support systems (DSS) and executive information systems (EIS) a useful one? Why or why not?

2. What factors do you feel were the most essential to the success of Lockheed-Georgia's MIDS?

3. How was the investment in MIDS justified? Would such an approach work in an organization with which you are familiar?

4. What led to the development of MIDS II?

References

1. Bennett, J. "User-Oriented Graphics, Systems for Decision Support in Unstructured Tasks," in *User-Oriented Design of Interactive Graphics Systems*, S. Treu (ed.), New York: Association for Computing Machinery, 1977, pp. 3–11.
2. DeLong, D. W., and Rockart, J. F. "Identifying the Attributes of Successful Executive Support System Implementation," *Transactions from the Sixth Annual Conference on Decision Support Systems*, J. Fedorowicz (ed.), Washington, D.C., April 21–24, 1986, pp. 41–54.
3. El Sawy, O. A. "Personal Information Systems for Strategic Scanning in Turbulent Environments: Can the CEO Go On-Line?" *MIS Quarterly*, vol. 9, no. 1, March 1985, pp. 53–60.
4. Friend, D. "Executive Information Systems: Success, Failure, Insights and Misconceptions," *Transactions from the Sixth Annual Conference on Decision Support Systems*, J. Fedorowicz (ed.), Washington, D.C., April 21–24, 1986, pp. 35–40.
5. Hogue, J. T., and Watson, H. J. "An Examination of Decision Makers' Utilization of Decision Support System Output," *Information and Management*, vol. 8, no. 4, April 1985, pp. 205–212.
6. Hogue, J. T., and Watson, H. J. "Management's Role in the Approval and Administration of Decision Support Systems," *MIS Quarterly*, vol. 7, no. 2, June 1983, pp. 15–23.

7. Keen, P. G. W. "Value Analysis: Justifying Decision Support Systems," *MIS Quarterly*, vol. 5, no. 1, March 1981, pp. 1–16.
8. McDonald, E. "Telecommunications," *Government Computer News*, February 28, 1986, p. 44.
9. Rockart, J. F. "Chief Executives Define Their Own Data Needs," *Harvard Business Review*, vol. 57, no. 2, January–February 1979, pp. 81–93.
10. Rockart, J. F., and Treacy, M. E. "The CEO Goes On-Line," *Harvard Business Review*, vol. 60, no. 1, January–February 1982, pp. 32–88.
11. Sprague, R. H., Jr. "A Framework for the Development of Decision Support Systems," *MIS Quarterly*, vol. 4, no. 4, December 1980, pp. 10–26.
12. Sundue, D. G. "GenRad's On-line Executives," *Transactions from the Sixth Annual Conference on Decision Support Systems*, J. Fedorowicz (ed.), Washington, D.C., April 21–24, 1986, pp. 14–20.

2.3

Choosing an Expert Systems Game Plan*

C. Lawrence Meador and Ed G. Mahler

In the world of baseball, there are many ways to score a run. The brute force of a power hitter can certainly do the job in dramatic fashion. But so, too, can the individual efforts of players working their way down the bases with infield hits and walks. By the ninth inning, it matters little how each team planned and plotted to rack up its runs. Only the total score—and who came out on top—really counts.

Choosing an expert systems strategy also involves making a series of choices from the beginning of the game. As in baseball, there is no right or wrong approach to winning with expert systems technology. But choosing a strategy that fits your company's culture and structure has a lot to do with your chances for ultimate success.

Five years ago, E. I. du Pont de Nemours & Co. opted to train its end users to develop their own small systems. Today, the more than 600 expert systems installed in DuPont's business units are cumulatively saving more than $75 million per year. By 1991, this expert systems program is expected to contribute more than $100 million annually to the bottom line.

Over the last 10 years, Digital Equipment Corp. has evolved an equally successful program following an entirely different strategy. To begin its expert system efforts organization, Digital established the Artificial Intelligence Technology Center (AITC) in Marlborough, Mass. AITC has become a strategic resource for training highly skilled knowledge engineers. The result is a fast-growing number of operational and strategic systems affecting all its business processes. Digital now has 50 major expert systems in place, contributing $200 million in annual savings.

DuPont and Digital share a fundamental expert systems goal: to improve decision making throughout the corporation by putting relevant information and knowledge into the hands of those making the decisions. But the routes the companies have chosen in achieving this goal are very different.

DuPont uses a "dispersed" approach to expert systems development. End users develop their own systems using standard, low-cost tools.

The "specialist" approach used by Digital typically involves a centralized development center where specially trained programmers or knowledge engineers use custom tools to create systems. Generally, the systems are more complex and are used by more people than those created under the dispersed approach.

Each approach can vary in the way that it's controlled and deployed, and many companies are evolving systems that use elements of both approaches. In choosing an expert system for your company, you should ask questions in the following areas:

Knowledge. What are the critical points of decision-making for the business? Is it critical to share knowledge between departments or is knowledge highly localized?

Resources. What is the state of your company's current information systems infrastructure? What is the computer literacy level of the employees? And what is your company's IS strategy?

At first glance, DuPont and Digital appear to have a lot in common. Both are global, highly decentralized organizations. Both have 120,000 employees and more than 100 plants worldwide. But that's where the similarity ends.

Digital's focus is on a single basic technology and a single architecture, with a primary emphasis on selling computer systems to end users. DuPont is a federation of businesses that produces products in almost every category found in a host of categories: fibers, plastics, chemicals, imaging systems, oil, coal, automotive products, electronics, agricultural products and medical products. DuPont offers an array of product types that are typically several sales away from the end user. For instance, the nylon it manufactures may ultimately end up in carpet made by Karastan and sold to the consumer by Sears Roebuck & Co.

The Knowledge Profile

The term "knowledge profile" describes the patterns of information flow throughout a company. Some companies require a tight integration of information between departments, while others function well with localized wisdom.

Although Digital also has a vast array of products—namely, 43 computer families comprise some 30,000 parts—most of these products must function under the constraints of a single computer architecture. That's a fundamental corporate totem, the basic strategy through which Digital tries to differentiate itself. Each part must plug and play with all the others, and the knowledge possessed by each function must be aligned with the others to create the final product.

Sales, for example, must be able to propose systems that are technically correct, manufacturing must be able to verify that an order can be produced and field service must know how and when to assemble the system at the customer's site.

At DuPont, the distribution of knowledge parallels the organizational structure—both are localized. The knowledge required to manufacture nylon in Seaford, Del., has nothing to do with the knowledge needed to sell Teflon in Hamburg, West Germany. Fiber production is a world away from coal mining.

Furthermore, enormous disparity exists within each product line. Most of the company's 1,700 product lines each contain several hundred subtypes. Some, such as the electronics connectors business, range up to 500,000 items. Even within a single plant, the individual assembly lines may differ.

Such dispersed knowledge pushed DuPont to its roll-your-own approach to expert systems. So did the organization's culture. DuPont *nurtures* fierce independence and technical excellence throughout *its* federation—a prerequisite for a company trying to stay on the leading edge in so many arenas.

Another DuPont characteristic begs for the dispersed approach. At DuPont, big is not necessarily beautiful. Large problems can be broken into small pieces that an individual expert can tackle. If care is taken to create standard interfaces—in this case, between expert systems—each of those solutions can be linked later to solve bigger problems. In one plant, for example, an expert system for process-control troubleshooting is actually an agglomeration of smaller systems designed for troubleshooting various components.

Understanding the resource profile of an organization is critical to devising a strategy for implementing expert systems, no matter which approach is followed. First, an effective resource profile dictates that the company's information systems infrastructure—the hardware platforms, the networks, the databases—must be in place. The decision makers, the users or user/developers of the systems, must also have an adequate level of computer literacy. Without such a foundation, success will take a long time to achieve.

The Resource Profile

Digital's resource profile is blessed with a staff that's largely computer literate. This literacy level contributes to the company's success in spreading the use of expert systems throughout its organization and beyond. AITC has already trained 500 knowledge engineers throughout the world.

Another key aspect of Digital's resource profile is an IS strategy to integrate at all levels—business process, applications and data. Driven by its need to align knowledge across functions, Digital's strategy mandates that expert systems adhere to all data and network standards. Like the products it sells, Digital's expert systems must be able to communicate with each other and with any databases and applications.

DuPont, in contrast, works with various hardware platforms and global networks. A degree of applications and database integration exists at each major organizational level—corporate, department and business unit—with most needs satisfied through four large IBM data centers. For example, an electronic mail system operates across all platforms: IBM mainframes, Digital and Hewlett-Packard Co. minicomputers, and PCs. The Digital VAXs and HP 3000s are used throughout DuPont's engineering and manufacturing facilities. And 15,000 IBM PCs and 15,000 Apple Macintoshes are used in DuPont offices worldwide.

More than 30,000 DuPont managers and professionals are Lotus literate today, a number that will grow to 60,000 before the decade is out. With this supporting infrastructure in place, DuPont's resource profile is naturally more oriented toward PC-based expert systems. More than 1,800 DuPont people are now using expert system shells as readily as they do spreadsheets, electronic mail and other tools.

The Specialist Approach

Being a high-cost/high-payback effort, the specialist approach requires many of the same attributes of any major system development effort: senior management sponsorship, adequate funding and rigorous management control when it comes to project selection, prioritization and development.

The human resource requirements can be a problem with the specialist approach. A knowledge engineer requires a mixture of normal programming skills, expert system language and tool skills and a firm understanding of subject matter. Digital says that, for complex systems, it can take a year before a trained individual is fully up to speed. The company's knowledge engineers are put through an apprenticeship program ranging from 13 weeks to nine months, depending on the business problem and the level of training required. In some instances, AITC consultants may continue to work with the trainees back at their home sites.

The development and maintenance of complex systems require more than a group of knowledge engineers working together. A group at Digital responsible for the XCON and XSEL programs, which are used to configure systems for customers, includes a program manager, software systems integration engineers and various experts providing information in terms of process and data content. For each quarterly release of these systems, Digital consults hundreds of experts in manufacturing and engineering. Moreover, 40% of the rules in the configuration systems change annually.

The possible options for getting started using the specialist approach are:

◆ Hire an outside firm to develop the first expert systems.

◆ Experiment internally, but team up with other companies to create a support group.

◆ Create a specialized shop.

In the late 1970s, when Digital decided on an expert system as the solution to its configuration problems, the technology was in its infancy. So the company joined with an academic artificial intelligence hotbed, Carnegie Mellon University in Pittsburgh, to produce what became XCON. The AI Technology Center grew out of this effort, and subsequently so did Digital's entry into the expert systems market, providing tools, training and consulting for customers wanting to leapfrog steps in the specialist approach.

AI Central

As its expert systems strategy evolved, Digital discovered that, in some cases, development and maintenance had to be controlled centrally. Yet this didn't prove to be true of the total expert systems program. Nor would the culture and organizational structure of the company allow for vesting such control in a single organization, says Jack Rahaim, manager of Digital's AI marketing and productivity shell programs. "From the beginning, we planned to disperse the technology throughout the organization," he says.

Digital's structure is not a simple one—a functionally decentralized organization integrated at the business process level and run under a matrix style of management. Even though the AI Technology Center is the locus for AI expertise at Digital, it doesn't run the entire expert systems show. Nor does its management plan or control the applications.

The Marlborough facility houses two basic expert systems groups. The first comprises 150 people involved in applications development for configuring systems, field service and manufacturing and engineering. These professionals report to line managers, as do other expert systems developers scattered throughout the company.

The second is the core staff under AITC management—also 150 professionals—who are involved in services and products for both internal and external customers. They are responsible for distributing the technology they develop throughout the organization and to customers via marketing, training and apprenticeship programs. They are also involved in establishing new training centers in Europe, Japan and the United States.

Rahaim emphasizes that line managers and their staffs control the selection of applications, the tools they use for development and even the skills-training process. (AITC offers training, but it's not mandatory for employees to go there.) The only rules are that applications meet the communications and data standards of the company if they are to be integrated at the business process, network and data levels.

In short, although AITC has enormous influence over the Digital program, it does not pull all the strings, a fact that Rahaim feels has contributed to corporatewide acceptance and commitment.

The Dispersed Approach

The issues involved in implementing the dispersed approach are quite different. The key questions to ask are the following:

- Who will be the target developers—the ultimate end user, the user in concert with an IS professional or a local guru?

- How can you build the user/developer's understanding and commitment?

- How can developers increase their programming skills?

- What standard tools should you select and sponsor, and how many of them will you need?

- How do you avoid reinventing the wheel?

- How do you find and maintain area management support?

The strength of this approach is that expert systems are often developed fast—from days to months—and for costs ranging from a few hundred to a few thousand dollars. At DuPont, training consists of a basic two-day course, plus a number of one-day, specialized courses.

Besides speed and low cost, the dispersed approach fosters user ownership and creates broad organizational support. If it's handled correctly, the successful user/developers will sell the concept to their colleagues.

To succeed in the dispersed mode, a company must move through three stages:

- **Maverick.** A few aggressive pioneers begin to create their own small systems.

- **Experimentation.** The mavericks' successes convince a group or a manager to address certain problems formally for a trial period.

- **Culture change.** A group decides to embrace the development of expert systems for a wide variety of applications.

With so many issues to resolve, don't expect shortcuts to culture change. Culture change means that many existing processes for resolving problems must be thrown out and new ones adopted. To make culture change work, the group must have a vision. And that vision must be supported by successful experiences, a sizable cadre of trained amateurs and a plan that specifies each milestone for achieving a completed system and the rewards at the end of each milestone.

It's taken five years for DuPont to evolve through the maverick and experimentation stages. Eighteen hundred people have been trained to use expert system shells, and several business units are now ready for the culture change that lies ahead. Two of them are developing several hundred expert systems this year.

Support From the Top

The dispersed strategy does not mean no corporate guidance or support. Back in 1985, DuPont did not simply scatter a few expert systems shells on users' desks and tell its people to play with them. An AI task force led by coauthor Ed Mahler examined the idea of letting the experts—the decision makers—develop their own systems using existing expert systems shells. The task force approved 40 different packages that would run on DuPont's installed workstations and personal computers.

Although shells were still in their commercial infancy, the task force decided there was enormous opportunity for improving front-line decision making through a dispersed approach. (See chart, "Experts at Everything.") Senior management agreed to experiment and provided $3 million in seed money.

Gradually, a consulting organization was put in place. The corporate AI group was to serve as the catalyst and change agent, selling the concept, selecting the standard tools and establishing training programs. Under this group, a cadre of site coordinators (now numbering 200) have been assigned to user locations, arranging for training and supplying help when needed.

Recognizing the culture of fierce independence at DuPont, the AI Group knew the expert system movement had to grow by word-of-mouth advertising, rather than by edict. Group members began by calling their colleagues throughout the

Experts at Everything

Expert systems are being used at every step of the product cycle, from customer order input to product shipment.

Activity	Expert System
Find the customer	Qualification adviser Product adviser (800#?)
Make the right offering	Product selection Pricing adviser
Take the order	Forms adviser Credit risk adviser
Schedule production	Scheduling adviser
Order raw material	Vendor Selection PO procedure assistant
Make the product	Machine setup adviser Control advisers Equipment diagnostics Maintenance advisers Process diagnostics Regulatory advisers Procedures advisers
Test the product	Quality assurance Test procedures
Package the product	Labeling adviser
Store and ship product	Warehousing adviser Carrier selection Routing adviser

business units and giving talks, and then waited for the word to spread. As the successes piled up, area management support increased.

The standard tools that were selected were not stipulated by law—users could opt to use any tool that would run on their microcomputers or VAX workstations. The initial tools sponsored were Insight + from New York City-based Information Builders Inc. and RS Decision from BBN Software Products, a division of Cambridge, Mass.-based Bolt Beranek and Newman Inc. Because no shell is suited to all applications, the number of standard tools in use today has grown. The only hard and fast rule was that each system had to have a standard interface for linking into the network and the data files.

It didn't take long for results to come in. Typically, trainees developed their first systems within a few weeks. DuPont tried several routes to avoid reinventing the wheel with these systems. The first idea, to create a database of expert systems, was soon discarded. Besides the technical complexity involved, the AI Group recognized that human nature would not cope with the centralized database idea. Could everyone be counted on to enter their expert systems into the central file? Not likely.

But people who were creating new systems could be counted on to find out if anyone had done a similar project. Fortunately, a vehicle for managing this type of fishing expedition was already in place. DuPont's global electronic mail network allows employees to put out a single call to all of DuPont's 1,800 expert systems developers.

The dispersed approach requires a lot of self help and self discipline. Novices will make mistakes, and they will sometimes develop systems that are not useful. Yet most mistakes quickly work themselves out, and whimsical projects usually fall into disuse because of the maintenance time involved. Just 50 systems have simply withered away at DuPont, while 600 have proven highly productive.

DuPont's expert systems generally fall into one of the following areas: troubleshooting and selection systems used from development to sales and delivery; production planning and scheduling; and remote process control.

Useful expert systems have been devised to help design products meeting specific customer needs. For example, the Packaging Adviser, used for designing rigid plastic food containers, helped DuPont break into the highly competitive barrier resin market. The company also tackled a critical problem, chemical spills occurring in transit, by developing a Transportation Emergency Response Planner to guide people in the field through the right procedures for diagnosing, controlling and cleaning up a spill. A Maintenance Finish Adviser is used at trade shows to answer questions on high-performance paints and obtain sales leads. And a Confidentiality Document Adviser is used for preparing sections of legal documents.

Expert systems are widely used throughout DuPont's manufacturing processes for troubleshooting and quality control. So far, the company has developed 50 expert systems for diagnosing and correcting process control problems. A 600-rule expert system, built by two people in concert with the business team, has been integrated into one unit's production planning and scheduling system.

The Three Steps to Knowledge Processing

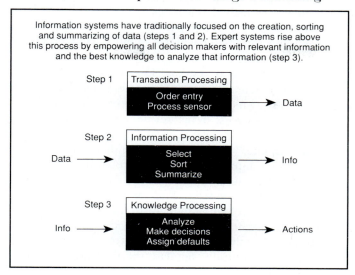

Information systems have traditionally focused on the creation, sorting and summarizing of data (steps 1 and 2). Expert systems rise above this process by empowering all decision makers with relevant information and the best knowledge to analyze that information (step 3).

Step 1 — Transaction Processing — Order entry / Process sensor → Data

Step 2 — Data → Information Processing — Select / Sort / Summarize → Info

Step 3 — Info → Knowledge Processing — Analyze / Make decisions / Assign defaults → Actions

While DuPont continues to decompose large problems into parts addressable through small expert systems developed by individuals, the company realizes that there are economies of scale in creating centers to help tackle generic problems, such as real-time process control and production scheduling. These groups, called competency centers, are composed of IS and network professionals who work with business units wanting to develop such systems.

17,000 Rules

At Digital, the configuration systems today include six systems totaling more than 17,000 rules: XCON, used to validate the technical correctness of customer orders and guide the assembly of these orders; XSEL, used iteratively to assist sales in configuring an order; XFL, for diagramming a computer room floor layout for the proposed configuration; XCLUSTER, to configure clusters; XNET, for designing local area networks; and SIZER, for sizing computing resources according to customer need.

Among the variety of other expert systems are inventory monitoring (CAN BUILD), truck scheduling (National Dispatch Router), manufacturing planning (MOC) and logic gate design (APES).

Digital's Rahaim notes that although enormous operational savings have been realized through the use of these systems, even greater benefits are evident, although difficult to quantify. "The configuration systems allowed us to pursue and extend our à la carte marketing strategy, which is what differentiates us."

The APES system has resulted in striking productivity gains. "Typically, a senior design engineer can create 200 logic gates per week," says Rahaim. "With APES, that number has gone to 8,000 per day. The first chip we designed this way sped up a computer introduction by six months. How do you quantify the strategic advantage of slashing the time to market?"

Besides day-to-day operational systems, Digital also has expert systems designed for senior management. One such system is called Manufacturing Operations Consultant (MOC), which helps managers examine the impact of major changes—in pricing, in resources, in market demand—on the capacity and work load of their plants worldwide. "That is an example of a strategic system and of a system that must integrate," says Rahaim. "You don't know about the plant in Ireland unless you can tap into the databases there on their production load, the cost structures, etc." MOC is used for short-range planning, but other expert systems are being devised for modeling long-range plans.

Systems integration is extremely important to the evolution of strategic expert systems at Digital. For instance, Rahaim foresees the day when systems such as APES will be integrated with other design systems and business processes so that management can electronically simulate the final product and estimate the manufacturing costs and time to market.

What's the right approach for your organization? There is no simple answer. Analyzing the business environment and the technology readiness of your business are critical steps that can lead to the use of either or both approaches described here. Whatever method is chosen, managing the evolution of the effort must be handled carefully if the program is to achieve broad organizational commitment.

Becoming a world-class organization requires putting world-class knowledge, not just information, into the hands of decision makers. Expert systems technology is far from mature, but we already have the tools, methods and approaches to use expert systems to begin to achieve that goal. Those still mulling over the question of whether to develop an expert system program will be outclassed by those already planning and implementing these systems.

Questions

1. What is the definition of an expert system?

2. Compare the approach used by Digital Equipment Corporation with that used by DuPont to bring expert systems into their firm.

3. Pick a company with which you are familiar or have studied in a case in one of your courses. Select an approach to bringing expert systems into that firm and defend your choice.

2.4

Information Technology in Marketing

John D. C. Little

Part I: Information Technology Is Everywhere

Information technology pervades marketing. When you answer the telephone, a computer may be calling with a sales message. If you buy shares of Intel, Microsoft, or other company listed with NASDAQ, you trade on an electronic market. NASDAQ has no physical location where traders meet. Instead, a network of securities dealers set bid and ask prices through connections to a common computer.

When I call Sears Roebuck to place a catalog order, the Sears operator asks me my phone number. Then she tells me my name and address. Obviously she is sitting in front of a video terminal. Later, when I go to the store to pick up my order, I find another terminal. It too wants my phone number and tells me my name. Then it gives me a slip of paper indicating the storage bin that holds my order. The whole system works smoothly and efficiently, providing quick service with low hassle and, important to Sears, little clerical labor.

Telemarketing is more evidence of information technology at work. This is a big business, about which you may have mixed feelings, if you are the recipient of many sales phone calls. But the technique reduces selling costs by screening prospects and saving travel. Unquestionably, it is a major success.

The phrase, *direct marketing*, applies to any activity in which individual prospects are pinpointed by name. Examples include mailed catalogs, other direct

SOURCE: "Information Technology in Marketing" by John D. C. Little, from *Information Technology and the Corporation of the 1990s: Research Studies*, edited by Thomas J. Ailen and Michael S. Scott. Copyright © 1993 by Sloan School of Management. Reprinted by permission of Oxford University Press, Inc.

mail selling, and telemarketing. As you are well be aware if you have a mailbox, direct marketing by catalog has exploded. Major catalog retailers like L. L. Bean and Land's End are totally dependent on information technology. Here are the essential ingredients:

- large, up-to-date, computerized mailing lists;
- toll-free 800 numbers;
- credit cards;
- rapid credit checks to computerized databases.

Then deliveries can be authorized and made quickly. Fast service has been a critical success factor in the rapid growth of direct marketing. It is easier and faster for me to buy computer equipment in New Hampshire or California by 800 number than to find time to shop at a computer store in Boston.

A friend of mine left a senior position in a consumer packaged goods company to become vice president of marketing in a large U.S. bank. The CEO hired him to lead the bank's charge into new financial services under deregulation. His focus was retail banking—i.e., services for individual customers. I saw him about a year later. He said, "I can design the new products. I can test them in the field and prove they are good and that people will pay for them. But the bank can't deliver them. It does not have the required computer systems and it cannot put them together in a reasonable length of time." Success in banking and other financial services has become critically dependent on good information technology.

In the 1960's, two management scientists working for an oil company discovered a fascinating marketing phenomena that applies to gas stations. Most people thought that, if you kept putting more Arco stations in the same city, they would soon start to cannibalize business from each other with rapidly diminishing returns for Arco. Hartung and Fisher (1965) discovered that, on the contrary, as you add stations in the same market, the gallons sold *per station* increase. The reasons are several. For example: (1) Each station is an outdoor advertisement for all stations of its brand; (2) People would rather have a credit card for a brand with many stations, rather than a few; (3) Local advertising is far more efficient if the company has many stations.

The same is true of most franchised outlets: Sales per outlet increase with the number of outlets in a city.

Now think about automatic teller machines.

In Massachusetts a few years ago, a holding company, BayBank, pulled together under a single umbrella many banks previously confined to individual counties by Massachusetts law. BayBank established a common name and logo across the state. It was not the first bank to have ATM's but it was the first to have them everywhere. Now it owns retail banking in Massachusetts and is awash in consumer deposits, the envy of the big Boston commercial banks. Information technology strikes again. And in this case it follows well-known laws of marketing.

FIGURE 1

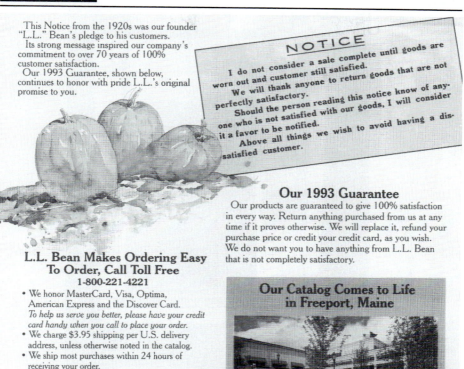

This Notice from the 1920s was our founder "L.L." Bean's pledge to his customers.

Its strong message inspired our company's commitment to over 70 years of 100% customer satisfaction.

Our 1993 Guarantee, shown below, continues to honor with pride L.L.'s original promise to you.

NOTICE

I do not consider a sale complete until goods are worn out and customer still satisfied.

We will thank anyone to return goods that are not perfectly satisfactory.

Should the person reading this notice know of any-one who is not satisfied with our goods, I will consider it a favor to be notified.

Above all things we wish to avoid having a dis-satisfied customer.

Our 1993 Guarantee

Our products are guaranteed to give 100% satisfaction in every way. Return anything purchased from us at any time if it proves otherwise. We will replace it, refund your purchase price or credit your credit card, as you wish. We do not want you to have anything from L.L. Bean that is not completely satisfactory.

L.L. Bean Makes Ordering Easy
To Order, Call Toll Free
1-800-221-4221

- We honor MasterCard, Visa, Optima, American Express and the Discover Card. *To help us serve you better, please have your credit card handy when you call to place your order.*
- We charge $3.95 shipping per U.S. delivery address, unless otherwise noted in the catalog.
- We ship most purchases within 24 hours of receiving your order.
- We ship Federal Express® to most of the USA for an extra fee.

Please check the order form in the center of the catalog for details.

For Customer Service Call Toll Free
1-800-341-4341

- Order status, returns and repairs

We guarantee prices and terms in this catalog through January 1, 1994.

Our Cover: Painting by Alfred Chadbourn.
4 *Source:* Barridoff Galleries, Portland, Maine.

Our Catalog Comes to Life
in Freeport, Maine

For over 80 years people from all over the world have come to visit our store on Main Street in Freeport. When they leave, we hope they have a better understanding of the outdoors and the feeling they've been someplace special. Stop by anytime. We're open 24 hours, every day.

Catalog sales have exploded because of the convenient, fast service made possible by 800 numbers, credit cards and computerized credit authorization.

More electronic markets: The Boston Computer Exchange runs an ad with a telephone number and a post office box. No physical address is given.

Video technology is big in marketing. Sales brochures on videotape are common—many schools send tapes to prospective students, for example. Buick will give you a diskette that you can run on a PC at home or in the showroom to view animated pictures of automobiles and examine models and options.

On the other hand, electronic home shopping has moved more slowly than expected. Several experimental systems have folded. The vision of people sitting at home and flipping through video catalogs has not yet materialized in a

FIGURE 2

Automatic teller machines not only enhance service and save labor but are robot soldiers in the battle for market share in retail banking.

substantial way. Videotext services such as Prodigy, Delphi, and the Source, however, offer computer shopping and usage may grow as the number of home computers equipped with modems increases. However, it may take another generation of higher resolution computer screens, greater communications bandwidth, and lower cost graphics to make home shopping widespread. For example, the way to do grocery shopping at home may be to push a video image of a shopping cart down store aisles on a screen, picking items off the shelves with a mouse along the way.

The sales force is an expensive and important part of an organization where any leverage in effectiveness can have large payoffs. Here information technology is providing new efficiencies in lead tracking, field reporting, and, perhaps most important, new services such as the analysis of customer problems on laptop computers. Moriarty and Swartz (1989) report examples.

An oft-cited case of the impact of information technology on marketing is the airline reservation system. American and United gained significant competitive advantages by putting their systems in the hands of travel agents. But, without as much publicity, something else is going on behind the scenes that uses information technology in combination with other activities, social and analytic, to place extra passengers on the planes. This is the overbooking system. Overbooking sounds bad, but perhaps it shouldn't. There is a hidden marketing triumph here. Here's why:

The airlines subsist on the business passenger. Business passengers need the service and pick up the tab. However, as queuing theory shows, if flights are working smoothly for the business passengers, there will be empty seats. Therefore, why not sell the extra seats at a discount to people who are willing to stand-by for last minute boarding? This is a good idea, but, when the airlines try to do this, various not-too-scrupulous individuals call up and make reservation under false names. Then they show up at the airport as stand-bys and, surprise, there are no-shows and plenty of seats available.

The airlines' answer is overbooking. This also helps with the no-shows arising from road traffic delays, late business meetings, and the like. But overbooking raises other problems. If you want a fight, try to eject a passenger with a confirmed reservation from an airplane. Needed is one more good idea and that is: buying people off the plane. Free market supply and demand are put to work. Every plane contains at least a few people who aren't in a big hurry. So offer them something that is valuable to them but not quite so valuable to the airline. What is that something? It's airplane tickets. This creates a win-win situation. What makes it all possible is: (1) the data provided by the reservation system, (2) some fine management science forecasting and seat inventory models, and (3) the basic strategic idea that you would be willing to do some marginal cost pricing. The whole system is a remarkably successful, if complex, informational and social operation that significantly increases capacity utilization.

A specialized workstation, called DesignCenter, developed by a Weyerhauser subsidiary, Innovis, targets the do-it-yourself market. Home improvement stores install a kiosk containing DesignCenter in their display area. A customer, usually with modest help from a sales clerk, can easily design a home deck by him/herself using the interactive system. The look and feel is somewhat analagous to a video game. The deck is visually displayed and easily manipulated to meet the customer's wishes about size, shape, type of wood, etc. After the design is finished, a push of a button brings a complete bill of materials with dimensions, costs, and other specifications for all parts. The customer can walk away with a drawing of the finished product and a hard copy of the bill of materials. Using the DesignCenter, do-it-yourselfers created $150 million in projects during the first eight months of operation. Much of this represents a market expansion of projects that home-owners would not otherwise have built.

DesignCenter typifies an important new class of applications of information technology in which the *customer* solves his or her own problem, thereby creating an increase in primary demand for the product. In presenting the workstation to retailers, Weyerhauser emphasizes the involvement of store sales people in assisting the customer, thereby, strengthening relations between manufacturer and retailer as well as ensuring that the customer can obtain any necessary information not contained in the computer program.

So a first point is that information technology is pervasive in marketing. We use it at every turn to gain a little or a lot of competitive advantage, improve our services, save money, and generally do a better job. Successful applications create new benefits at one or more stages along the chain of added value in the product or service. A hierarchy of improvements is:

1. *Labor displacement.* This is a traditional computer role. Among the examples above, the Sears catalog order system clearly falls in the category. So does the automatic teller machine. One can also include videotape presentations.

2. *Service enhancement.* Surprisingly, just about every example of labor displacement includes service enhancement, which, in fact, may be more important. Automatic tellers are open 24 hours a day and appear in more places than branch banks. Machines lack the personal touch often associated with good service, but they bring timeliness, convenience, and the up-side of being impersonal: you can discover in privacy that your account is overdrawn. Some of the cited examples, for instance, catalog retailing, have blossomed because of service enhancements and then have maintained competitiveness through labor efficiencies.

3. *Improved market intelligence.* An important source of value from information technology lies in understanding and pinpointing your markets better. Direct marketing benefits from computerized lists of names spun off from other activities. Screening of lists by pre-specified criteria is often possible; for example, you can restrict a mailing to people who have bought more than $100 worth of goods by mail in the last six months. Analysis of customer records reveals individual tastes and preferences so that people can be sent information only on goods that might interest them. One of the biggest new adventures is taking place with an explosion of marketing data in consumer package goods. This will be probed in depth below.

4. *Creation of new entities.* Some organizations and services could not have existed before an enabling information technology came into being. The electronic markets, like NASDAQ, are examples. DesignCenter is completely dependent on modern computer technology. Certain financial services also fall in the category. In principle they seem simple, but in practice they are remarkably difficult to implement and require sophisticated hardware, software and communications.

Part II: Consumer Packaged Goods: A Discontinuity in Marketing Information

A striking example of the information age at work is taking place in the consumer packaged goods industry. Packaged goods consist primarily of the grocery business (i.e., food) along with health and beauty aids (e.g., shampoo and aspirin). The largest quantities of packaged products go through supermarkets, which therefore become the primary focus of the manufacturers' marketing attention. Supermarkets sell 280 billion dollars of goods per year—20% of all retail sales.

The main information technology activity in packaged goods today is behind the scenes. A rush is going on to use new information to understand better which marketing actions work and which do not, so as to improve marketing efficiency and effectiveness. The changes are taking place so rapidly as to warrant calling them a discontinuity in marketing practice. There are lessons here for other information-intensive industries.

Some of the forces at work are: large quantities of new data, dropping hardware costs, improved software, new marketing science models, and expert systems. As we shall see, these have led to the founding of new companies, organizational change within manufacturers, and power shifts in the distribution channels.

Early history of information use

To go back sixty years into the 1930's, Arthur C. Nielsen invented a scorecard for package goods companies—market share. He did this by collecting data on retail grocery sales in a national sample of stores. Teams of people called auditors were sent into the stores every two months. They counted inventory and went over invoices for hundreds of products in each store. The auditors took the amounts on the invoices, adjusted them for the change in inventory and thereby determined bimonthly sales through the store. An acre of starched-collar clerks in Chicago added all this up with hand-crank calculators. Another roomful drew bar chart reports and the Nielsen Food Index was born. Marketing stars at Proctor and Gamble and General Foods rose and set based on Nielsen market shares.

By the 1960's, new sources of data had appeared and a typical consumer packaged goods company ran its business with up to four kinds of numbers: its own factory shipments, Nielsen shares, warehouse withdrawal data provided by Selling Areas Marketing, Inc. (SAMI), and consumer purchase histories collected by national diary panels. As may be seen in Figure 3, these data sources represent different places to look at the distribution pipeline. Each source tells a story about a different actor in the system. Everything was in hard copy, but, it should be noted, the IBM 370 had arrived and management information system (MIS) departments were learning how to master the large systems that handled ordering, billing, and other high volume jobs.

Decision support systems

In the 1970's came the initial flowering of decision support systems (DSS's). The original technological impetus was time-sharing. Then database management systems came in, along with fourth generation languages. Most of the fourth generation languages that found favor in financial analysis were not suitable for

FIGURE 3

In the 1960's data was available for measuring sales at each stage of the product pipeline but reporting was all in hard copy.

marketing because they could not handle large databases. However, the few that could became widely used and marketing data slowly inched its way on-line.

The really significant accomplishment of information technology in this era was putting companies in control of their own shipments data. In the early 70's I recall a sales crisis with one of Nabisco's flagship brands. As a result, the director of marketing wanted to make comparisons of the most recent six months sales with the corresponding period a year ago in the midwest region. His chief lieutenant for doing this, the head of marketing research, was told by MIS that he would have to have, besides a budget—which was no problem—special priority and, even then, it would take 4 to 6 weeks to do the programming and make the runs.

A colleague and I were visiting the company at the time. Contemplating the development of on-line systems, we asked the marketing research director whether he would be willing to pay $100 to have the answer in ten minutes. He pulled out his wallet and said he would pay for it himself. The great irony of the story, however, occurred two months later when he received his report. He glanced at it for a few moments and the numbers looked peculiar. Then he realized he had forgotten that a teamsters' strike in Chicago had disrupted sales during a month of the previous year. The print-out was meaningless. He immediately knew how to fix it, but that took another week.

Market response reporting

By the early 1980's the days of the MIS bottleneck were gone in most large companies as modern DSS databases and on-line systems for marketing information went into place. Indeed, starting in the late 70's people began to raise their sights and differentiate between *market status reporting* and *market response reporting*. Figure 4 makes the distinction. Prior to this time most marketing decision support systems had supplied what may be called status information: what are company and competitive sales volumes? shares? prices? etc. This is key information for running the business, but of equal and often greater importance are answers to market response questions: What is the effect of price changes on sales? How profitable are promotions? What is the impact of advertising? With the data going into the on-line systems of the early 80's, companies began to scratch at these questions and learn enough to whet their appetites.

All this was good, but it was mostly doing what people had been doing laboriously in batch systems prior to DSS. It was quicker, better, and in greater quantity but not a discontinuity.

The universal product code

Optical scanning of bar codes on grocery packages started in 1974 with the goal of saving labor by speeding up checkouts. Implementation of the *Universal Product Code* (UPC) represented a remarkable achievement of cooperation among manufacturers and retailers. However, growth of installations was slow, and, as late as 1980, less than 15% of national grocery sales were being scanned. Al-

FIGURE 4

Conventional Decision Support Systems provide
  MARKET STATUS REPORTING
  ◆ sales

  ◆ share

  ◆ price

  ◆ promotion

  ◆ advertising

New systems should also provide
  MARKET RESPONSE REPORTING
  ◆ price elasticity

  ◆ promotional effectiveness

  ◆ advertising impact on sales

Improved data and analytic methods permit the measurement of market response and hold the promise of reporting it on a regular basis.

though there was much talk about using scanning information for "soft savings", i.e., marketing purposes, nothing much happened because there were too few scanning stores. But in 1979 a pair of entrepreneurs in Chicago decided not to wait any longer. They simply bought and installed scanners themselves. The company, Information Resources, Inc. (IRI), developed what it calls Behavior-Scan and may generically be called *laboratory markets*.

Figure 5 describes the idea. IRI initially put scanners in all the supermarkets in two small cities, Pittsfield, Massachusetts, and Marion, Indiana. This gave them sales and price data as a direct spinoff from the scanners. In addition, they started recording all the newspaper ads and all the special displays in the stores. In each market they recruited a panel of 3,000 to 4,000 households whose members identify themselves at checkouts so that their purchase records could be set aside in the store computer and accumulated. The two markets were chosen for high cable television usage and the panelists on the cable had specially modified television sets so that different groups of people could be sent different commercials in test and control fashion. Thus was introduced a powerful testing laboratory for new products, television advertising and other marketing activities. The whole system was extremely successful and grew rapidly until now there are about 8 such markets.

In instrumenting the markets IRI made a look-ahead move. It extracted the data directly from the stores electronically, polling the stores at night by telephone from Chicago. Although more expensive than sending tapes by UPS, it is obviously faster and is also more reliable. (UPS doesn't lose the tape, but the stores may lose data if it sits around too long.) As happens so often in information technology, there are unexpected fringe benefits from the electronic delivery.

FIGURE 5   The Laboratory Market

- small to medium sized city

- scanners in all supermarkets

- voluntary panel of 3000 households

- identification of panelists in stores

- controllable TV ads to households

- observation of in-store conditions

- store and panel data
   purchases
   price
   promotion
   advertising
   coupons
   display

Laboratory markets are ideal for testing new products, TV advertising, and other marketing activities.

Here is an example of one such benefit. In late 1985 it became apparent that a drought in Brazil would very likely ruin the coffee crop and send world coffee prices skyward. A major food company contacted IRI and said, "How fast can you give us coffee prices and sales movement at retail?" The answer was nine days after the close of the store week for the IRI laboratory markets. This compared to an average age of 4 to 8 weeks for top line reports from more conventional syndicated sources. The data arrived by diskette to run under flexible DSS software on a personal computer.

The drought did indeed devastate the coffee crop, and, starting in late December, a coffee task force of senior managers in the food company met weekly to review the latest data on what the consumers and retailers were doing in the market. Out of these meetings came the company's pricing policy.

Figure 6 shows some of the data, which is fascinating. It shows how your household was buying coffee that January. The top curve is the price. It is steady on the left, suddenly runs up in January, and then tapers down during 1986. The lower curve shows total coffee sales. We see some seasonality on the left— people switch to iced tea and soft drinks in summer. But notice the spike. When the price started to rise, people stocked up on coffee, but stopped well before the price peak. Very smart. It also appears that during 1986, with coffee prices considerably higher than the previous year, overall coffee purchases were down. Such data permits easy calculation of price elasticity for the product category.

FIGURE 6

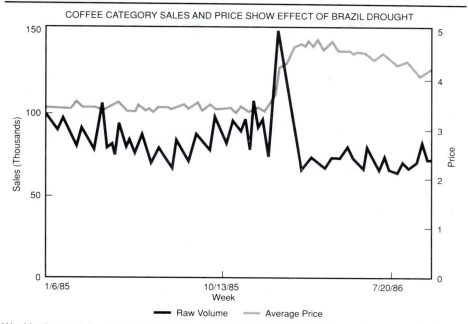

COFFEE CATEGORY SALES AND PRICE SHOW EFFECT OF BRAZIL DROUGHT

■ Raw Volume   ■ Average Price

Weekly data, quickly reported, has high value in fast-breaking marketing situations. A drought in Brazil caused a run-up of coffee prices and a rush to stock-up by households. Then, under high prices, sales fell below pre-drought levels.

Note that this whole managerial scenario is a far cry from the frustrated marketing research director described earlier who had to wait a month to obtain an analysis of last year's data. The incident illustrates how advances in information technology speed up and improve the quality of marketing decision making. But it is just the start of the discontinuity that is taking place.

The data explosion

A new generation of tracking and status reporting services has been created. Scanner stores now represent most of the sales volume through supermarkets and it is therefore possible to design a valid national sample of 2000–3000 scanner stores and develop a data service based on them. The two major players are Information Resources and Nielsen Marketing Research. Their services provide coverage of individual major markets as well as the total U.S. Both companies include, besides basic sales and price data, specially collected information on store displays, newspaper advertising in the market, and coupon drops, all classified and broken out in a great variety of ways.

FIGURE 7   Marketing Along the Distribution Pipeline

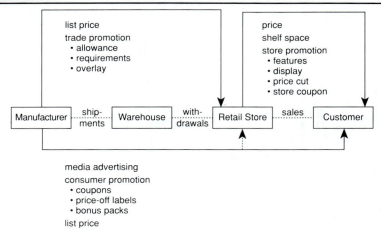

Each actor along the distribution pipeline influences others through its set of marketing activities. Each activity is a target for a measurement of marketing effectiveness using the new data sources.

The distribution pipeline in Figure 7 illustrates the potential value of the new data for learning market response. Each actor in the system influences sales to the others by means of the marketing variable shown. Scanner data opens the possibility of measuring virtually all the response relationships along the pipeline.

All this sounds wonderful. But there is a hitch. The amount of data is overwhelming. Consider the new detail now available: *weeks* instead of 4 weeks or bimonths (this increases data by a factor of 4 to 8), *UPC's* instead of aggregate brands (a factor of 3 to 5), *top 40 markets* instead of broad geographic regions (a factor of 4 to 5), *new tracking measures* (a factor of 2 to 3), and *chain breakouts* (a factor of 1 to 3).

Multiplying out these factors reveals that roughly 100 to 1000 times as much data are at hand than previously. Furthermore, any analysis that requires going to individual stores or to panel households brings in new, equally large databases. Let's take 100 as a conservative multiplicative factor for the data that many companies are now bringing in-house for everyday use.

This kind of change is not easy to comprehend. In terms of a report, it means that, if a report took an hour to look through before, the corresponding document with all the possible new breakouts would take 100 hours to look through. In other words, the new detail won't be looked at.

Solutions will come in stages

What should be done about this data explosion? Certainly there is value and competitive advantage to be found amid the detail, but how do we get at it? There is no single answer; solutions will come in stages:

Stage 1: *Get access.*

This is well underway. Manufacturers have set up systems that permit them to get their arms around the new databases. Since they must continue to run their businesses at the same time, they have given high priority to recreating aggregate numbers similar to those they have used before so as to make a smooth transition into new modes of operation.

Stage 2: *Automate the analysis.*

Whatever people were doing to examine data previously is almost certainly inadequate now, at least as far as obtaining the new value. The old way consisted of an individual analyst, often an assistant product manager or management scientist, putting the data into a spread sheet or a statistical package and manipulating it to look for relationships and try to solve particular problems.

Although individual analysis continues, of course, no company is willing to hire 100 times its present staff in order to pour over the new data and find out what is in it. Some other solution must be found. Part of the answer lies in automation. Although the required software will have to be developed, market response analysis often follows identifiable rules and can be approached through expert systems techniques.

By analyzing market response, I mean going over historical events to determine the effectiveness of marketing activities. Trade promotions, coupons, price changes, store merchandising, etc. are all fair game for evaluation. There are thousands of such events when you break them out by brand, geographical area and time period. Much work is already underway to automate this type of analysis and obtain its benefits. Here are examples:

Promotion evaluation. Package goods manufacturers run trade promotions. These are temporary wholesale discounts and usually include a contract with the retailers for merchandising activity, for example, putting the product on special display at the end of an aisle for a week. Or the retailer may agree to advertise the product in the local newspapers. Ordinarily the store temporarily reduces the shelf price. The net result is often a big bump in retail sales. You can see an example in Figure 8, which shows sales peaks for several successive promotions.

Now, how do you know whether a promotion was profitable for the manufacturer? Well, you would like to know what sales would have been without the promotion. The usual way to determine this is, essentially, to draw a line through the data points for which there were no promotions. Such a line is called a *baseline*. But, as it turns out, drawing a baseline offers many pitfalls. Abraham and Lodish (1987) have developed a set of procedures and a computer program for drawing a baseline and determining the difference between the baseline and actual sales. This gives the incremental sales for the promotion, from which its profit can be calculated.

The baseline program makes extensive use of expert systems ideas. That is, it mimics the hands-on processes of the authors, a pair of skilled marketing scientists, and employs their heuristics for handling the many issues that come up in working with the data. To give the flavor of this, we quote from the authors'

FIGURE 8

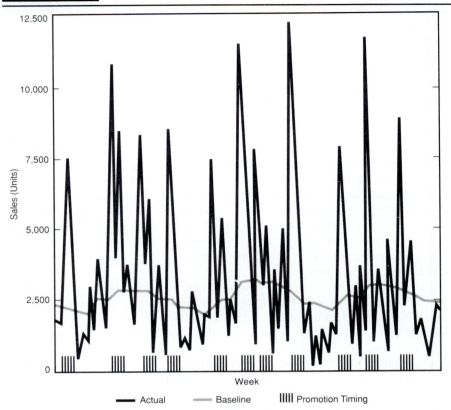

Weekly shipments to retailers show sharp peaks corresponding to manufacturers' promotions. The evaluation program constructs a baseline to represent what sales would have been without the promotion.

flow diagram. They use such phrases as "contaminated points are removed from the data," "non-normal points are diagnosed," and "corrective actions." Such words are more in the realm of human judgment than mathematical technique. The work is a good example of combining statistical methods and expert system ideas in an automated analysis. The methodology has since been hardwired into efficient code for high volume commercial processing.

Coupon evaluation. Manufacturers in 1988 distributed about 220 billion cents-off coupons. Approximately 3.2% were redeemed at an average face value of about 42 cents. The cost of this, plus distribution and handling, produced a total bill of $4.7 billion. In the past people have had only the number of redemptions (cashed-in coupons) with which to evaluate coupons. This was inadequate because no one knew how many of the customers redeeming coupons would have bought the product anyway. The money at stake suggests a large payoff from a valid measurement of coupon profitability.

Today this can be routinely done using panel data—the purchase histories being collected from 60,000 households in 25 markets. These, and copious computer time, permit the building of a model that will predict the brand purchase probability for each household in the panel. The model is calibrated over some time period, say, a year, before a coupon drop. Then the model projects ahead to forecast what the households would have purchased in the absence of the coupon. An example is shown in Figure 9. The difference between forecast and actual sales appears as the shaded area. This measures the extra sales attributable to the coupon and becomes the basis for a report card of coupon effectiveness for each coupon dropped.

The model underlying the evaluation comes from university research. The basic technique is the multinomial logit as adapted by Guadagni and Little (1983) for scanner panel data. In commercial practice, the process is partially auto-

FIGURE 9

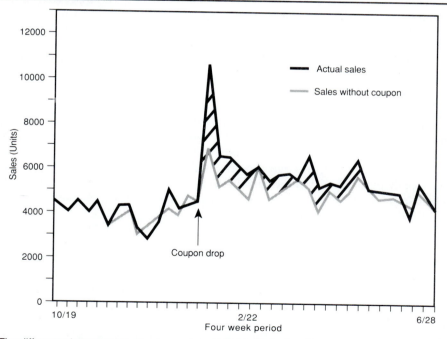

The difference between actual sales and predicted sales in the absence of the coupon measures the effect of a coupon and appears as the shaded area. Predicted sales are calculated from a product choice model based on 60,000 households.

mated. Full automation is needed and will require building further intelligence into the program because real markets of real customers are full of unexpected (though understandable) events.

Derived databases. Promotion and coupon evaluations themselves accumulate into valuable new databases. Some of these are big, not in the sense of megabytes, but in terms of people absorbing what they mean. Over a thousand coupons have been evaluated and hundreds of new ones are analyzed each year. Promotion response differs by event by market and by brand, adding up to tens of thousands of numbers.

These are *market response databases* and contain much valuable information. By analyzing them we can develop norms about what to expect and detailed understanding about why certain marketing actions worked and others did not. For example, by looking across many different coupons, we can determine whether high face-values are more profitable than low ones, full-page ads better than half-page, etc. There is competitive advantage for the companies who understand these results first. It seems likely that, except for day to day tracking purposes, internal analysts in companies will spend more time on market response databases than on the raw scanner data itself.

Stage 3: *Find the news.*

Suppose a half dozen new computer tapes have just come in with the latest four weeks of scanner data for our product category. What important thing has happened? Who has gained share? Where did it come from—what regions, what brands? Who has lost share? Perhaps there is a rumor that a major competitor was promoting heavily in Los Angeles. How heavy was it really? How much did it affect us?

These are typical highlights people want to know early. In many companies, top line reports of latest results are distributed on a regular basis. They contain fairly detailed tables, breakouts and graphs, but, almost always, they start with a cover memo that reports major happenings. The memo is traditionally written by the analyst who prepares the report. Significant changes in the market are noted—perhaps a substantial increase in category volume, a share loss for a key product in an important geographical area, etc. The tables and charts provide detail for the reader who wants to follow up.

A computer should write the cover memo. In a project at MIT a few years ago, some students built a prototype that did this (Stoyiannidis, 1987; Little, 1988). Since then, the ideas have been picked up and further developed into a commercial product, CoverStory, by Information Resources (Schmitz, Armstrong, and Little, 1990). An example of the output appears in Figure 10.

Because the process is automated, you can easily generate the memo for any brand or category or segment of a category, depending on managerial interests. You can even look at the market through the eyes of your competitors by running their brands. Or you can run the report for a district sales manager, where instead of pulling out highlights by market you do it by key retail account.

FIGURE 10

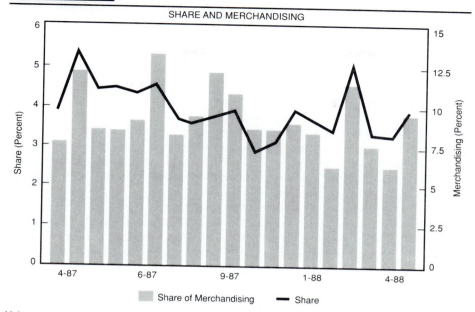

Using expert systems techniques, a computer can go through a large database, identify important news, and report it in a natural language memorandum.

This application also provides an important lesson for DSS architecture in the 1990's. Many companies have built DSS's that are basically retrieval systems. A file server holding the data is accessed over a local area network by a workstation that is essentially a PC. Design has focused on smooth user interfaces at the front end and standardized database management at the back. This is an ideal architecture for the marketing DSS's of the *1970's*, when most applications involved people retrieving a few numbers to look at personally and analyze by hand.

But automated analyses and expert systems working against large databases require real processing power not available on a PC. They need what might be called MIPS in the middle between PC and database. Computer architecture for this is not difficult to devise but probably will not happen unless marketing management identifies the need.

Knowledge delivery

Automated analysis is necessary for dealing with the data flood but it is not enough. There is, I believe, too much *response* information. The issue is not what the computer can hold, but rather how much a person can organize and assimilate just by looking at it. Needed are structures to turn the information into knowledge and techniques to deliver it. The former will come from people. For the latter, technology will help.

Knowledge delivery will evolve through phases, typically: "What happened?" then, "Why did it happen?" and, finally, "What do we do about it?"

Today people are focusing mostly on "What happened?" and the beginnings of "Why did it happen?" Prospects for rapid progress are good because many people inside and outside of packaged goods companies are working with scanner data to solve day-to-day marketing problems. As successful applications emerge, they can be generalized and packaged for automatic on-line delivery. Expert systems technology is not the bottleneck but rather the development of marketing knowledge. Likely near-term applications are, for marketing, the diagnosis of brand performance and, for sales, the development of fact-based selling points for salespeople's presentations to key accounts.

The application of expert systems to scanner data is an active topic for a number of academic researchers. McCann and Gallagher (1988) have an ambitious program in progress. Bayer and Harter (1989) report a PC-based system.

Looking ahead, I see a general problem and, out of it, a goal. Market response analysis is done today by internal staff groups, essentially internal consultants, and by external consultants. At the culmination of a study, they make a presentation to management. In the course of an hour's presentation the consultant summarizes the results of an effort that took, perhaps 3 to 6 man-months. If the consultant is lucky the audience will become really interested and the meeting will run over its allotted time by a half hour or so. But no matter how well things work, a standard presentation provides a very narrow bottleneck through which to transmit information. Under these circumstances, there is great pressure to produce tight, top-line summaries and to uncover immediately actionable implications. This is all to the good, but much information is lost and never becomes available to product management because it doesn't happen to fit into the current need at the time the information was created.

A goal, therefore, is to find structures that will organize the market response information that will soon be generated and to develop methods for delivering relevant portions of that information to the decision maker at the time that he or she is thinking about the problem. I call this *Stage 4* of the answer to the information glut.

As an example, consider a product management team planning its promotional program for the coming year. A brand has some set of current circumstances. It has a share and a rank in its product category. The category itself is characterized by an overall sales rate, a percentage of households using such products, a certain history of competitive activity, etc. The brand may have specific current concerns, such as falling share, or low distribution or a new competitor. One would like a support system that could systematically bring to bear the distilled experience of hundreds of past marketing activities on the brand's problem at hand.

This seems doable. Many companies have long had how-to-do-it handbooks on promotions, coupons, media, etc. These handbooks contain rules of thumb for what to do in various brand and market circumstances. Although the rules need extension and updating with the new knowledge being generated, they represent a worthwhile starting knowledge base. Based on such information, Van Arsdell and Weise (1986) developed a prototype promotion advising system. It asks you questions about your product and then recommends actions. Although the system would require an order of magnitude more effort to become a practical tool, it suggests that, with the output of automated market response analysis that is to come, we should be able to build a generation of electronic marketing advisors that would really be helpful.

Impact of information technology on the packaged goods industry

So far I have focussed on behind-the-scenes data and its evolving utilization. Now let us stand back and assess the overall impact this is having on the packaged goods industry, including its effect on organization and industry structure. Figure 11 provides an overview.

First of all, in the marketing function generally, we are seeing *increased efficiency and effectiveness*. This is what we have been discussing.

Next, a major opportunity lies in using the new data to gain *regional marketing* advantage. Historically, the evolution of the grocery industry saw the emergence of giant companies like General Foods, Nabisco, and Proctor and Gamble in the first half of this century. Such companies invented national brands by producing uniform, high quality goods, backed by national advertising budgets and reinforced with economies of scale in manufacturing, distribution and marketing. Although national brands usually ended up being somewhat stronger in one part of the country than another and some local tailoring of the marketing was done, this was largely left to the sales force. The major elements of the marketing program: price, promotion, advertising, packaging were set at the home office.

Now with information costs dropping drastically, companies have data on a market by market basis for the top 40 or 50 markets, and, potentially, can act on the information. But you cannot reproduce the central staff in 50 regions. That's

FIGURE 11   **Information Technology Impact on Packaged Goods Industry**

- ◆ In the marketing function
  —increased efficiency and effectiveness
  —shift to regional marketing

- ◆ In the manufacturer's organization
  —sales and marketing move closer

- ◆ In the grocery industry as a whole
  —shift more power to the retailer

New knowledge about marketing effectiveness is bringing changes at both the company and industry levels.

not the answer. You can, however, create small, *sales and marketing teams* in prin-cipal sales regions and give them strong DSS support. Several manufacturers are now implementing such an organizational change. The step represents a major rethinking of the product management system that has been operating in the packaged goods industry for the last 50 years.

However, this is not likely to be the end of the changes. The new information signals a *shift in power toward the retailers*. Initially, retailers have not been as well situated as the manufacturers to gain value from the UPC data. They suffer from lack of scale. A large food manufacturer deals with a few hundred or a thousand items. These are clustered into brands, each of which might represent sales in the range of 10 to 100 million dollars. Therefore, a manufacturer deals with large entities and can afford to spend considerable money collecting and analyzing data for them. Consider, however, a retailer. A large supermarket may carry 20,000 items, whose sales might range from a few hundred to a few thousand dollars a year. Even when you multiply these figures by the number of stores in a chain, a retailer cannot afford to lavish as much attention on an individual item as a manufacturer. However, the cost of processing information is plummeting and already the retailers are beginning to find actionable content in their data, espe-cially by analyzing it at the category level, which is the most meaningful unit for them. Analysis of the data by retailers will certainly increase. One implication of this is that strong brands will get stronger whereas weak ones will be in trouble. This is not a matter of market power but rather increased efficiency in the mar-ketplace. It also sounds like something that is, on net, a good outcome.

What can we conclude? A huge new database has arrived in consumer package goods and, lagging a little, the ability to extract useful information from it. The totality of the data has not been absorbed yet but soon will be. The data permit measurements and understanding that reveal inefficiencies in the system and opportunities for improvement. As a result, companies will stop doing a lot of things that don't work well and do some better things. By and large the market will become more efficient. We are seeing changes in roles and in organization.

Part III: Will Information Technology Make Marketing Obsolete?

Paradoxically, while marketing is almost universally regarded as essential to modern organizations, marketing departments have come under increasing fire.

Charges of inadequacy and inefficiency are common. The U.S. automobile industry receives regular abuse, being accused of failing to provide the cars peo-ple want. Critics assert that the supermarket shelves are filled with products that differ from one another only in hype. Trade promotions in the packaged goods industry have created striking distribution inefficiencies by pushing products through distribution channels in big lumps—the promotional discounts offered by manufacturers cause retailers to "forward buy", that is, stock up at the low price to meet future needs. The large, lumpy orders not only require manufacturing plants to run in a stop-and-go manner but lead the retailers to build new warehouses just to accommodate the promotional merchandise. A potentially smooth production and distribution process has been made inefficiently erratic.

One hears other criticisms: "Marketing is too important to be left to the marketers." A case in point is the "house of quality" methodology in manufacturing (Hauser and Clausing, 1989). In this planning and communication process, the "voice of the customer" permeates engineering design, parts specification, manufacturing process planning, through to production itself. Although the voice of the customer and the house of quality epitomize the fundamentals of marketing, the methodology originated in manufacturing at a Japanese shipyard and is sponsored within most U.S. companies by engineering, not marketing.

One may reasonably ask: Will information technology alleviate or accentuate these difficulties? What is the role of marketing as business becomes increasingly information centered? Before answering, we examine some of the forces that the information age is placing on the firm and thence marketing. As Glazer (1989) and Braddock (1989) point out, information technology blurs the classic strategies of cost leadership (seeking market share through low cost) and differentiation (targeting special market segments). Traditionally, low cost is achieved by standardization and economies of scale. Then broad markets can be approached competitively. Differentiation, on the other hand, focuses narrowly on meeting the needs of a specific customer group. But information technology offers the possibility of achieving both. This is because it facilitates not only rapid and flexible design but also targeted delivery of products and services.

Therefore, it is increasingly feasible to pursue a market niche strategy in many niches at once. As databases grow and provide increased knowledge of customers, we can determine better their wishes and how to communicate with them. With the help of information technology we shall often be able to handle large groups of customers with remarkable individuality.

The opportunities for product flexibility have been widely recognized by the financial service industry with its proliferation of cash management accounts, different mutual funds, money market accounts with checking privileges, CD's, credit cards, debit cards, etc. Citicorp, for example, sees itself as being in the information business. Braddock (1989) stresses the close connection between providing information-intensive services to customers (automatic tellers, automated voice interrogation of account data, varied kinds of accounts) and using the resulting databases to understand customers' wishes and cater to them.

The ability of information technology to permit large scale operations and yet provide individual attention is only just beginning to be tapped. As part of its information-oriented strategy, Citicorp plans to build a scanner database of grocery purchase histories for 20 million households. This is customer information on a grand scale. That many households is 100 times the number currently monitored by market research companies. The goal, of course, is different: it is operational—to provide new services to the household, such as "frequent buyer" programs that reward brand loyalty or store loyalty with a kind of electronic green stamps, or to deliver coupons to individual households based on their historical buying patterns.

Such an undertaking is but one example of a rapidly growing field of direct marketing to customers, sometimes known as "database marketing." As Roscitt (1988) observes, there are dozens of commercial databases providing remarkable detail about various characteristics of the American consumer, from demographics, to product ownership and purchase habits. Many of these are broken out by small geographic areas, such as zip codes or neighborhoods, and even by household. Often the data can be combined with a firm's own customer transaction histories to understand better what products might be of interest. The process will lead to far more efficient and effective marketing programs than possible by indiscriminate mailings or broadcast media.

Yet, such direct marketing, with its dependence on large systems of data collection, processing and analysis, looks more like operations than marketing and calls into question the traditional marketing function.

To be competitive, companies will organize to get close to their customers. An example that we saw earlier was packaged goods manufacturers moving to regional organization of marketing and sales teams. Such teams know the local conditions, receive up-to-date tracking data via workstations, and, increasingly, can perform automated analyses, such as generating potential selling points for use with key accounts. Certain kinds of activities have long been local, for example, community-oriented public relations, but increasingly one sees television commercials for national products that show the local city in the background. This all fits with the concept of flat organizations and fast response to the customer, but it weakens the traditional national marketing planning function at headquarters.

As one looks through the marketing-mix in modern information-intensive customer relationships, one finds a blurring of lines once thought rather separate (Glazer, 1989). For example, when we buy from a catalog using an 800 number and a credit card, and have the product sent directly to our home, the benefits of the product itself are almost swamped by the benefits we receive in the form of information and information processing. The fact that the catalog came to us in the first place, the presentation of the product within the catalog, the telecommunications by 800 number, the financial credit transaction, the prompt delivery by UPS or Federal Express (traceable at any point in time), all of these information-intensive operations are key service attributes that we see as benefits and help lead us to make the purchase in this manner rather than at a store. One can call the catalog, a communications medium, UPS, a distribution channel, and the credit card, part of the price transaction, but we would be artificially disassembling the essential unity of the system.

Returning to our question: Will information technology make marketing obsolete? If we think of marketing in conventional, compartmentalized, planning-back-at-headquarters terms, separate from operations, sales and R&D, the answer is likely to be yes. But, the answer is no, if we think of marketing as distributed throughout the organization, bringing in the voice of the customer through appropriately collected information and helping to define and communicate a bundle of benefits in an integrated way with R&D, operations and sales. Then information and information technology will play a transformational role in strengthening marketing throughout the organization.

References

Abraham, Magid and Leonard Lodish (1987), "PROMOTER: An Automated Promotion Evaluation System," *Marketing Science*, Vol. 6, No. 2, p101–23 (Spring).

Bayer, Judy and Rachel Harter (1989), "SCAN*EXPERT: An Expert System for Analyzing and Interpreting Scanning Data," Working Paper, Carnegie-Mellon University, Pittsburgh PA (October).

Braddock, Richard S. (1989), "Keeping the Customer at the Fore," 1989 Marketing Conference, Conference Board, New York NY (October).

Hartung, Philip H. and James L. Fisher, "Brand Switching and Mathematical Programming in Market Expansion," *Management Science*, Vol. 11, No. 10, B-231-43 (August).

Glazer, Rashi (1989), "Marketing and the Changing Information Environment: Implications for Strategy, Structure, and the Marketing Mix," Report No. 89–108, Marketing Science Institute, Cambridge MA 02138 (March).

Guadgni, Peter M. and John D. C. Little (1983), "A Logit Model of Brand Choice Calibrated on Scanner Data," *Marketing Science*, Vol. 2, No. 3, p203–38 (Summer).

Little, John D. C. (1988), "CoverStory: An Expert System to Find the News in Scanner Data," Sloan School, M.I.T., Cambridge MA 02139 (September).

McCann, John M. and John P. Gallagher (1988), "The Future of Marketing Systems: From Information to Knowledge Systems," Report from The Marketing Workbench Laboratory, Duke University, Durham NC (September).

Moriarty, Rowland T. and Gordon S. Swartz (1989), "Automation to Boost Sales and Marketing," *Harvard Business Review*, Vol. 67, No. 1, p 100–9 (January-February).

Roscitt, Rick R. (1988), "Direct Marketing to Consumers," *The Journal of Consumer Marketing*, Vol. 5, No. 1, p. 5–14 (Winter).

Schmitz, John D., Gordon D. Armstrong, and John D. C. Little (1990), "CoverStory—Automated News Finding in Marketing," in Linda Volino, ed., *DSS Transactions*, The Institute of Management Sciences, Providence, RI, May 1990.

Stoyiannidis, Demosthenes (1987), "A Marketing Research Expert System," Sloan School Master's Thesis, M.I.T., Cambridge MA 02139, June 1987.

van Arsdell, Heidi (1986), "Expert Systems in Marketing: A Promotion Advisor," S. M. Thesis, Sloan School of Management, M.I.T., Cambridge MA 02139.

Weise, Stephen L. (1986), "An Expert System Decision Support System for Marketing Management," S. M. Thesis, Sloan School of Management, M.I.T., Cambridge MA 02139.

Questions

1. What is the hierarchy of improvements from using IT in support of marketing efforts?

2. Explain why information technology moves marketing power from the distributor to the retailer.

3. The author ends the article with a brief statement that he believes that information technology will not make marketing obsolete. Expand on his argument, giving examples of specific new roles that you see marketing playing in the future.

2.5

Let the Customer Do It

Jerry Kanter, Stephen Schiffman, J. Faye Horn

Remember the scene in *The Adventures of Tom Sawyer* in which Tom gets his friends to do his whitewashing chore by convincing them that it's a privilege? Today, companies are exercising that same approach by using technology to get customers to do their work for them.

Maturing technologies, such as personal computers, networking, and electronic data interchange, hold the promise of improving customer service while managing the growing labor cost of customer transactions. The new approach? Let the customer do it.

Examples of do-it-yourself point-of-sale (POS) technology are becoming more common each day: In addition to using the ubiquitous automated teller machine (ATM), travelers can now do self-ticketing of airline flights and use self-actuated kiosks to buy insurance policies and mortgage options. You can also design your own deck or price a new car, all by keying in your requirements.

In certain areas, fully automatic gas stations enable you to pump your own gas and pay by credit card—without a human attendant. Citicorp has developed a telephone with a built-in screen to facilitate banking at home. Home buying services, such as Compuserve, Inc.'s Compuserve, which has been in business for years, are being joined by new competitors.

Yet the idea of letting the customer do transaction processing is not new. Users have been dialing telephone calls without operator assistance since the 1920s.

Today, two major factors are driving the rapid growth of self-service systems: improved technology and business pressures. Until recently, transaction processing was handled exclusively by large mainframe systems. The advent of mini-

SOURCE: "Let the Customer Do It" by Jerry Kanter, Stephen Schiffman, and J. Faye Horn, from *Computerworld*, August 27, 1990, pp. 75–78. Copyright 1990 by CW Publishing, Inc., Framingham, MA 01701. Reprinted by permission from *Computerworld*.

computers and PCs, along with better, more reliable networks, has changed all that. Tied to bar-code scanning and other POS devices, these electronic links have been extended from the retail store directly to customers.

The bottom line is that today's technology allows the capture of transactions at the point of sale, integrating them electronically with a company's billing and order-replenishment systems.

And organizations everywhere are under great pressure to make technology investments pay off.

Not Just an Option

Letting the customer do it may be more than just an option. Research company American Demographics points out that a fast-growing elderly population, declining numbers of young adults, and a record low population growth rate will put the nation in a demographic vise in the 1990s. Nationally, the 20 to 29 age group is projected by the U.S. Census Bureau to drop 12.5 percent during the next decade. With the continued growth of a service-oriented economy, there may not be enough people to satisfy the demand for retail clerks and service attendants.

These demographic shifts are forcing retailers, financial service providers, and other firms that deal directly with consumers to take a hard look at customer self-service systems. The approach could become a key determinant of survival for some industries.

Beyond survival, many businesses implement self-service systems for other reasons. Cost leadership, product differentiation, bigger market share, or strategic advantage are among the possibilities.

For example, an ATM can help a bank reduce its labor expenses and thus provide a cost leadership position in the industry. As a technology, ATMs can help distinguish a bank's services from its competitors. Sears, Roebuck and Company, for instance, may support Prodigy Services Company's Prodigy to exploit a market niche not currently addressed through catalog or showroom sales channels.

Self-service systems can also help customers with various stages of the buying cycle. Weyerhauser Company's design-a-deck system, for example, helps the customer establish requirements. Prodigy allows the customer to select, order, pay for, and acquire a product. ATMs let customers acquire cash and monitor their accounts. Avis, Inc.'s ATM-like machines allow customers to expedite car-rental returns. The biggest payoffs come from applications that support many buying steps.

However, it is clear today that competitive advantage gained through information technology is not necessarily sustainable. Even small banks eventually responded to the ATM challenge and joined regional and national bankcard networks. This in turn forced leading banks to evolve their ATM services in order to stay ahead of the competition. Baybanks, Inc., for instance, has introduced a service that allows the customer to keep an eye on which of their checks have cleared most recently.

Looking at three technologies—ATMs, automatic checkout machines, and the Prodigy home buying service—provides a good insight into the current state of the do-it-yourself movement.

ATMs: More for the Money

In the 20 years since their introduction, money machines, or ATMs, have become an accepted method of convenient access to cash. Financial institutions originally intended ATMs to provide customers with convenient banking services at lower costs than tellers' salaries. By 1988, approximately 65,000 ATMs were in use in the United States, handling nearly half a *trillion* transactions. Nearly half of all cash withdrawals are made from ATMs. In fact, ATMs are so common today that, for most of the United States, automated banking is no longer a differentiator between financial institutions. ATMs have become a commodity service as common as telephone booths.

As a result, banks are looking at two major strategies to increase ATM profitability. One is to join nationwide network systems, such as Cirrus, that permit users to access cash outside of the bank's regional area. The other is to increase the range of services and their attractiveness to ATM users and generate revenue from new fees.

The new challenge for bankers is twofold: Offer profitable services and convince customers that automation is the most effective way to conduct their financial affairs. Some innovative options are within one or two years of implementation. These will require rethinking the role of automation in financial institutions, and, in some cases, the nature of the banking business itself. Institutions will probably rely heavily on frequent use bonuses and other use incentives.

Dale L. Reistad, president of the Electronic Funds Transfer Association, predicts that ATM cards will evolve eventually into "supersmart cards" with key pads, readouts, and a small battery. These cards will be used not only for personal banking but also for stock transactions, worldwide special-interest electronic mail systems, and accessing a variety of databases.

Reistad suggests that the end result in the United States will be that customers will have their own "individual bank" custom-designed to meet their personal banking, investment, and transactional needs.

Checkrobots: New Wave Market

A different twist on customer self-service systems has less to do with dollars than with doughnuts. The Automated Checkout Machine (ACM) System, a product of Florida-based Checkrobot, Inc., enables shoppers to check out their own merchandise before paying a centrally located cashier. It incorporates a security system to ensure that each item departing the store has been scanned and paid for. Laser scanning, local-area networks, and database management systems are combined to produce a user interface with the store's central computer.

Checkrobot claims that ACM System offers the perception of improved customer service because the automated checkout machine is easy to use, decreases shopping time, and increases customers' control over their shopping environment. It also says the system provides a high return on investment, primarily because of decreased labor costs. While the current target market is supermarkets, the company plans to expand to retail organizations in general.

ACM System consists of automated checkout machine stations, a central computer linked to the stations, and a POS computer. The automated stations are made up of five parts: a laser scanner, which reads bar-code labels; a color video touch screen, which displays a complete description of the items being purchased, along with their prices and a running subtotal; a produce key pad and produce video screen for handling produce and other variable-weight bulk items; a proprietary and patented merchandise security system; and a conveyer belt that moves through the merchandise security system to the bagging area.

Checkrobot developed ACM System as a response to the evolving retail market and shrinking labor pool. The company claims that automated checkout machines can not only cut down on staffing needs but also lower costs and increase profitability. Checkrobot estimates that one cashier is needed for every three to four automated checkouts, plus one optional bagger (usually working for a lower wage than checkout operators) for every one to two checkouts.

Beyond cost savings, the system also offers the promise of a competitive advantage. Increasingly, customer service in supermarkets is becoming a big differentiator in a competitive industry. By far the most important factor is efficient, speedy checkout.

Customers seem to think that automated checkout machines work. Independent research found that more than half of the users surveyed said that the systems were "much faster" than conventional checkouts; two thirds preferred the automated checkout machine to a conventional checkout, perceived self-scanning as an additional service offered by the store, thought overall service was better than in stores without automated checkout, and thought their overall checkout time was shorter than prior to the installation of the machines. In addition, five sixths of the respondents labeled the automated checkout machines as easy to use.

Why does this high-tech system cause a perceived improvement in a low-tech area such as customer service? In general, it is because customers judge service quality perceptually, not quantitatively. There are four possible reasons for this perception.

First, autoscanning responds to shoppers' No. 1 complaint: waiting in line. Automatic checkout machine-equipped lines are always open, regardless of the number of checkout operators working at the time. (The actual time spent scanning is longer, however.) Customers do not operate the scanning system as fast as trained employees. But the longer real time does not affect their perception of faster checkout.

Second, customers perceive autoscanning as more accurate than staff-operated scanning systems. As they scan, the customer can see the item listed with its price on the video screen and then verify its accuracy.

Third, customer research indicates that automatic checkout machines are readily accepted across demographic lines of age, sex, or income.

If the financial benefits of ACM System are firmly established, autoscanning may become a familiar everyday part of life—just like ATMs.

Self-Serve Success

What makes some self-service systems become part of everyday life quickly, while others never seem more than expensive, awkward monstrosities?

- *A perception of benefit:* Customers are willing to operate a transaction processing system if they perceive a benefit greater than the effort of doing it themselves. Prodigy may not shorten delivery time, but customers may still view it as a sales aid. If transaction processing does not appeal to some buyers' purchase criteria in a meaningful way, it may well fail to gain acceptance.
- *Rapid response and a good interface:* High bandwidth is key here. Transaction speeds—and thus satisfaction—are affected by communications between the customer's input device and the rest of the transactional system.

  High bandwidth allows for both rapid response time and the use of a user friendly graphical or video interface, such as the one currently found in Checkrobot's ACM System.

  There are limitations, though. Prodigy's user interface certainly yields much higher bandwidth than text-oriented videotex systems, which have fared poorly in the past, yet Prodigy still cannot compete with the high-bandwidth environment of a glitzy, live display of merchandise in a store or even with television advertisements.
- *Ease of use:* Beyond a good interface, ease of use also depends on the complexity of information exchanged between the customer and the transaction processing system. For example, when a customer wants cash, he decides to withdraw an amount—say $50—and tells the ATM.

  Compare this with a novice ordering a fly-fishing rod through Prodigy. A good salesperson would know that certain rods are suitable for saltwater fishing, others for river fishing and still others for lake fishing. If the customer is not prompted for specific requirements, he could well end up with the wrong rod.
- *Native intelligence:* Built-in artificial intelligence or other "smart" capabilities can make self-service systems more useful, because such systems can aid in the interchange of complex information between the customer and the system. For example, the leading producer of elevators, Otis Elevator Com-

pany, provides its customers with PCs and the required software to guide them in selecting, ordering and scheduling the construction of elevators.

New Ideas for Self-Service

Several promising technologies are emerging that will allow customers to handle more of the ordering burden:

- *Multimedia:* A host of devices now coming to market will transmit video, voice and even three-dimensional pictures to potential customers. For example, a real estate office can simulate a walk through a house, or an architect can superimpose a home or garden addition to an existing property.
- *Automatic scanning devices:* In a Milan, Italy bank, for example, a customer can stack his U.S. bills in a device that returns lire and an itemized record of the transaction. The device handles 16 different currencies. And the scanner reportedly does a much better job than the human eye of detecting counterfeit bills.
- *Voice recognition:* Like optical scanning, this is another powerful option. It works on the premise that most people are more comfortable speaking than keying or typing. A few working applications are in the field, and research continues. One system employs a chip in an ATM card that will verify the voice of the cardholder. This can be considered a "voice print" and offers voice withdrawals as opposed to the current method of using a key pad.
- *Handwriting recognition:* Akin to optical scanning are machines that can read printed writing. Their use would allow office workers and customers to record information in the same way they always have—by filling in the blanks and checking off boxes. The potential also exists for processing handwriting in foreign languages with automatic translation.

Prodigy: A Promising Infant

Prodigy Services, a joint venture combining IBM's technological expertise and Sears' retailing expertise, offers PC owners an "on-line electronic mall of information and shopping services." Operating from telephone networks connecting 22 minicomputer centers around the country, Prodigy provides shopping, banking, news, and database access to an estimated 160,000 subscribers.

Prodigy's launch in October 1988 was greeted with skepticism because of the earlier failures of similar ventures. In particular, home banking services were expected to be widely accepted when they first became available in the mid-1980s. But earlier technology was not user-friendly, and applications were not geared to the mass market. Thus, those systems disappeared.

Prodigy faces stiff competition. Not only do 1.3 million computer owners subscribe to similar systems, such as Compuserve, but telephone companies are also starting information ventures of their own. However, according to Sears chairman

Edward Brennan, Prodigy's edge is that it is broader and less expensive than its competitors.

To meet mass-market appeal, Prodigy is menu-driven and friendly and costs $9.95 per month for unlimited use. Subscribers can order from Sears, J.C. Penney Company, and 45 other direct-mail retailers. They can also bank with more than a dozen affiliates, including Manufacturers Hanover Corporation, and make plane reservations through American Airline's Sabre system. A wide range of news, financial and entertainment sources are also available.

The deliberate mass nature of Prodigy's marketing appeal has another advantage: It provides an attractive advertising medium. Almost 200 companies, including American Express and J.C. Penney, pay Prodigy every time an advertisement is accessed, a lead is generated or a product is sold.

Edward Papes, Prodigy's chief executive, says he doesn't expect Prodigy to break even for another few years. However, IBM and Sears say they consider Prodigy a long-term project. If Prodigy continues to upgrade its electronic package for a growing market, it could change how Americans acquire a wide variety of goods and services.

Letting the customer do transaction processing is not a fad. It is driven by such factors as population demographics and industry competition.

As with the introduction of any new technology, some will fail, and some will succeed. Technological improvements in computing hardware and software and in the telecommunications infrastructure will allow for the introduction of new customer-driven systems. The successful ones will provide a perceived benefit to customers by convincing them, as Tom Sawyer did, that "it's a privilege."

Questions

1. Give four examples of self-service transaction processing systems. Which of these have you operated yourself?

2. What are the advantages and disadvantages to the user of the checkrobots discussed in the article? Consider both the technical and human factors.

3. List all the information items that are required to run a secure ATM. Assume that the ATM can handle withdrawals from several accounts and can check for erroneous input.

Electronic Data Interchange

The Elements of Implementation

James A. Senn

Electronic data interchange (EDI) is one type of interorganization system; others include electronic mail, electronic funds transfer, and videotext. All types of interorganization systems are increasing in number as business processes are modified so that corporations can respond to new opportunities as well as to the constant pressures for greater responsiveness to the needs of customers and trading partners.

Drivers of Interorganization Systems

Although there are numerous information technology alternatives available to facilitate the communication of business documents between organizations, information technology by itself is not the principal force behind the spread of these systems. Depending on the industry, the following factors are the driving forces.

SOURCE: "Electronic Data Interchange: The Elements of Implementation" by James A. Senn, from *Journal of Information Systems Management* (New York: Auerbach Publications), Winter 1992, pp. 45–53. Copyright © 1992 Research Institute of America Inc. Used with permission.

Customers determine business actions

Across virtually all industries, customers (not dealers or suppliers) determine which products and services will be successful. Whether at the individual or corporate level, buyers are stating what they will accept, when they will accept it, and under what conditions. Mass-produced goods of the past are being replaced by customized products.

Quick response is becoming the retailing standard

Time is increasingly being recognized as a barrier to business. Delays are caused in addressing market opportunities if the elapsed time between the need for a product and its fulfillment is excessive. Time requires decisions to be made far in advance of the point at which their impact will be noticed. Quick response methods are redefining the way business is transacted by shortening the time periods around which commercial activities are arranged.

The just-in-time manufacturing technique has gained increased popularity

The barrier of time also forces businesses to accumulate inventories and stockpile goods to ensure that demand can be accommodated when it occurs. Manufacturers are revising their strategies so that plenty of materials are on hand and that the materials arrive in time for manufacturing, but not so far in advance that they accumulate as inventory.

Essential information technology is available

Hardware, software, and communications networks provide the ability to link organizations and transmit business documents electronically. The level of information technology needed for interorganization systems is generally available and component reliability and cost levels are acceptable.

Standards have been formulated

For customers, suppliers, and other business partners to be linked, each party must use an agreed-on format for communication. Standards for such transmission have been established and are used in many industries. They serve as a foundation on which to build interorganizational relationships.

The global nature of business

At one time, the notion of a global business community was of concern only to international or multinational companies. Today, there is a truly global market for sales and sources of materials.

Even if an organization does not directly market its products in another part of the world, it may interact with a distributor or representative who does. Material and service sources may also be internationally based. The capability to transmit and receive business communications over long distances and between distinct time zones is usually the reason interorganization systems are created. Electronic data interchange systems in particular are of increasing importance because they link trading partners and redefine the way business is transacted.

Features of EDI

Electronic data interchange is a form of electronic communication that allows trading partners in two or more organizations to exchange business transaction data in structured formats that can be processed by computer applications software. EDI is fundamentally a data processing concept that spans multiple businesses. It does this by relying on data communications methods and standard formats for the transmission, acceptance, and understanding of business data (see Exhibit 1).

The basic features of EDI include the following:

- ◆ Intercompany communications—EDI links trading partners (e.g., organizations and their customers and suppliers) in a cooperative relationship that offers the potential for improved levels of profitability, service, and productivity.
- ◆ Computer-to-computer linkage—Data is exchanged electronically, in machine readable form, and without the need for manual intervention in the

EXHIBIT 1   **Intercorporate Transactions Using EDI**

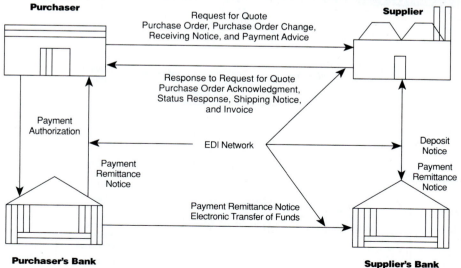

data entry or manipulation process. Networks link computers within the departments of participating organizations.

◆ Transmission of business documents—Business documents, rather than messages or narrative reports, are the substance of EDI transmissions. Typical business documents include purchase orders, purchase order acknowledgments, request for quotations, quotes, invoices, bills of lading, and shipping notices.

◆ Formatted data—To ensure that the data is received and properly understood, carefully defined formats specify the order of data items in a transmission and the characteristics of each item.

◆ The capability to overcome technological differences—Distinctions in the computer technology used by communicating parties are overcome through translation. Thus, hardware, protocol, and data format differences do not limit participation in EDI activities.

Exhibit 2 describes the flow of information between the EDI trading partners. The EDI network interconnects the partners, either directly (i.e., computer to computer) or indirectly through the use of electronic mailboxes. Located within the network, the mailbox holds documents transmitted from a source authorized to add to its contents. Documents remain in the mailbox until they are checked and retrieved by the intended recipient.

The network capabilities include more than just transport capacity. Routing and security is an essential feature that protects against unauthorized access to potentially sensitive data. Built-in mechanisms for recovery protect against loss of data if the network fails. As these characteristics suggest, EDI consists of much more than electronic transmission of orders.

EXHIBIT 2   EDI Links Trading Partners

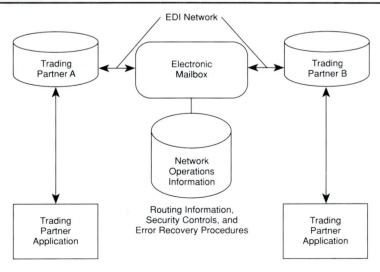

Reasons to Adopt EDI

Organizations migrating to EDI are driven mostly by business needs. Improved productivity for the entire organization and the need to reduce the number of paper documents used are the broadest objectives.

An organization should consider itself a candidate for EDI when the following conditions exist:

- Loss of time due to paper flow is substantial.

- Management of paper flow consumes excessive personnel or financial resources.

- Tracking of specific sales or manufacturing orders is essential.

- The cost of an out-of-stock condition is high or unacceptable.

- Trading partners are concentrated.

- Customer service expectation is high.

- Current internal systems are effective and adaptable to EDI.

The business case is typically made using one or more of the five strategic and operational reasons discussed in the following sections.

Strategic reasons

The drivers of EDI point to two strategic reasons (i.e., strategic in that they change the way an organization competes) to consider adoption.

Compresses Business Cycle

Electronic transmission of business data compresses time. Details of transactions are sent, received, evaluated, and processed in a fraction of the time usually associated with business processes and with enormous benefits. Evidence is growing: One manufacturer, Lithonia Inc, Conyers GA, has become a leader in the lighting industry by developing applications that incorporate EDI to cut in half the time it takes to receive and fill orders from its customers. The company is now able to receive, process, package, and ship orders in the same amount of time it takes competitors just to receive orders from their field locations. This industry leader also releases its invoices as the orders are shipped, providing an additional cash flow advantage over its competitors.

An IBM industry consultant study of the textile industry, which is notorious for long lead times in its order-to-manufacture-to-ship cycle, has demonstrated lucrative benefits from speed-of-business improvements. The cycle has been reduced by 25% and overall industry savings are projected to exceed $12 billion annually. In addition, both buyer and manufacturer share the benefits.

Implements Just-in-Time Practices

Just-in-time inventory management, which involves shipping parts to factories and assembly facilities as they are needed and thereby eliminating the need for large inventories of safety stock, is dependent on rapid and accurate transmission of shipping notices. Ordinary mailing of documents is virtually out of the question. Delay in receiving the shipping notice, for any reason, or an error in specifications could lead to the shutdown of a production line. It is even conceivable that the parts could be on the receiving dock, even though the organization's records would not indicate that.

More businesses are developing systems to send shipping notices through EDI and route them directly into the recipient's computer for evaluation. The supplier's computer remains online to the recipient while the specifications are verified. This promising method is an alternative to leaving notices in an electronic mailbox, which recipients may not check for several hours. It compresses the time interval because the document is both transmitted and accepted in a matter of moments. Chrysler Corp, Highland Park MI, is continually evaluating the method for enhancing its just-in-time inventory practices. Chrysler management anticipates that soon all transactions with its more than 2,000 suppliers are or will soon be handled through EDI.

Operational reasons

Potential strategic benefits often drive many organizations to use EDI as a basis for formulating external linkages with traditional partners. They are important because they change the way the organization competes. At the same time, there are significant internal benefits which improve operational performance. Three operational benefits include the elimination of errors, the rapid detection of document errors when they do occur, and the reduction of business document costs.

Eliminates Errors

The Electronic Data Interchange Association reports that 70% of computer output becomes input to another computer somewhere else and that 25% of the cost of a business transaction is in data entry and reentry. Each time data is manually entered into a system, there is a chance of error. Computer-to-computer transmission of business documents not only eliminates costs, it also eliminates errors.

Detects Errors Quickly

Errors may not be due to data-entry, but a result of differing business records, for the price charged versus the price quoted for a product. The following example illustrates how EDI can help managers detect errors of this nature and correct them immediately.

A select group of grocery suppliers and their customers are testing a direct-to-store EDI system. For example, Frito-Lay Inc, the Dallas-based snack food manufacturer, worked with Ralph's Grocery Company of San Francisco to develop such a system. The route salesperson in the Frito-Lay truck uses a hand-held computer which contains daily delivery information for the driver. By simply plugging into the in-store computer, the driver is able to transfer the delivery information from the hand-held device into the store's computer (product and quantity details are coded in a previously agreed upon data format).

In only a few moments, the receiving manager electronically compares the delivery information with the records that describe the expected shipment, including prices. If they agree, the driver's entry becomes a document of record. Disagreements are detected and resolved on the spot. Having the store computer accessed directly eliminates the need for checking every delivery transaction and eliminates the need for paper. The company anticipates that the prototype will prove itself, and the process will become common throughout the industry within a five-year period.

Reduces Document Costs

The levels of costs savings resulting from EDI use can be substantial. A widely publicized study performed by Arthur D. Little Inc for the grocery industry concluded that if only one-half of the industry's businesses implemented EDI, the industry would save in excess of $300 million per year. This level of cost saving is particularly significant because of the low profit margins that characterize the grocery industry.

RCA recently estimated that each purchase order it processes costs approximately $50. EDI, it estimates, reduces the cost to approximately $4 for the same purchase order ($1 of which is communications costs).

Most significantly, the cost savings are not one-time. They continue for every transaction that follows, growing as business volume increases. A bottom-line impact is likely.

Responding to strategic imperative

A decision within an organization to develop its EDI capability may not always be a deliberate choice. Instead, it may be the result of pressure placed on it by other events in the industry in which the organization competes. Such pressures create strategic imperative, and therefore, are a strong driving force.

In these settings, EDI is not an alternative but a requirement for remaining competitive. In some industries, such as pharmaceuticals, transportation, and automobiles, EDI is already the standard conduit for business transactions. In others, the message is rapidly spreading to link up or lose out. The threat of losing business is indeed a very convincing argument.

Some organizations have told their suppliers in no uncertain terms what is expected: "Not developing EDI capabilities will undoubtedly lead to fewer orders from us." Others have emphasized the effect on revenue: "If you begin transmitting business data to our firm electronically, you may take an additional 1% cash discount on all orders." Or to suppliers: "Your participation in our EDI project should noticeably increase the amount of business the company does with you annually."

Technology Requirements

EDI relies on widely used computer networking and information systems technology. However, several key activities and decisions are essential to ensure that its advantages are obtained.

Industry standard for product identification

Although fundamental in concept, the establishment of a standard method for identifying and marking products is an EDI requirement. Proprietary identification systems limit the number of organizations with which a corporation may interact for electronic trading. Partners may be unwilling to adopt the particular system requested if they are unwilling to use product identification or information-handling procedures dictated by another organization. Or they may be unwilling to use multiple systems, one for each major partner with which they interact.

Some industries currently struggling with the development of an identification system are finding that the process is by no means quick or without controversy. It is clear that the universal product code (UPC) in the grocery industry has been a major enabler of EDI. Because the standard bar code is printed on more than 95% of all products handled by the industry, all participants can use a common code (often in ways not previously anticipated). There is little question that industry standard coding systems, such as the UPC code, will be a fundamental element in the successful development of EDI at both the individual organization and the industry level.

Standard format for exchange of data

Business documents transmitted by EDI methods are included in an envelope (Exhibit 3) that contains both the data itself as well as identification and routing details. The communications transport protocol indicates the method by which the document is sent (e.g., SDLC, ASC, or BISYNC), which enables the coordination of transmission between sending and receiving computers. Interchange control segments delineate a set of documents transmitted between organizations at one time. Within each group, headers and trailers separate the transaction sets; that is, the actual business documents themselves.

Standard data formats, which prescribe the contents of a business transaction (e.g., order number, quantity required, and shipping dates), tell trading partners what to expect in the contents, order, and form of data transmitted through EDI. A family of standard formats, known as the X.12 format, is widely promoted.

Among its attractions is the existence of a variety of transaction subsets that specify the content of electronic purchase orders, packing slips, invoices, and payments. Each subset identifies the contents of the transactions (i.e., the data items to be included), the order in which each item is presented, and the spec-

EXHIBIT 3 | EDI Data Transmission Format

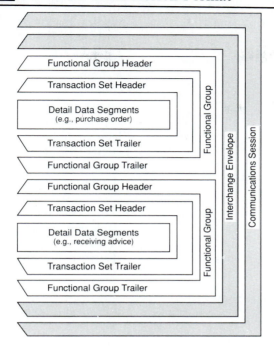

ifications for the data. Both sender and receiver must expect and use a particular format containing data in a specific order or an exchange will not occur.

The following is a list of current and proposed industry transaction subsets and data formats:

- Purchase order.
- Purchase order acknowledgment.
- Purchase order change request.
- Purchase order change acknowledgment.
- Invoice.
- Payment and remittance advice.
- Request for quote.
- Reply to request for quote.
- Shipping notice.
- Receiving notice.
- Receiving advice.
- Planning schedule with release capability.
- Price and sales catalog.
- Data element dictionary.

Exhibit 4 identifies several industries that have developed unique transaction formats.

EXHIBIT 4   Status of Industry EDI Formats

Industry Segments Using EDI Formats	Industry Segments Planning to Use EDI Formats
Using Standard (X.12) Transaction Formats	Metals Electronics Petroleum Aerospace Hospital Supplies Electric Utilities Federal Government Procurement (Department of Defense and General Services Administration) Federal Government Taxation (Internal Revenue Service, Treasury Department, and Customs Bureau)
Electrical Equipment Telecommunications Equipment Chemicals Textiles Textile and Apparel Linkage Fabric and Suppliers Linkage Automotive Industry Action Group Retail Merchants Paper	
Other Industry Formats (Not Using X.12 Standard)	
Medical and Surgical Suppliers Oil and Gas Retail Hardware Health Insurance Claims Insurance Wholesale Pharmaceuticals Trucking Optometrists Retail Grocers Warehousing	

EDI software

Several levels of software are used in EDI networks (Exhibit 5). The communications software connects the sender and receiver systems to the transmission network. Working in conjunction with the carrier source (e.g., a value-added carrier), the software provides for the proper protocols and speeds.

The existence of the communications software is usually taken for granted and thus reference to EDI software includes the components responsible for translation and application activities. Translation software is any computer code that transforms data from one form to another as a way of facilitating the exchange of data. The sender, for example, may use an internal proprietary format whereas the receiver may rely on an X.12 specification. Translation software would handle the conversion between the formats.

Application software performs the typical transaction-processing activities (e.g., preparing purchase orders, acknowledging receipts.) However, in an EDI envi-

EXHIBIT 5   EDI Software

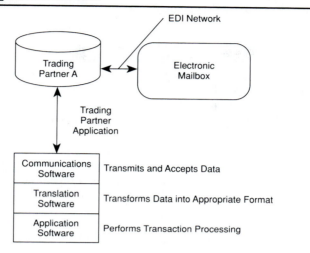

ronment it also includes the capability to interact with the translation software and to use agreed-upon data formatting guidelines.

Common data dictionary

Standard transmission formats must agree with internal data standards in an organization. The responsibility for setting and maintaining these standards falls within the IS department.

A data dictionary records the number of characters or digits allowed for each item. This is an essential element for ensuring that data transmissions will be understood. Therefore, any organization or industry must not only maintain a common data dictionary of data elements, but must also ensure that the dictionary is constantly brought up to date, usually on a quarterly basis. Each partner must always know or be able to determine the makeup of each electronic messaging format it sends or receives.

Network transportation source

The transmission network may be proprietary, consisting of transmission lines established for the sole use of the trading partners, or for general use, involving public data networks. Although the trend is moving away from proprietary systems, this does not mean that organizations will use only a single network. Many corporations, particularly those that are involved in several industries, are finding that they must seriously consider using multiple commercial telecommunications networks. Each trading partner may use a different network for data transmission.

The following list identifies the most widely used EDI networks and their providers in order of market share:

- GEISCO (GE Information Services Co)—Industry focus includes apparel, automotive, petrochemical, electronics, steel, and international trade.
- British Telecom/Tymnet—Industry focus includes grocery, transportation, chemicals, and electronics.
- Sterling Software/Ordernet—Industry focus includes pharmaceutical, warehouse, medical, transportation, and grocery.
- IBM Information Network—Industry focus includes insurance, retail, apparel, and electronics.
- Kleinschmidt—Industry focus includes transportation, grocery, warehouse, electronics, and chemicals.
- Control Data Corp—Industry focus includes automotive, manufacturing, and chemicals.

Other specialty providers include:

- CompuServe—Electronic network provider, seeking to provide niche EDI services.
- Harbinger—Providing selected services for banking, utilities, and electronics industries.
- Sears Technologies—Commercial service is an outgrowth of its internal EDI network; it provides new insurance interface traffic for the IVANS insurance network.
- Regional Bell Operating Companies (RBOCS)—Seeking to develop services that will leverage their telephone customer network.
- Western Union—Seeking to provide services in the distribution, electronics, and petrochemicals industries.

Financial partner

The electronic funds transfer component of EDI involves a banking partner. The originator bank concept has caused financial institutions to increase their consideration of EDI. General Motors initiated this practice when it said it would make electronic payments to any of eight specified banks (the originator banks) in the US. Trading partners are paid only if they make arrangements to receive payment from one of the eight banks. Facing the possibility of being left out of other corporate EDI systems if not included as an originator bank, many financial institutions began to take EDI seriously.

Yet while some have established services, most others are still creating an EDI strategy, often very slowly. To date, it appears that many institutions are taking a wait-and-see stance, not having established an EDI program.

Formulating an EDI Strategy

Organizations evaluating EDI alternatives face several key concerns. The strategy itself will be most successful if it results from an evolutionary, rather than a revolutionary, process.

Key concerns

When general management and the IS department in an organization formulate their strategy for moving ahead on electronic data interchange, the following concerns must be addressed.

How to Encourage Trading Partners to Participate?

A decision by management to invest in EDI does not mean that trading partners will go along. For example, Hewlett-Packard Co, Palo Alto CA, recognized as a pioneer in EDI within the electronics industry, found that even after seven years of EDI experience only nine of its trading partners were participants.

In What Ways Will the Organization Be Required to Change the Way It Does Business?

The question of whether or not to adopt EDI is essentially a business issue. The technology for EDI is in place and well-proved, and any remaining technical issues have been identified and are correctly being addressed. Standards are available to support EDI. The essential question is whether an organization wants to change the way it does business (or whether there is even a choice). The other question to consider is should it change the way it handles business transactions, at least during the initial phases of implementing EDI?

Can the Bank Provide Services?

Can the organization's bank handle the volume of its remittance data? Many banks do not yet have the capacity to handle the high volume of activities that full-time EDI use will require. The banking industry recognizes the problem; an individual corporation must decide whether it can afford to wait for its bank to solve the problem and ensure adequate capacity.

In some instances, the banks are still deciding how to manage EDI as a revenue source and at the right profit level. They are also caught up in debates about whether to handle non-bank data fundamental to their clients' activities.

Some organizations may decide they can no longer wait and will take steps to initiate the service. For example, the National Wholesale Drug Association recently decided it could no longer wait for the banks. Consequently, it established its own task force, which created a record structure that a third-party clearinghouse could handle and circulated details of the format for evaluation.

Can the Organization's Accounting Software Accommodate EDI?

Accounting software is an essential component in electronic data interchange, although most discussions of EDI do not address this element. Among the concerns are the ability of the software to match orders and requisitions against invoices and orders received, and the capability for line-by-line reconciliation of quantity received and quantity billed. These concerns transcend data coding and go to the heart of procedural control.

Should Standard or Proprietary Methods Be Used?

Some organizations have developed their own proprietary, corporate EDI formats. Among the largest are J.C. Penney, K-Mart Corp, McKesson Corp,

Wal-Mart Stores Inc, General Motors Corp, and Ford Motor Co. However, many organizations using proprietary formats are rethinking their strategy as they increasingly find that partners are refusing to use a proprietary standard. (In some cases, organizations are adopting a second format that meets the X.12 standard, while also maintaining their proprietary format.)

Other implications for the IS department

The information systems department in an organization is a key player in the development of an effective EDI strategy, as the preceding discussion indicates. In addition, unexpected challenges can arise, including inadvertent overselling to management, restructuring of business elements, managing maintenance requirements, and underwriting costs.

Overselling to Management

Electronic data interchange often has an immediate appeal to business managers when it is presented to them, particularly when it is emphasized that the underlying technology already exists and has been perfected. Unfortunately, the attraction can lead to expectations that will not be met in the time frame most business managers anticipate. Once the enthusiasm is generated, it is difficult to explain that almost a year may pass before full implementation occurs. The peculiarities of testing data formats, communications links, and interconnection of multiple vendor systems are lost on most business managers.

When the system is conceptually understandable, it is a challenge to explain why the service cannot be delivered immediately. Initial applications should be selected to demonstrate the impact of EDI while testing procedures at both ends of the communications link. The most successful organizations will be those in which business procedures are not modified right away, but evolve through experience. Starting with current transactions is the safest route, with enhancements to follow.

Restructuring Business Elements

EDI is not another layer of technology that is added to existing applications. Instead it often involves a restructuring of key elements of business systems. Applications systems become increasingly interdependent through the sharing of product and process information. Accounting, shipping and receiving, inventory, manufacturing, and sales support (even compensation) systems become intertwined.

Data standards take on a new level of importance because all applications must expect the same details. Ownership of information and the authorization to change details becomes a particularly sensitive subject. All parties must have a clear understanding of their responsibilities for providing and maintaining operating information.

Managing Maintenance Requirements

The development of interorganization systems is a continuing process. EDI activities cannot be installed and then left to operate unattended. Rather, like information systems in general, they require ongoing support, either because processing requirements change or because new business partners must be accommodated. In addition, ongoing changes in transaction systems linked to the EDI process continue their typical evolution. On both the customer and the supplier end of the link, the implications are the same: Changes must be accommodated.

Organizations experienced in EDI typically find that they have underestimated the level of maintenance and support required. Many of these organizations today have as many staff members focused on EDI maintenance as they do on new systems development.

Underwriting costs

The decision to proceed with interorganization systems is also a decision to invest additional resources in information processing. The internal IS development costs are often recognized and dealt with according to typical resource allocation guidelines (e.g., chargeback to the functional unit). Other costs, however, may be questioned (e.g., how is the cost of the value-added carrier providing the EDI network charged?).

Frequently, organizations must underwrite the costs associated with bringing their trading partners into their EDI environment. It is quite common for an organization to provide the software the partner needs to get started; in some instances, personnel are sent to the trading partner's site to help with startup. Although these costs are not insurmountable, they are internal issues to be addressed. Often they do not fit within existing IS operating policies in most organizations.

Conclusion

The growing emphasis on compressing business time, enhancing the linkage between customers and suppliers, and improving the effectiveness with which businesses operate, for both strategic and tactical gain, has brought fundamental change to business as usual. The potential of EDI as a vehicle for interorganizational business is substantial. It can enhance both local and international commerce.

However, the full perspective of the business change must not be overlooked. EDI alters the way organizations do business and therefore management must be willing to adjust fundamental activities, such as when and how orders are processed or funds transferred, to participate successfully. Above all, EDI is not a technology change but a restructuring of business practice.

Questions

1. Give some examples of transactions for which electronic data interchange is commonly used.

2. What are the advantages and the disadvantages to a major firm (such as an automobile manufacturer or an airplane manufacturer) of following international EDI standards?

3. What are the strategic advantages and disadvantages of adopting EDI?

2.7

Applications of Global Information Technology:

Key Issues for Management

Blake Ives and Sirkka L. Jarvenpaa

Introduction

Globalization reveals an imposing future for the managers of many firms. In numerous industries, globalization has already produced dramatic changes in key markets, major competitors, and products. Many of North America's biggest firms have become relatively small players in the new global markets (i.e., "the Global 1000"), with industry leaders increasingly headquartered in Asia or Western Europe (*Business Week*, 1989). Firms operating in these new world markets will increasingly be at a serious strategic disadvantage if they are unable to firmly control their worldwide operations and manage them in a globally coordinated manner (Bartlett and Ghoshal, 1989).

Exciting opportunities

Investments in information technology (IT) can give firms a basis for increased coordination and control or can provide direct competitive advantage in world markets. For example, a large computer vendor uses its worldwide network to ensure that products designed in the U.S. are appropriate for customers throughout the world. Lawyers for a large oil firm use the firm's worldwide office system to prepare international contracts in a fraction of the time previously

SOURCE: "Applications of Global Information Technology: Key Issues of Management" by Blake Ives and Sirkka L. Jarvenpaa, from *MIS Quarterly*, Vol. 15, Number 1, March 1991. Copyright 1991 by the Society for Information Management Systems Research Center at the University of Minnesota. Reprinted by special permission.

153

required. In a large merchant bank, a global integrated trading system helps the dealers manage their currency risk and calculate profits, while it also permits the firm to operate in a virtual 24-hour currency market. Moreover, traders conducting business through the Australian or Japanese subsidiaries, which are located across the international date line from the U.S., enjoy a full extra business day before they must settle with North American and European trading partners.

As these examples demonstrate, information technology on a global scale compresses time and space and permits the duplication and sharing of scarce corporate expertise. Such capabilities provide firms with an opportunity to leverage advantages in both market size and geographical scope while they simultaneously provide the means to respond rapidly to the unique requirements of national markets.

Difficult challenges

Misalignment of information technology with global business strategy can severely hamper a firm's efforts to seek global pre-eminence. For instance, a decentralized financial services firm catering to globetrotting customers found it very difficult to enlist the support of its foreign subsidiaries in a worldwide customer database. Subsidiary managers were reluctant to endorse an integrated corporate solution for fear that in the short-run it would adversely impact their earnings and in the long-run reduce their autonomy. Similarly, a manufacturing firm sought to rationalize production across plants in different countries, but found that systems incompatibilities severely restricted the range of products that could be moved from one factory to another.

Harnessing IT on a global scale presents management with problems that are far more challenging than those encountered in sharing systems across domestic divisions. In fact, it is likely that insights gained in studying IT on an international level will provide solutions applicable to large, domestic-distributed IT operations. Unfortunately, progress in the other direction—the exportation of domestic systems solutions—often proves to be less rewarding. Cash, et al. (1988) note problems related to language, currency, culture, national infrastructure, availability of IT staff, data export control, and trade unions. Hardware, software, and communications costs and availability also pose major challenges—challenges for which domestic solutions are often inappropriate. For instance, a centralized hardware solution may provide the best economics in the U.S. where communications costs are low. Elsewhere in the world, however, the high costs of telecommunications may favor a decentralized or distributed solution.

Information technology vendors are often poorly prepared to support global information requirements across national boundaries. For instance, a multinational decentralized petroleum company chose to install a worldwide electronic mail system to better leverage its personnel in 45 countries. Management was disheartened to learn that they would require 14 different versions of the hardware vendors' office productivity system, each tailored to a particular language and each varying in functionality. Regional data centers were required to support multiple versions of the software, and for some Asian countries, there was no appropriate language version available.

Key issues for management

This article identifies the key issues that a manager charged with managing global IT applications for U.S. multinational is likely to face—issues that must be mastered if the firm is to use IT successfully in the new global markets. The primary objective of this article is to provide a rich description of global IT applications and some tentative generalizations.

The following definition for an application of global information technology serves as the framework for our discussion of the key issues:

A global information technology application

- contributes to achieving a firm's global business strategy
- by using information technology platforms
- to store, transmit, and manipulate data
- across cultural environments.

Hence, in this article we identify key issues for the following four elements of global IT: (1) the linkage of global IT to global business strategy, (2) information technology platforms, (3) international data sharing, and (4) cultural environments. Previous work pertaining to applications to global IT and to each element of global IT is first reviewed.

Global Information Technology in the Literature

The rapid globalization of business and the increased role of IT in shaping corporate strategy indicate that global IT is a topic of considerable importance to information systems practitioners. Our review of previous work suggests that the information systems research community has generally neglected this important area. Cash, et al. (1988) call international IT "a major, largely unreported, unstudied IT story" (p. 212). Feeny, et al. (1990) argue that the role of information technology in supporting and enabling the globalization of business has been "understated and certainly under-explored" (p. 36). When international topics have been addressed by the information systems research community, it has often been as a *replication* of American research in a different country. This type of work has focused on countries or cultures as the primary unit of analysis. By contrast, the focus of this article is *applications* of information technology that transcend national boundaries.

A few case studies consider global IT applications. These include the development and implementation of a worldwide sales management information system at Du Pont's Polymer Products Department (Kneitel, 1980), the strategic use of IT at a paper company with 100 worldwide sales offices, agents, and distribution centers and headquartered in Finland (Reponen and Copeland, 1986), and two case studies (Selig, 1982) illustrating strategic planning approaches for information resources in a multinational organization. Keen, et al. (1982) discuss the implementation hurdles of an integrated bank transaction processing system in 40 worldwide locations.

The literature, however, offers little guidance for choosing between local versus common applications. Keen, et al. (1982) argue that the more standardized the business process across home and foreign locations, the larger the fraction of the system will consist of the "common core." The larger the core, and therefore, the smaller the need for local tailoring, the more sense a common global application makes. But, Keen, et al. (1982) warn that relatively minor differences in local markets can mean major requirements for local tailoring. Viewing the issue from a higher level, Reck (1989) concludes that a firm should structure its information systems function to operate in a "mixed mode." Reck recognizes that different suites of applications will support different business strategies and will therefore require varying degrees of commonality across borders.

Global business strategy

Some business strategies are more dependent than others on timely, accurate, and complete information on overseas operations (Egelhoff, 1982). For instance, in the past, home offices typically conceded considerable autonomy to their foreign businesses (Bartlett, 1986). Worldwide reporting and information requirements were minimal under these "country-specific" strategies. As information technology advanced into foreign facilities, it was primarily used to serve local information needs. It is not surprising then that in 1985, Freeman (1985) found that IT activities were relatively decentralized to company units for most U.S. multinationals.

More recently, firms have begun to adopt globally integrative strategies in response to increasingly competitive global markets. Among these pressures are the search for global economies of scale and scope, the development of global products, and the increasing requirement to satisfy the needs of worldwide customers. The consequent increased need for global coordination and control has placed greater demands on information and communication between headquarters and subsidiaries (Carlyle, 1988). In search of global efficiencies, many firms have started to move away from a geographic focus and toward a business operations orientation. Carlyle (1988) suggests that these changes in corporate strategy and structure may be precipitating more centralized global IT activities: one common telecommunications network, shared databases, and standardized reporting and planning systems. But, writing in 1987, Keen was unenthusiastic about the pace of the transition to global information systems. He concluded that, "It is absurd that so many international firms have global business strategies but no corresponding strategy for managing information technology internationally" (p. 1). Others fear that a poorly crafted IT strategy will limit organizational options. Thompson and Taylor (1988), discussing the organizational repositioning that will be required when Europe unifies in 1992, warn that, "inflexible minds presiding over installed bases of unconnected applications software and incomparable data will retard the organization's ability to redraw its map of Europe" (p. 6).

IT can propagate new business strategies, but a more common goal is to effectively harness IT to an existing global business strategy. Such alignment requires a shared understanding of the firm's overall global strategy. Various authors have presented models of global business strategy (e.g., Levitt, 1983; Perlmutter, 1969; Rowe, et al., 1986), but usually with little or no attention to information processing requirements. For example, Porter (1986) positions a firm's global business strategy along a spectrum ranging from *multidomestics*, whose off-shore operations independently set strategy and handle production, marketing, and administrative functions, to *global multinationals*, who integrate their activities on a worldwide basis to capture the linkages between countries, while still maintaining some single-country perspective. Shanks (in Freeman, 1985), Carlyle (1990), and Runyan (1989) all agree that some amount of centralized IS is critical for global multinationals.

The global business strategy models of Bartlett and Ghoshal (1989) are among the most developed because they tie business strategy to a set of organizational forces faced by the firm. Bartlett and Ghoshal identify four broad strategies that a multinational firm may pursue. The firm following a *multinational* strategy operates its foreign subsidiaries nearly autonomously or in a loose federation so as to quickly sense and respond to diverse local needs and national opportunities. The requirement for local responsiveness is the driving organizational force. The firm following a *global* strategy closely coordinates worldwide activities through central control from headquarters so as to capitalize on the economies associated with a standardized product design, global scale-manufacturing, and centralized control of worldwide operations. In this strategy, the firm is organized around a requirement for global efficiencies. The firm following an *international* strategy exploits parent company knowledge through worldwide diffusion and adaptation. Rapid deployment of innovation is the prime operating principle. The firm following a *transnational* strategy seeks to retain local flexibility while simultaneously achieving global integration and efficiencies as well as worldwide diffusion of innovations. According to Bartlett and Ghoshal (1989, p. 69), "Dynamic interdependence is the basis of a transnational company—one that can think globally and act locally."

The transnational model appears to be similar to the global multinational model of Porter (1986) and also resembles the global model of Ohmae (1989). According to Ohmae, the global model prevails today because customer "needs have globalized and the fixed costs of meeting them have soared" (p. 161). Ohmae (1989) cautions that this does not mean that firms should necessarily pursue universal products. He argues that the businesses that are most likely to succeed in global markets are those that can devise a short list of *lead-country* models—a product tailored to the dominant and distinct markets—and can adapt these lead-country models to local preferences at low cost. Ohmae's lead-country models have implications for IT. The common global systems need to be designed to efficiently accommodate local add-ons for local responsiveness. The add-ons might reflect differences in underlying product or marketing and distribution strategies (e.g., sold direct or through shared or exclusive channels), local resource or legal requirements, or the strategic importance of subsidiaries to headquarters.

Information technology platforms

Keen (1987) contends that ". . . the telecommunications architecture is generally the strategic driver for evolving a truly international capability" (p. 9). He suggests that management fund the *backbone* global communications network as "a corporate business asset, rather than allowing local case-by-case, cost-based decisions about communications facilities" (p. 2). But he warns that the builder of a global communication system must tread carefully when designing the infrastructure or seeking out international standards for IT. For example, Japan, Germany, Brazil, and France have used information policy to protect their national computer and telecommunications concerns (Lerner, 1984). To operate in such countries, Wiggin (1987) suggests that senior management "finds friends in the PTTs"—the state-owned post office and telecommunications operators that closely regulate the telecommunications industry. Buss (1984) suggests that corporate contacts with the PTT "show a corporate concern for the issues and a willingness to comply with both the letter and the spirit of the law" (p. 118).

Worldwide variations in hardware and software features, i.e., availability and quality, force firms to use different vendor products in different parts of the world. This causes major obstacles in integrating communication networks, hardware, and disparate systems software for global applications. Vendors' protectionist policies for their products are cited as the major barrier for agreements on standards such as Open Systems Interconnection (OSI) (Cash, et al., 1988). Keen (1987) argues that "the fastest way that standards emerge is through the power of key market players" (p. 5). Although vendors are usually considered as key market players (Quinn, 1987), there have been other suggestions that appropriate IT standards will only develop if the user organizations coordinate their demands and play an active role in "international pressure groups" (*Datamation*, 1988). In the area of electronic data interchange (EDI), standards have been developed jointly by the United Nations and ANSI. Harrington (1988) projects that 400,000 companies will have implemented international EDI standards (EDIFACT) by 1995.

International data sharing

The international flow of data has received attention both in the literature and from various legislative bodies. Much of this has been focused on the issues of data privacy and transborder data flows (TDF). TDFs have been defined as "movements of machine-readable data for processing, storage, or retrieval across national boundaries" (Chandran, et al., 1987, p. 75), and have been classified by Lerner (1984) into four types: (1) operational data including orders, accounting statements and records, or management directives, (2) personally identifiable data that pertain to credit records, travel reservations, or employment records, (3) electronic transfers of money, and (4) technical and scientific data that include instructions for operating machinery in a plant. TDF laws usually concern the second category, although many countries also restrict transfer of technical and scientific data (Smith and Healy, 1987).

TDF laws originated in the 1970s from concerns about the integrity and confidentiality of personal data. Since then, several countries have extended privacy laws to protect "legal persons" such as associations and corporations. As of 1988, 24 nations had privacy legislation on transborder data flows (McCrohan and Lowe, 1988). The impact of these laws was predicted to be devastating for U.S. multinationals. Buss (1984) argued that "legislation is now being strengthened to the point where it may hamper or even completely stall a company's important operations" (p. 111). A study conducted in 1985 involving 370 service companies reported that 63 percent considered TDF regulations to be a serious potential problem, although only 31 percent reported problems at the time (Kane and Ricks, 1988).

Global applications present other data management challenges. Because users of global applications often access the same worldwide database or because data from different foreign locations are intended to be shared and consolidated, global systems require well-defined and standard data definitions. In fact, Keen, et al. (1982) argue persuasively that commonality in global systems should be established primarily through standardization of data rather than standardization of programs.

Cultural environment

Finally, global applications of information technology must be developed for and operate in a heterogeneous cultural environment. Levitt (1983) proposes that consumers have become alike in all parts of the world through the homogenization of needs and desires. This homogenization has resulted from the "proletarianization of communication and travel" (p. 83). It suggests that cultural differences across international user communities may, to some extent at least, be converging.

Nonetheless, cross-cultural IT research has found major cultural disparities that warrant attention in developing global IT applications. Dagwell and Weber (1983) conclude that Australian and Swedish systems designers favor a Theory Y orientation in assessing user needs, whereas U.S. and U.K. designers lean instead toward a Theory X view of users. Kumar and Bjørn-Andersen (1990) found similar differences in values across Canadian and Danish systems designers. Couger and Motiwalla (1985) found major demographic differences between U.S. and Singaporean IS professionals; Singaporean IS professionals were younger, less experienced, and better educated than their U.S. counterparts. Research on group decision support systems has also detected that the assumptions underlying specific information technology features are culture sensitive (Ho, et al., 1989).

Global Information Technology in Practice

Our exploratory study sought to identify the key problems and opportunities facing managers responsible for developing global applications of information technology. These were assessed in terms of (1) the linkage to business strategy, (2) information technology platforms, (3) international data sharing, and (4) cultural environments. We interviewed 25 senior managers responsible for the implementation of global applications of information technology in *Fortune 500* industrial and service firms. The managers were drawn from 19 organizations that represented a variety of industries including petroleum, computers and electronics, chemicals, motor vehicles, financial services, and management consulting services (see Table 1). The firms in the sample were not randomly chosen. Selections were based on our ability to gain access to a firm's senior management; many of the firms were associated either with the information systems programs at the University of Texas or Southern Methodist University.

The typical interviewee was either a project sponsor from the user organization or the individual responsible for project delivery. In seven cases, he or she was either the head of information systems or responsible for a particular suite of applications—e.g., director of worldwide manufacturing systems. Other typical titles included: vice-president for systems development, senior partner (of a large consulting firm), manager of corporate office automation and information services, coordinator of telecommunications planning, and so on.

The applications discussed ranged from the worldwide spare parts network of a computer vendor, a global risk management system of a financial services firm, a reservation system of an airline, a worldwide manufacturing planning and control system implemented by a manufacturer, to the corporate-wide general ledger systems of a petroleum firm and a computer company. Most applications had been completed within the previous two years, though some were still being implemented. All involved at least two countries in addition to corporate headquarters—many spanned several continents including a petroleum application implemented in over 50 countries. Among the applications, some were running on a mainframe at headquarters, some were duplicated for use at multiple regional data centers, and some standalone systems were housed on local PCs or mainframes. Others were housed on different-sized hardware, ranging from PCs to mainframes, depending on the business need within the foreign subsidiary. There were applications developed outside the U.S. and subsequently implemented in the U.S. Others had been exported from the U.S., then severely modified by foreign subsidiaries. In this exploratory study, we sought variety in the application set, industry, and international settings to ensure that we were thoroughly exposed to the phenomenon of global information technology.

TABLE 1 Companies in the Study

COMPANY	INDUSTRY	1988 REVENUES IN BILLIONS	% REVENUE FROM OVERSEAS	COUNTRIES OPERATING IN (PLANTS OR SALES OFFICES)
1	Computers/electronics	>$25	>50%	>50
2	Financial services	$11–25	11–25%	11.25
3	Petroleum	>$25	>50%	>50
4	Petroleum	>$25	>50%	>50
5	Petroleum	>$25	26–50%	>50
6	Manufacturing	>$25	>50%	26–50
7	Computers/electronics	$1–10	11–50%	11–25
8	Transportation	$1–10	11–50%	11–25
9	Computers/electronics	$1–10	>50%	26–50
10	Financial services	$1–10	25–50%	11–25
11	Management consulting	—	—	150 offices worldwide
12	Chemicals	$1–10	<10%	<10
13	Consumer goods	$25–50	<10%	26–50
14	Chemicals	$1–10	25–50%	11–25
15	Manufacturing	$1–10	25–50%	11–25
16	Banking	$1–10	11–25%	11–25
17	Manufacturing	$1–10	>50%	<10
18	Petroleum	$11–25	11–25%	11–25
19	Freight forwarder	<$1	—	26–50

Key Issues for Global IT Management

In this section the interview results for the four elements of global IT applications are reported. The key issues detailed at the end of each subsection summarize the main management concerns expressed in the interviews.

Linking global applications to corporate strategy

The search for systems economies was the initial driving force for global IT applications in many firms. One interviewee recalled being told by the CEO, "We have invested so damn much money in these home office systems—let's get some additional use out of them." Based on their hard won experience, however, the interviewees were nearly unanimous in endorsing the need for a compelling business reason to coordinate and standardize information technology. Many interviewees agreed that they had initially erred by assuming application requirements were similar, when the underlying business processes were later revealed to be different in sometimes subtle but significant ways. For instance, an engineering firm wished to use a common engineering database to share project work between its U.S. and European offices. In addition to anticipated variations in engineering codes and the relative costs of materials, management soon discovered that the European project requirements demanded far more detailed specifications for contractors than had traditionally been required of their U.S. counterparts.

Our interviewees offered a range of business drivers for their global applications. Some of these drivers were strongly linked to the needs of the marketplace—e.g., a global customer or a constrained resource—whereas others were driven by regulatory requirements. Many still mentioned the search for system economies as a driver for global applications. Table 2 summarizes the global business drivers for the applications discussed.

Except for the economies of scale for systems, similar drivers were often mentioned by respondents in the same industry. Hence, it appeared that at least some of the business drivers for global IT are related to an industry in which the firm competes, although others vary by firm, or even by a strategic business unit.

Although the interviewees were typically able to readily identify the business drivers, particularly the industry-based drivers, for the global application under discussion, few were able to state the firm's overall approach or strategy for managing global information technology. Consequently, from the discussions on applications of IT and from the interviewees' comments on their firm's global business strategy, we attempted to infer the *emerging* patterns of managing IT in the respondent firms. Four generic patterns emerged that seemed to be aligned with the four business strategies proposed by Bartlett and Ghoshal (1989). These four strategies, discussed previously, were multinational, global, international, and transnational.

TABLE 2   Business Drivers for Global IT

1. Global consumer/ customer	Firms that serve traveling customers— airlines, hotels, rental car, and credit card companies—find it necessary to have worldwide customer databases. A similar requirement is increasingly being imposed by corporate customers with global operations that more and more are demanding integrated worldwide services.
2. Global product	The product is either the same thoughout the world (e.g., Coca Cola) or is assembled from subsidiaries throughout the world (e.g., security, currency exchange, or real estate). Information systems can provide the ability to manage worldwide marketing programs.
3. Rationalized operations	Different subsidiaries build different parts of the same product based on availability of skills, raw materials, or favorable business climate. For example, a computer manufacturer might build software in the U.K., monitors in South Korea, and circuit boards on the West Coast of the U.S. IT is used to coordinate the operations.
4. Flexible operations	Operations are moved from a plant in one country to a plant in another. For instance, a computer vendor moves production of personal computers between plants in response to labor strife or raw material shortages. Common systems exist across plants, which facilitates the move.
5. Joint resource	National subsidiaries may share certain facilities or people. For instance, the European subsidiaries for a petroleum company jointly own tankers or storage tanks. A material resource system is implemented to track the location of joint resource.

Continued

TABLE 2 (*Continued*)

6. Duplicate facilities	A chemical company uses nearly identical plants to produce gases in different countries. Software supporting that production facility can be readily shared.
7. Scarce resources	A chemical firm requires that high-cost gas compressors be available in case of breakdowns in its identical worldwide plants. High costs prohibit storing them at each facility. A parts logistics system coordinates the compressor's use and distribution.
8. Risk reduction	Risks associated with currency conversions, multiple global markets, and multiple traders are alleviated. For instance, a petroleum company develops a global system for bidding on crude oil contracts, or a multinational bank implements a global risk management system for currency trading.
9. Legal requirements	Information requirements mandated by laws in one or more countries are consolidated. For instance, financial or environmental regulations imposed on a subsidiary may necessitate corporate-wide information requirements if the subsidiary intends to sell or use products manufactured elsewhere.
10. Economies of scale for systems	One corporate-wide system is used to reduce data center requirements, duplicate development activities, and maintenance resources.

Approaches for managing global IT

Independent Global IT Operations

For a few firms in our sample, subsidiaries continued to pursue independent system initiatives, often mirroring a relatively independent *multinational* strategy. Common systems were few and largely exceptions in these firms. Technology choices reflected the influence of local hardware and software vendors as well as the prevailing national communication standards and offerings. For these firms, headquarter's systems personnel rarely traveled abroad on business and had little knowledge or interest in their subsidiaries' system initiatives. Local profit and loss responsibility, coupled with reliance on local information systems departments and local technology, resulted in non-integrated technology platforms, databases, and applications. This lack of integration appeared at times to severely impede efforts to implement global business strategies. For instance, a computer vendor who had neither a global ordering or billing system had a difficult time meeting the needs of a headquarters-based client who sought to design a worldwide system in New York for subsequent implementation in 50 country facilities, with payments to be made from regional offices located in London, Tokyo, Rio, and New York. The independent global IT operations best supports the multinational strategy of Bartlett and Ghoshal. The focus is clearly on local responsiveness, and the applications portfolio is strongly oriented toward local requirements.

Headquarters-Driven Global IT

A number of firms have imposed corporate-wide IT solutions on subsidiaries, at least for some applications. For many firms the headquarters-driven approach was not only desirable but required. These are Bartlett and Ghoshal's (1989) *global* firms that strive for worldwide efficiencies, usually in support of global products. Here the compelling business need and the opportunity to harvest worldwide economies of scale force the firm toward a global systems solution. For instance, large semiconductor manufacturers with global customers and products, rationalized production, and stiff international competition have little choice but to seek global efficiencies. Centralized IT may provide some efficiencies of its own, but, more importantly, it provides the coordination and control necessary for efficient operations throughout the firm.

Headquarters-driven global IT appeared to run into problems without a strong global business need. Efforts resulted in overt or covert resistance to the "ugly American" who suddenly appeared at the subsidiary's data center. This was often a frustrating period for a U.S. systems manager assigned overseas. One interviewee assigned to the U.K. confessed to us that "after a year I had finally learned enough to be useful and not to be bluffed—then I was recalled to the States." For some firms, applications brought over from the U.S. were successfully implemented, but many died later from neglect or unmaintainability after the U.S. emissary departed. In other firms, this approach had ended with a recognition that "their business really is different from ours," followed by a hasty retreat to independent global IT operations. For these firms, the only benefit was unplanned—organizational learning emerging from face-to-face contacts between the subsidiaries' and headquarters' systems people and their major users.

Intellectual Cooperation in Global IT

For some of the firms in our sample, strong links existed between the home office and foreign subsidiaries, but the linkages were those of cooperation and mutual assistance rather than management fiat. In these organizations, headquarters personnel attempted to influence rather than control the information technology choices of their foreign subsidiaries. Personnel were exchanged regularly, and joint application development efforts were initiated. If headquarters had already developed an application that the subsidiary now required, the subsidiary might ask for a copy to modify. Alternatively, they might choose to send a group to the U.S. to study the application thoroughly before developing their own version. One interviewee described the objective that he and his European IT director shared as an attempt to develop "intellectual synergy" between their two groups. This approach to managing IT seems to fit well with Bartlett and Ghoshal's (1989) *international* strategy. The objective in this case is to rapidly disseminate corporate innovation while continuing to provide the flexibility required to be responsive to local business entities.

Integrated Global IT

Bartlett and Ghoshal (1989) have proposed that a *transnational* strategy will supersede the multinational, international, and global strategies currently pursued by different firms. According to Bartlett and Ghoshal, firms will seek this transnational status to permit them to simultaneously be globally efficient, provide local responsiveness, and quickly diffuse organizational innovation. The companies in the study had yet to reach the truly transnational status. Feeny, et al. (1990) have proposed that firms pursuing a transnational strategy will require applications of information technology that reach across national borders to meet the firm's diverse objectives. Here systems solutions would be integrated using international standards and a planned common architecture that will meet the needs of various-sized organizational units operating in diverse environments. Multinational development teams would ensure that organization-wide IT solutions also meet the needs of local business units with applications modules divided into common and locally tailored code. Global database design teams would ascertain the data entities that would be shared across the worldwide organization and develop universal data dictionaries and appropriate databases. Innovation in this case would be a two-way street, with headquarters benefiting from the knowledge of subsidiaries. Several of the firms we talked with, who had previously based their IT strategy on intellectual cooperation or headquarters-driven global IT, had recently recognized the necessity of moving toward the cooperative development of globally integrated applications.

Table 3 lists the key issues resulting from the interviews related to the linkage between IT strategy and business strategy. If no deliberate global IT strategy is deemed necessary or viable at present, management may wish to assess how important such a linkage might become in the future and how to best prepare for that eventuality.

Information technology platforms

Data center consolidation, location operations, vendor relations, and software availability were commonly mentioned concerns related to IT infrastructure. The

TABLE 3   Linking IT and Business Strategy: Key Issues

- ◆ Understand each business unit's global business strategy.
- ◆ Determine the appropriate global IT management approach or IT strategy to align with the global business strategy.
- ◆ Identify the fundamental objective or objectives driving the global IT strategy and global IT applications.
- ◆ Classify and prioritize applications based on their contributions to global business strategy.
- ◆ Assign responsibility for developing and implementing the global IT strategy.
- ◆ Assist senior management to understand the potential impacts of global IT on corporate strategy.

interviewees infrequently discussed data networks and telecommunications as either barriers, if they had fallen behind their competitors, or competitive advantages, if they perceived themselves as leaders.

In many firms, additional data centers were located outside the U.S. These centers were used to meet national or regional needs and sometimes to balance international workloads via satellite communications. According to our interviewees, establishing locations for international data centers presents several challenges: overlapping working hours; local computing and labor regulations; potential theft; sabotage and terrorism; unreliable power sources; availability of completely redundant network backup capability; and the like.

Our interviewees complained that equipping a local data center can be problematic because of high prices for local hardware, the lack of local service for products, the absence of an authorized distributor, and long lead times in acquiring both equipment and spare parts. Interviewees complained that in Japan, for instance, local distributors hold monopoly positions and charge rates nearly double the price of comparable products purchased in the U.S. Economic and technical barriers set by national governments include higher prices for computing equipment and communication lines, restrictions on the importation of equipment and services, and rigid hardware and software standards. Severe import limitations on assembled hardware in countries such as Brazil forced one firm to enter the computer assembly business to outfit their foreign subsidiaries. Even in countries with open trade policies, new hardware models or software versions may take a year or two to be released to the market because the vendor may not have the resources available to quickly adapt the product, documentation, and support to local conditions. To support languages such as Japanese requires that a single character from the language be stored in two, rather than the customary one, bytes of computer storage, often necessitating vendors to make costly and time-consuming modifications to software packages.

According to our interviewees, purchased software packages present unique problems in an international setting. Packages designed to run in Europe may

be incompatible with their American or Asian counterparts, even when purchased from the hardware vendor. Packages from software houses are even less
universally available than those from hardware vendors—no matter how well known
in the U.S. Software houses often rely on licensing agreements with local personnel to handle the sales, distribution, and support of their product. In some
countries, local disregard of copyright restrictions has caused vendors to completely ignore or retreat from a particular market. As a consequence, several firms
have restricted package choices to those provided and supported by their hardware vendor. Others buy PC packages in the U.S. and distribute them to their
subsidiaries. Firms dealing in developing countries face even more challenging
problems. A firm with operations in China first selected a hardware platform that
they could legally import into the country and then searched for applications that
potentially might be of some use to their Chinese business.

Table 4 lists the key issues related to technological infrastructure.

Data

In 1988, McCrohan and Lowe (1988) predicted increasing regulation of transborder data flows (TDF), claiming that "the control of transborder data flows will
be the trade war of the 1990's" (p. 8). Our interviewees tell us that McCrohan
and Lowe's war was never fought. One manager claimed that "transborder data
flow is a myth." Another said that "TDF looked very exciting in the 70s, but
proved to be a non-event in the 80s." One expert explained that many transborder data laws are vague and therefore difficult to follow and to enforce. He explained his policy for dealing with the regulators: "The officials charged with
enforcement are often as confused about these complex laws as we are and they
are not anxious to spend much time interpreting them. We don't ask their permission. Instead, we tell them what we intend to do and ask them to let us
know if there are any problems."

Two application categories seemed most vulnerable to TDF or privacy legislation. The first is payroll systems, which generally do not lend themselves to

---

TABLE 4   **Information Technology Platforms: Key Issues**

- Determine the number and locations of regional data centers.
- Ensure 24-hour system availability and support for global applications op-
  erating from global data centers.
- Select vendors who can provide support in dispersed locations.
- Select hardware and software appropriate for shared data or processing re-
  quirements.
- Expect delays and incompatibilities from vendors operating outside their
  own home markets.
- Anticipate a reduced set of hardware and software alternatives.
- Identify reliable local IT distributors and service providers.

global use. The second is personnel-record systems. Typically, the firm must commit to providing the same level of security and access to personnel data stored abroad as is required by privacy legislation locally. Although our IT experts acknowledged the difficulty of transporting personal data from some countries in Europe to the U.S. or from Canada to the U.S., some questioned whether "we even really need it [personal data] in the U.S." Few companies expressed need for a skills inventory system that spans national boundaries. However, as corporations continue to institute truly transnational corporate strategies, the need for worldwide personnel systems—at least for senior managers and professionals—is likely to surface.

Although transborder data laws and regulations were not perceived to be a major obstacle to global IT, worldwide data management and data standardization within the firms were perceived to present significant barriers for international data sharing. Defining common data names presents unique problems when multiple languages are used. But, even within countries sharing a language, the same word or phrase may take on quite different meanings. Differing national standards, rules of thumb, or differences in technology platforms also present problems when, for instance, common part codes are desirable. Data modeling presents further challenges as real world entities and relationships among data entities, as well as day-to-day plant and field operations, vary from country to country. According to one executive, "People suddenly just forgot how to speak English" when confronted with standards that threatened cherished local operating procedures.

To find an organizational body within the firm that is willing to lead the standardization effort may be difficult. A major manufacturer of farm equipment, for example, installed a worldwide manufacturing system in its plants. The corporate finance group was responsible for developing common standards for general ledger accounts, but nobody was willing to take action to standardize part numbers. Finally, the project manager from the corporate IT group developed a new standard coding scheme for parts. Local personnel complained, but not enough to catch the ear of top management. The project manager commented: "The systems group became a catalyst for changes that should have been done long before."

The key issues related to international data that were uncovered in the interviews are listed in Table 5.

Cultural environment

"Not Invented Here" and "Unsuitable for Our Environment" were commonly identified barriers that severely hampered attempts to standardize on a global or regional application. Several interviewees acknowledged that these concerns had been well founded in the past. We found some signs of them still. One respondent, for instance, was disappointed when system users in his Japanese subsidiary balked at data fields containing dollar signs ($) as substitutes for the yen sign (¥). Nevertheless, the Japanese were recognized as being more

TABLE 5   International Data Sharing: Key Issues

- Weigh the desirability of transborder sharing and standardizing against the requirements for local flexibility.
- Understand your responsibilities, limitations, and exposures vis-a-vis TDF and privacy laws.
- Assign responsibility for data standardization.
- Involve subsidiary users and IT groups in the standardization of common data names and data modeling activities.
- Design and develop a global data architecture around global business objectives.
- Physically locate databases based on business requirements, legal considerations, relative costs, vendor support, organizational politics, etc.

accepting of "parachuted" solutions than the Europeans. According to several interviewees, the Japanese, once convinced that an application met their needs, were quick to embrace it. Several firms interviewed had chosen to distribute development between the U.S. and European subsidiaries to neutralize subsidiary resistance to an imposed outside solution. This appeared to provide some short-run advantages, but in the long run reduce opportunities for full integration.

Variations in work values were perceived across cultures, some no doubt stereotypic. One interviewee claimed that employees in one European subsidiary were half as productive as their American counterparts (they were also paid approximately half as much). In another country, where skilled jobs were at a premium, workers were seen as highly protective of their personal knowledge. The interviewee had found that employees there were generally unwilling to share knowledge with others and considerably overstated their own proficiency. Another interviewee had been delighted to discover that although Japanese systems personnel were in short supply, women were more readily available than men. After the interviewee encouraged her Japanese systems manager to hire several women, she was later chagrined to discover that he had "turned them into tea ladies." Religion is often another important factor. Prayer breaks and long holidays must be accommodated. Obviously, the cultural stereotyping goes both ways; managers from the European subsidiary of a U.S. firm described their American counterparts as "inclined to do something fast, but likely to have to later sow the seeds of the storm they planted."

The firms' subsidiaries also varied in systems skill sets. Several interviewees noted that the French were skilled in data modeling and in the more theoretical aspects of systems development. Other interviewees reported the English to be well trained in the use of structured development methodologies, while the Germans were seen as excellent project managers. Singaporeans were described by one interviewee as extremely hard working, skilled, and willing to take on any task assigned. Another manager described them as the consultants of Asia. Australia, on the other hand, was seen as lacking in systems skills. Where such observations reflect real rather than perceived cross-cultural differences, there may be opportunities for creatively allocating systems work or for fostering organizational learning across subsidiaries.

The key issues related to cultural environment are summarized in Table 6.

Developing Global Applications of Information Technology

Some of the cultural, infrastructure, and data issues that can impede the successful employment of global information systems were described above. The importance of tightly linking information technology to the firm's global business strategy was also highlighted. Next, some additional, but more specific, issues expressed by the interviewees about the development and maintenance of individual global applications are described. A few generic approaches used to overcome these specific development-related issues are also presented.

The most commonly mentioned challenges in the development of global applications were the determination of global versus local requirements and the maintenance of high levels of local user involvement and ownership. One interviewee estimated that it takes five to 10 times more time to reach an understanding and agreement on system requirements and deliverables when the users and developers are in different countries. This is partially explained by travel requirements and language and cultural differences, but technical limitations also contribute to the problem. In many developing countries, outdated or unreliable communications systems can restrict or totally preclude regular phone calls, fax transmissions, or dial-up computer connections. One interviewee, who faced a 12-hour time difference in reaching some subsidiaries, claimed that it typically took nearly an hour to establish a phone link and that the line would often go dead during the call.

Ongoing maintenance of a functioning application presented problems for many respondents. Our interviews suggested that global systems face similar, but

---

TABLE 6   Cultural Environment: Key Issues

- Identify critical systems applications or skills competencies (or weaknesses) possessed by foreign subsidiaries.
- Provide opportunities for global organizational learning related to these areas of unique competency.
- Recognize the sensitivity of foreign subsidiaries to imposed solutions and seek mutually acceptable alternatives.
- Seek new ways to sensitize managers sent abroad (or brought to the United States) to cultural, religious, and political differences.

usually more extreme, maintenance problems than do distributed domestic systems. If the global system is run from one centralized data center serving different markets, time-zone differences pose problems for preventive and file maintenance. An interruption during a third shift in New York City will present midday service interruptions in Tokyo. One respondent recalled a decision he had made earlier in his career that eventually came back to haunt him. "For various reasons we had designed the system so that it had to be down for one day each year. I had chosen the Fourth of July [U.S. Independence Day] because everyone would be on vacation that day."

If the global system is to be run on multiple host computers, a decision must be made whether to develop a single system reflecting all the variations required for its target countries or to develop multiple sets of code, each tailored to a particular environment. The first option ensures a more consistent evolution of the system, but may cause performance degradation and slow response to local maintenance requests. Even within one single system, if run from multiple data centers, there tends to be an evolution to multiple local systems. "Without strong central supervision in maintenance," one of our interviewees argued, "there is a natural affinity for local solutions, no matter how similar the business."

The interviews surfaced three approaches for overcoming problems in developing and implementing global systems. The most common approach is to transform the home office or "best in firm" application into a global system. Some respondents reported better success in bringing a European system to the U.S. than the other way around, because the European systems were already designed to deal with multiple languages and currency conversions. Having identified the system, it is then modified to meet worldwide requirements. A smaller version of the system may be created for developing countries where both the required functionality and technological resources are modest. Almost without exception, the worldwide roll-out of the application has been gradual. Typically, the system is first modified to meet the requirements of the European subsidiaries. Later, the requirements of the Far Eastern operations might be added, followed by the requirements from South American subsidiaries, and so on.

A second development approach requires assembly of a multinational design team. Systems and user personnel from headquarters and from local subsidiaries are posted to one design location, often for months at a time. Costs for this approach were reported as high. One respondent noted that the costs to maintain a U.S. systems manager in Japan are approximately 2.5 times greater than the U.S. fully costed rate. Some countries restrict the number of foreign personnel assigned to a firm's local office, and the procedures to gain approval for staff can be time-consuming. Development outside the U.S. need not always be expensive, however. For instance, one firm reported that a U.S.-based software engineer costs three times as much as an Indian with similar qualifications.

Whatever their costs, multinational design teams ensure that appropriate decisions are made concerning allocations of system functionality to common versus local code, adherence to international standards, and, over time, the development of common tools. The approach also develops personal networks across borders and exposes the home office personnel to the environment of foreign operations (and vice versa).

Parallel development is the third approach. Here, the project is broken into components, with each component developed by a different home office or subsidiary development team. One firm included in the study was using this approach with a system currently in the requirements stage. The location of particular development sites was selected based on the availability of appropriate expertise and resources. The home office was scheduled to develop one significant module of the global system, while a European systems group was scheduled to develop a second. Each was expected to assist the other with requirements determination. The respondent hoped that common development methodologies, shared software engineering tools, electronic mail, and consistent definitions of data would ensure close coordination and consistency in the resulting application.

Few of the firms had considered a common methodology for systems development projects to facilitate cooperation in global projects, and there was little activity in implementing common automated development tools across subsidiaries. Interestingly, several of the manufacturers we interviewed already used common, automated design tools within their product or process engineering groups in different countries, but shared software development tools appear to lag far behind their engineering equivalents.

In summary, management must realize that global applications are expensive and difficult to develop and operate. Even when a home office system is transformed into a global system, designers must fully understand the similarities and differences in the underlying business processes across countries. The applications must also often be designed with 24-hour, seven-day-a-week support and operational requirements in mind. Maintenance must be closely orchestrated for duplicated systems. To allow development in centers in different parts of the world, common development approaches, tools, and methodologies must be agreed upon. But perhaps of most critical importance is the need to align the global applications and application approaches with global business objectives.

Future Research Directions

The purpose of this study was to outline some of the key management issues in global information technology and broadly examine the phenomenon of global IT through semi-structured interviews with a relatively small number of senior managers. This broad brush approach is appropriate given both the complexity of the area and the lack of previous literature. Future researchers may find it advantageous to focus on some of the specific "key management issues" identified here.

We have several practical recommendations for conducting global IT research. First, we encourage researchers to be creative and opportunistic in studying some of the naturally occurring experiments such as Europe 1992 or the opening up of Eastern Europe. "Living" with a multinational development team for a few months provides another fascinating natural laboratory for studying project management and team management issues in a global area. Moreover, voice mail, electronic mail, and fax messages so common in these international interchanges provide artifacts of considerable potential value to the interested researcher. Finally, researchers should involve scholars located throughout the world in their projects to reduce the costs of research while fostering global learning. Our own global messaging systems give us the infrastructure for coordinating global efforts, while providing us with experience participating in and managing our own global enterprise.

There are also limitations of this research that may suggest additional opportunities for future investigators. Our sample size was small (only U.S.-based), and selected partially on the basis of convenience. Our conversations with the interviewees, though far ranging, were relatively short and were biased by the interviewees' current concerns and faulty memories. Our starting point was business applications rather than either the corporation or a specific business unit within that corporation. For a large, multinational firm with multiple diverse business units, it is likely that one would find a diversity of both global business strategies and corresponding IT management approaches.

Conclusion

By the year 2000, firms with worldwide operations will use advances in communications and computer technology to leverage their distinctive competencies. This may mean providing multinational customers with a singular worldwide identity or being able to quickly adapt products to the requirements of different cultures and nationalities. It may mean being able to shift production schedules from one country to another or producing lead-country products with common components and tools. Implementing any of these strategies will require a major upheaval for existing IT applications and architectures—most of which were initially designed to support single geographic markets and homogeneous hardware environments. These new business needs will require software and documentation that can be quickly enabled for particular national languages so that products available in one part of the world are nearly simultaneously made available throughout the world. Top management will demand instant access to meaningful data from around the world. Engineers of global products will require global information on legal requirements, professional codes, product performance, and customer needs. These new strategies will require us to leverage scarce intellectual resources on a worldwide basis using knowledge systems, databases, and various communication systems.

In the future, many global applications will be interorganizational. Multinational firms will require immediate access to information systems residing in the computer systems of national customs departments, freight forwarders and consolidators, brokers, carriers, bankers, and insurers as well as their customers, suppliers, and channel partners. Participation in such networks will require firms to have carefully integrated their own internal processing systems using internationally recognized standards. Firms who fail to build those global and interorganizational information bridges will be increasingly at a competitive disadvantage.

Acknowledgements

We want to thank Peat Marwick Main Foundation for financial assistance on this project. We are also grateful to Siddik Badruddin for his able research assistance and Michael Vitale for comments on a previous draft.

References

Bartlett, C. A. "Building and Managing the Transnational: The New Organizational Challenge," in *Competition in Global Industries*, M. E. Porter (ed.), Harvard Business School Press, Boston, MA, 1986.

Bartlett, C. A. and Ghoshal, S. *Managing Across Borders: The Transnational Solution*, Harvard Business School Press, Boston, MA, 1989.

Business Week. "The Global 1000—The Leaders," July 17, 1989, pp. 139–145.

Buss, M. D. J. "Legislative Threat to Transborder Data Flow," *Harvard Business Review* (62: 3), May–June 1984, pp. 111–118.

Carlyle, R. E. "Managing IS at Multinationals," *Datamation*, March 1, 1988, pp. 54–57.

Carlyle, R. E. "The Tomorrow Organization," *Datamation*, February 1, 1990, pp. 22–29.

Cash, J. I., McFarlan, F. W., and McKenney, J. L. *Corporate Information Systems Management: The Issues Facing Senior Executives*, Irwin, Homewood, IL, 1988.

Chandran, R., Phatak, A., and Sambharya, R. "Transporter Data Flows: Implications for Multinational Corporations," *Business Horizons* (30:6), November–December 1987, pp. 74–81.

Couger, J. D. and Motiwalla, J. "Occidental Versus Oriental IS Professionals' Perceptions on Key Factors for Motivation," *Proceedings of the Sixth International Conference on Information Systems*, Indianapolis, IN, December 1985, pp. 105–112.

Dagwell, R. and Weber, R. "System Designers' User Models: A Comparative Study and Methodological Critique," *Communications of the ACM* (26:11), November 1983, pp. 987–997.

Datamation. "International Users: What the World Needs Now," May 1, 1988, International Section, 48:1–4.

Egelhoff, W. G. "Strategy and Structure in Multinational Corporations: An Information-Processing Approach," *Administrative Science Quarterly* (27), 1982, pp. 435–458.

Feeny, D., Earl, M. N., and Stevenson, H. "Information Technology and Global Strategy: From Trade-offs to Simultaneities," working paper, Oxford Institute of Information Management, Templeton College, Oxford, OX1 5NY, England, 1990.

Freeman, D. H. "Managing Information Systems at the Multinational," *Infosystems* (32:1), January 1985, pp. 58–62.

Harrington, L. "Global EDI Language May Have Finally Arrived," *Traffic Management* (27), April 1988, pp. 17–18.

Ho, T. H., Raman, K. S., and Watson, R. T. "Group Decision Support Systems: The Cultural Factor," *Proceedings of the Tenth International Conference on Information Systems*, Boston, MA, December 1989, pp. 119–129.

Kane, M. J. and Ricks, D. A. "Is Transnational Data Flow Regulation a Problem," *Journal of International Business Studies* (19:3), Fall 1988, pp. 477–482.

Keen, P. G. W. "An International Perspective on Managing Information Technologies," An ICIT Briefing Paper, International Center for Information Technologies, Washington, D.C., 1987.

Keen, P. G. W., Bronsema, G. S., and Zuboff, S. "Implementing Common Systems: One Organization's Experience," *Systems, Objectives, and Solutions* (2), 1982, pp. 125–142.

Kneitel, A. M. "Evolving and Implementing a Worldwide Management Information System (IMS/MIS)," *MIS Quarterly* (4:3), September 1980, pp. 31–40.

Kumar, K. and Bjørn-Andersen, N. "A Cross-Cultural Comparison of IS Designer Values," *Communications of the ACM* (33:5), May 1990, pp. 528–538.

Lerner, E. J. "International Data Wars are Brewing," *IEEE Spectrum* (21:7), July 1984, pp. 45–49.

Levitt, T. "The Globalization of Markets," *Harvard Business Review* (61:3), May–June 1983, pp. 92–102.

McCrohan, K. F. and Lowe, L. S. "Non-Tariff Barriers to International Data Flow," *Industrial Management and Data Systems*, May/June 1988, pp. 8–11.

Ohmae, K. "Managing in a Borderless World," *Harvard Business Review* (67:3), May–June 1989, pp. 152–161.

Perlmutter, H. V. "The Tortuous Evolution of the Multinational Corporation," *Columbia Journal of World Business* (4:1), January–February 1969, pp. 9–18.

Porter, M. E. *Competition in Global Industries*, Harvard Business School Press, Boston, MA, 1986.

Quinn, E. "Global Push for OSI Standards," *Euromoney*, Special Report, August 1987, pp. 31–33.

Reck, R. H. "The Shock of Going Global," *Datamation*, August 1, 1989, pp. 67–69.

Reponen, T. and Copeland, D. "Finnpap/Finnboard," Harvard Business School, Case No. 9-186-130, December 1986.

Rowe, A. J., Mason, R., and Dickel, K. *Strategic Management: A Methodological Approach*, Addison-Wesley, Reading, MA, 1986.

Runyan, L. "Global IS Strategies," *Datamation*, December 1, 1989, pp. 71–72, 78.

Selig, G. J. "Approaches to Strategic Planning for Information Resource Management (IRM) in Multinational Corporations," *MIS Quarterly* (6:2), June 1982, pp. 33–45.

Smith, K. A. and Healy, P. E. "Transborder Data Flows: The Transfer of Medical and Other Scientific Information by the United States," *Information Society* (5:2), 1987, pp. 67–75.

Thompson, J. and Taylor, S. "Europe in 1992: Winning Through Technology," *Indications*, Index Group, Five Cambridge Center, Cambridge, MA 02142, 1988.

Wiggin, G. "The Golden Rules of Global Networking," *Datamation* (33:19), October 1, 1987, pp. 68–73.

Questions

1. Compare the four approaches to managing global information technology discussed by the authors.

2. Suppose a company has divisions in the United States, in France, and in Japan. How would cultural differences among the three countries affect the information technology managers?

3. What are the advantages and disadvantages of creating a multinational design team?

2.8

Applications of the Future

Raymond Kurzweil

Scenarios

Since the founding of the computer industry almost half a century ago, one of its most salient and consistent features has been change. Functionality per unit cost has been increasing exponentially for decades, a trend that shows no sign of abating. When I attended MIT in the late 1960s, thousands of students and professors shared a *single* computer, an IBM 7094 with 294,912 bytes of core storage (organized as 65,536 words of 36 bits each) and a speed of about 250,000 instructions per second. One needed considerable influence to obtain more than a few seconds of computer time per day. Today, one can buy a personal computer with ten times the speed and memory for a few thousand dollars. In *Metamagical Themas*, Doug Hofstadter cites an actual job that took 10 people with electromechanical calculators ten months to perform in the early 1940s, was redone on an IBM 704 in the early 1960s in 20 minutes, and now would take only a few seconds on a personal computer.[1] David Waltz points out that memory today, after adjustment for inflation, costs only one one-hundred millionth of what it did in 1950.[2] If the automotive industry made as much progress in the past two decades, a typical automobile today would cost about two dollars (the doubling of price performance every 22 months on average has resulted in an improvement factor of about 2,000 in 20 years; this is comparable to the difference between the 7094 of the late 1960s and a personal computer with a Intel 80386 chip today).[3] If we go back to the first relay-based computers, a

SOURCE: "Scenarios" from *Intelligent Machines*, Richard Kurzweil, Editor, MIT Press 1991, pp. 401–416. Reprinted by permission of the MIT Press.

[1] Douglas R. Hofstadter, *Metamagical Themas: Questing for the Essence of Mind and Pattern*, New York: Basic Books, 1985, p. 128.

[2] David Waltz, "The Prospects for Building Truly Intelligent Machines," *Daedelus*, Winter 1988, p. 204.

[3] The preface in Tom Forester's *The Information Technology Revolution* examines similar issues. Cambridge, MA: MIT Press, 1985.

personal computer today is nearly a million times faster at a tiny fraction of the cost. Many other examples of such progress abound.[4]

In addition to the basic power of computation as measured by speed and memory capacity, new hardware and software technologies have greatly improved our ability to interact with computer devices. Through the 1940s and 1950s most communication with computers was through boards with plug-in cables; through the 1960s and 1970s, with reels of punched paper tape, stacks of punched paper cards, and print-outs from line printers. Today the advent of high resolution graphic displays, the mouse, graphics tablets, laser printers, optical cameras, scanners, voice recognition, and other technologies have provided a myriad of ways for humans and machines to communicate.

Advances in software have harnessed these increasingly potent hardware resources to expand the productivity of most professions. Twenty years ago computers were used primarily by large corporations for transaction processing and by scientists (occasionally by computer scientists to explore the power of computing). Today most workers—professionals, office workers, factory workers, farmers—have many occasions to use methods that rely on the computer. I can recall that fifteen years ago even thinking about changing my company's business projections was regarded as a very serious endeavor; it would take the finance department days to grind through the numbers to examine a single scenario. Today with spreadsheet programs it is possible to consider a dozen alternative plans and determine their implications in less than an hour. Twenty years ago the only people interacting with computers were computer experts and a small cadre of students learning the somewhat arcane new field of computation. Today computers appear ubiquitously on office desks, in kitchens, in play rooms, in grocery stores, and in elementary schools.

Will these trends continue? Some observers have pointed out that an exponential trend cannot continue forever. If a species, for example, happens upon a hospitable new environmental niche, it may multiply and expand its population exponentially for a period of time, but eventually its own numbers exhaust the available food supply or other resources and the expansion halts or even reverses. On this basis, some feel that after four decades, exponential improvement in the power of computing cannot go on for much longer. Predicting the end of this trend is, in my view, highly premature. It is, of course, possible that we will eventually reach a time when the rate of improvement slows down, but it does not appear that we are anywhere close to reaching that point. There are more than enough new computing technologies being developed to assure a continuation of the doubling of price performance (the level of performance per unit cost) every 18 to 24 months for many years.

With just conventional materials and methodologies, progress in the next ten years, at least in terms of computing speeds and memory densities, seems relatively assured. Indeed, chips with 64 million bits of RAM (random access mem-

---

[4] In the fall of 1987 an entire issue of *Scientific American* was devoted to this topic. In particular, see Abraham Peled, "The Next Computer Revolution," *Scientific American*, October 1987, pp. 56–64.

ory) and processor chips sporting speeds of 100 million instructions per second are on the drawing board now and likely to be available in the early 1990s. Parallel-processing architectures, some including the use of analog computation, are an additional means of expanding the power of computers. Beyond the conventional methods, a broad variety of experimental techniques could further accelerate these trends. Superconducting, for example, while challenging to implement in a practical way, has the potential to break the thermal barrier that currently constrains chip geometries. As I mentioned earlier, the resulting combination of smaller component geometries with the effective utilization of the third dimension could provide a *millionfold* improvement in computer power. A variety of new materials, such as gallium arsenide, also have the potential to substantially improve the speed and density of electronic circuits.[5] And optical circuits—computing with light rather than electricity—may multiply computing speeds by factors of many thousands.[6]

Will software keep up? It is often said that the pace of advances in software engineering and applications lags behind that of the startling advance of hardware technology. Advances in software are perhaps more evolutionary than revolutionary, but in many instances software techniques are already available that are just waiting for sufficiently powerful hardware to make them practical. For example, techniques for large-vocabulary speech recognition can be adapted to recognize continuous speech but require substantially greater computational speed. Vision is another application with the same requirement. There are many techniques and algorithms that are already understood but are waiting for more powerful computers to make them economically feasible.[7] In the meantime, our understanding of AI methods, the sophistication of our knowledge bases, the power of our pattern-recognition technologies, and many other facets of AI software continue to grow.

Where is all this taking us? People in the computer field are accustomed to hearing about the rapidly improving speed and density of semiconductors. People in other professions inevitably hear reports of the same progress. Numbing are the extremely small numbers used to measure computer timings and the enormous numbers used for memory capacity, time measured in trillionths of a second and memory in billions of characters. What impact are these developments going to have? How will society change? How will our daily lives change? What problems will be solved or created?

One can take several approaches in attempting to answer these questions. Perhaps most instructive is to consider specific examples of devices and scenarios that have the potential to profoundly change the way we communicate, learn, live, and work. These concrete examples represent only a few of the ways that

---

[5] See James D. Meindl, "Chips for Advanced Computing," *Scientific American*, October 1987, pp. 79–81 and 86–88.
[6] See Mark H. Kryder, "Data-Storage Technologies for Advance Computing," *Scientific American*, October 1987, pp. 117–125.
[7] Such as massively parallel processors based possibly on superconductors. See Peter J. Denning, "Massive Parallelism in the Future of Science," *American Scientist*, Jan.–Feb. 1989, p. 16.

computer and other advanced technologies will shape our future world. These examples are based on trends that are already apparent. In my view, it is virtually certain (barring a world calamity) that all of these scenarios will take place. The only uncertainty is precisely *when*. I will attempt to project current trends into the future and estimate when we are likely to see each example.

Obviously, the further into the future we look, the more uncertain the timing of these projections become. The history of AI is replete with examples of problems that were either underestimated or (less often) overestimated. A great irony in early AI history is that many of the problems thought most difficult—proving original theorems, playing chess—turned out to be easy, while the "easy" problems—pattern-recognition tasks that even a child can perform—turned out to be the most challenging.[8] Nonetheless, I believe that we now have a more sophisticated appreciation of the difficulty of many of these problems, and so I will attempt the thankless task of making specific projections. Of course, by the time you discover that my predictions were altogether wrong, it will be too late to obtain a refund for the purchase price of this book.

As I mentioned, these projections are based on trends that are already evident. What is most difficult to anticipate are *breakthroughs*. Any attempts to have predicted the future at the beginning of this century would have almost certainly overlooked the computer, as well as atomic energy, television, the laser, and indeed, most of electronics. In the following chapter I offer a discussion of the overall impact these developments are likely to have on our educational, social, political, medical, military, and economic institutions.

The Translating Telephone

Koji Kobayashi, chairman of the powerful Japanese corporation NEC, has a dream. Someday, according to Kobayashi, people will be able to call anyone in the world and talk, regardless of the language that they speak. The words will be translated from language to language in real time as we speak.[9]

Three technologies are required to achieve Kobayashi's dream: automatic speech recognition (ASR), language translation (LT), and speech synthesis (SS). All three exist today, but not nearly in sufficiently advanced form. Let us consider each of these requirements.

ASR would have to be at the "holy grail" level, that is, combining large (relatively unrestricted) vocabulary, accepting continuous speech input, and providing speaker independence (no training of the system on each voice). Conceivably, the last requirement could be eased in early versions of this system. Users of this capability may be willing to spend fifteen minutes or so training the system

---

[8] Marvin Minsky discusses this problem in "Easy Things are Hard," *Society of Mind*, p. 29. New York: Simon & Schuster, 1985.
[9] Koji Kobayashi, *Computers and Communication: A Vision of C & C.* Cambridge, MA: MIT Press, 1986, pp. 165–166.

on their voice. Such enrollment would be required only once. Combining the first two elements—large vocabulary and continuous speech—will take us to the early to mid 1990s. Adding speaker independence will take us another several years.

LT requires only the ability to translate *text*, not speech, since ASR technology would be translating speech input into written language. The LT capability would not require literary-quality translations, but it would have to perform unassisted. LT systems today require human assistance. Completely automatic LT of sufficient quality will probably become available around the same time that the requisite ASR is available. It should be noted that every pair of languages requires different software (going from French to English is a different problem from going from English to French). While many aspects of translation will be similar from one set of languages to another, LT technology will vary in quality and availability according to the languages involved.

SS is the easiest of the three technologies Kobayashi requires. In fact, it is available today. While not entirely natural, synthetic speech generated by the better synthesizers is quite comprehensible without training. Naturalness is improving, and SS systems should be entirely adequate by the time the necessary ASR and LT systems are available.

Thus, we can expect translating telephones with reasonable levels of performance for at least the more popular languages early in the first decade of the next century. With continuing improvements in performance and reductions in cost, such services could become widespread by the end of that decade. The impact will be another major step in achieving the "global village" envisioned by Marshall McLuhan (1911–1980) over two decades ago.[10] Overcoming the language barrier will result in a more tightly integrated world economy and society. We shall be able to talk more easily to more people, but our ability to misunderstand each other will remain undisturbed.

The Intelligent Assistant

You are considering purchasing an expensive item of capital equipment and wish to analyze the different means of financing available. Issues to consider are your company's current balance sheet, other anticipated cash flow requirements, the state of various financial markets, and future financial projections. You ask your intelligent assistant to write a report that proposes the most reasonable methods to finance the purchase and analyzes the impact of each. The computer engages you in sufficient spoken dialogue to clarify the request and then proceeds to conduct its study. In the course of its research, it accesses the balance sheet and financial projections from the data bases of your company. It contacts the Dow Jones data base by telephone to obtain information on current financial markets. It makes several calls to other computers to obtain the most recent financing

---

[10] See Marshall McLuhan, *Understanding Media: The Extension of Man*. New York: McGraw-Hill, 1964.

charges for different financial instruments. In one case, it speaks to a human to clarify certain details on a lease-repurchase plan. It speaks with your company's vice president of marketing to obtain her level of confidence in achieving the sales projections for the following two years. It then organizes and presents the information in a written report complete with color charts. The report is presented to you the following day, since it took that long to reach the two humans involved. (Had it been able to conduct the research through communication only with other computers, it would have required only a few minutes.) Other services provided by your computerized assistant include keeping careful track of your schedule, including planning your travel from one appointment to another. The system plans your work for you, doing as much of it itself as it is capable of and understanding what portion of it you need to do yourself.

When we shall see the above system depends on how intelligent an assistant we would like to have. Crude forerunners exist today. Large-vocabulary ASR has been integrated with natural-language understanding and data-base-management programs to provide systems that can respond to such commands (posed by voice) as, "Compare the sales of our western region to our three largest competitors." Such systems are, of course, highly limited in their problem-solving ability, but efforts to integrate ASR with data-base access have already begun.

The most challenging aspect of the vision is problem solving, having sufficient commonsense knowledge and reasoning ability to understand what information is required to solve a particular problem. Required are expert systems in many areas of endeavor that are less narrowly focused than the expert systems of today. One of the first intelligent assistants is likely to be one that helps get information from data bases through telecommunications.[11] It has become clear to a number of software developers that a need exists to improve substantially the ease of accessing information from such data-base systems as Compuserve, Delphi, The Source, Dialog, Dow Jones, Lexis, Nexis, and others. Such data-base systems are greatly expanding the volume and diversity of information available, but most persons do not know where to find the appropriate information they need. The first generation of office-assistant programs are now being developed that know how to obtain a broad variety of information without requiring precisely stated requests. I expect that within several years such systems will be generally available, and some of them will take ASR for input.

Thus, in the early to mid 1990s we shall see at least part of the above vision in use: flexible access to information from increasingly varied information services around the world, accessed by systems that understand human speech as well as the syntax and (at least to some extent) the semantics of natural language. They will support their own data bases and be able to access organization-specific knowledge. You will be able to obtain information in a flexible manner without having to know which data-base service has what information or how to use any particular information utility. As the 1990s progress, these systems will be inte-

---

[11] For a vision of an office system interfacing with a public communication network, see Koji Kobayashi, *Computers and Communication*, chapter 10. See also Roger Shank and Peter G. Childers, "The World of the Future," in *The Cognitive Computer*, pp. 227–230. Reading, MA: Addison-Wesley, 1984.

grated with problem-solving expert systems in many areas of endeavor. The level of intelligence implied in the above scenario describing a capital-equipment purchase will probably be seen during the first decade of the next century.

The World Chess Championship

As noted earlier, the best machine chess players are now competing successfully at the national senior-master level, regularly defeating all but about 700 players.[12] All chess machines use some variant of the recursive algorithm called minimax, a strategy whose computational requirements are multiplied by some constant for each additional move ahead that is analyzed. Without a totally new approach, we thus need to make exponential progress in computational power to make linear gains in game-playing performance (though we are indeed making exponential progress in hardware). The analysis I gave before estimated that the requisite computer power to achieve world-championship chess playing should become available between 9 and 54 years from now. This estimate was based on the continuing gains anticipated in the speeds of individual microprocessors. If we factor in the increasing popularity of parallel-processing architectures, the result will be much closer to the short end of this range. Some of the other scenarios in this section require significant advances in both hardware power and software sophistication. In my view, the ability of a machine to play championship chess is primarily a function of the former. Some of the possible breakthroughs in electronic hardware discussed below will be directly applicable to the chess issue. For example, if we are successful in harnessing the third dimension in chip fabrication (that is, building integrated circuits with hundreds or thousands of layers of active circuitry rather than just one), we will see a major improvement in parallel processing: hundreds or thousands of processors on a single chip. Taking into consideration only anticipated progress in conventional circuit-fabrication methodologies and continued development of parallel-processing architectures, I feel that a computer world chess champion is a reasonable expectation by the end of the century.

What will be the impact of such a development? For many, such as myself, it will simply be the passing of a long anticipated milestone. Yes, chess is an intelligent game (that is, it requires intelligence to play well), but it represents a type of intelligence that is particularly well suited to the strengths of early machine intelligence, what I earlier called level-2 intelligence (see "The Recursive Formula and Three Levels of Intelligence"). While level-3 intelligence will certainly benefit from the increasing power of computer hardware, it will also require substantial improvements in the ability of computers to manipulate abstract concepts.

---

[12] David N. L. Levy, *All about Chess and Computers*, Rockland, MD: Computer Science Press, 1982. See also M. M. Botvinnik, *Computers in Chess: Solving Inexact Search Problems*. Trans. Arthur A. Brown. New York: Springer-Verlag, 1984.

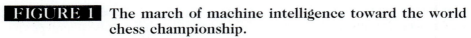

FIGURE 1 The march of machine intelligence toward the world chess championship.

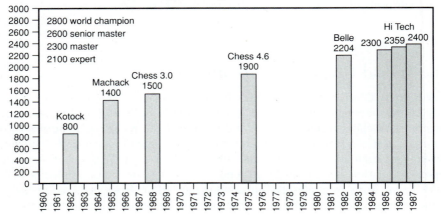

Defenders of human chess playing often say that though computers may eventually defeat all human players, computers are not able to use the more abstract and intuitive methods that humans use.[13] For example, people can eliminate from consideration certain pieces that obviously have no bearing on the current strategic situation and thus do not need to consider sequences of moves involving those pieces. Humans are also able to draw upon a wealth of experience of previous similar situations. However, neither of these abilities is inconsistent with the recursive algorithm. The ability to eliminate from consideration branches of the expanding tree of move-countermove possibilities not worth pursuing is an important part, called pruning, of any minimax program. Drawing upon a data base of previous board positions is also a common strategy in the more advanced chess programs (particularly in the early game). It is estimated that human chess masters have memorized between 20,000 and 50,000 chess boards.[14] While impressive, it is clear that this is again an area where machines have a distinct edge. There is little problem in a computer mastering millions of board positions (each of which can have been analyzed in great depth in advance). Moreover, it is feasible for computers to modify such previously stored board positions to use them even if they do not precisely match a current position.

---

[13] An intriguing study of the relevance of comments made by master chess players during play can be found in Jacques Pitrat, "Evaluating Moves Rather than Positions," in Barbara Pemici and Mareo Somalvico, eds., *III Convegno Internazionale L'Intelligenza Artificiale ed il Gioco Degli Scacchi* (Federazione Scacchistico Italiana, Regione Lombardia, Politecnico di Milano, 1981).

[14] Evidence of this are early board-game programs modeled on master players' strategies. The 1959 checkers program of Arthur Samuels, for example, had 53,000 board positions in memory. See Peter W. Frey, "Algorithmic Strategies for Improving the Performance of Game-Playing Programs," in *Evolution, Games, and Learning: Models for Adaptation in Machines and Nature*, Proceedings of the Fifth Annual International Conference of the Center for Nonlinear Studies at Los Alamos, NM, May 20–24, 1985, p. 355.

It may very well be that human players deploy methods of abstraction other than recalling previous board positions, pruning and move expansion. There is little evidence, however, that for the game of chess such heuristic strategies are inherently superior to a simple recursive strategy combined with massive computational power.[15] Chess, in my view, is a good example of a type of intelligent problem solving well suited to the strengths of the first half century of machine intelligence. For other types of problem solving (level-3 problems), the situation is different.

Not everyone will cheerfully accept the advent of a computer chess champion. Human chess champions have been widely regarded as cultural heroes, especially in the Soviet Union; we regard the world chess championship as a high intellectual achievement. If someone could compute spreadsheets in his head as quickly as (or faster than) a computer, we would undoubtedly regard him as an amazing prodigy, but not as a great intellect (in fact, he would actually be an idiot savant). A computer chess championship is likely to cause a watershed change in how many observers view machine intelligence (though perhaps for the wrong reasons). More constructively, it may also cause a keener appreciation for the unique and *different* strengths (at least for the near future) of machine and human intelligence.

The Intelligent Telephone-Answering Machine

The intelligent telephone assistant answers your phone, converses with the calling party to determine the nature and importance of the call (according to your instructions), interrupts you if necessary, and finds you in an emergency. The latter may become relatively easy once cellular-phone technology is fully developed. If cellular phones become compact and inexpensive enough, most people would be able to carry them, perhaps in their wristwatches. This raises some interesting issues of privacy. Many people like the ability to be away from their phones; we do not necessarily want to be accessible to phone calls at all times. On the other hand, it could be considered irresponsible to be completely unavailable for contact in the event of an emergency. But addressing this issue will be more a matter of evolving social custom than artificial intelligence.

The other aspects of the above scenario require the same machine skills as the intelligent assistant: two-way voice communication, natural-language understanding, and automated problem solving. In some ways this application may be more challenging than the office assistant. For a cybernetic assistant that we interact with, many people would be willing to spend time learning how to use

---

[15] Recursiveness and massive computational power allow for subtle (and hence enormously varied) solutions to algorithmic problems. See, for example, Gary Josin, "Neural Net Heuristics" BYTE, October 1987, pp. 183–192; and Douglas Lenat, "The Role of Heuristics in Learning by Discovery," in R. Z. Michalski, J. J. Carbonell, and T. M. Mitchell, eds., *Machine Learning: An Artificial Intelligence Approach*. Palo Alto, CA: Tioga Publishing, 1983. Also see Monroe Newborn, *Computer Chess*. New York, Academic Press, 1975, pp. 8–15.

such technology if it really helped them to accomplish their work. We might not mind if it failed to handle every interaction gracefully, so long as it provided an overall productivity gain. On the other hand, we might set a higher standard for a machine intended to interact with our friends and associates.

The Cybernetic Chauffeur

When will computers drive our cars? Without major changes in the methods of traffic control, the advent of the self-driving car is not likely for a long time. Unlike character recognition, factory vision, and similar tasks that involve limited visual environments, driving on existing highways requires the full range of human vision and pattern-recognition skills. Furthermore, because the consequences of failure are so serious, we would demand a high level of performance from such a system before relying on it. (On the other hand, with 50,000 traffic deaths each year on American highways, the human standard of performance is far from perfect.)

Yet there is a simpler form of the cybernetic chauffeur that is easier to build and could still accomplish a sharp reduction in driving fatalities as well as substantially reduce the tedium of driving. If specially designed sensors and communication devices were placed in major thoroughfares, cars could communicate with the road as well as with other cars. They could then be placed on automatic pilot. Highways would essentially become electronic railways that our cars could join and leave. The communication system required would be similar to the complex one already in place for cellular phones. Algorithms built into each car and into the roads would maintain safe distances between cars and would handle a variety of situations.[16] Although no specific system has been developed, the underlying technology exists today to deal with the steady-state situation of cars driving on a highway and maintaining proper speed and distance. But the situation gets more complicated when several other contingencies are considered. First, we need to be able to get our car *onto* a computer-controlled road. Presumably, we would drive to an access road, where our computer driver would lock onto the road's communication system, which would take over (in conjunction with the intelligence of our own car computer). Getting *off* the road is perhaps trickier. The system has to consider the possibility that the driver has fallen asleep or is otherwise not ready to resume manual control. The best protocol might be for the system to bring the car to a halt at an exit position at which point the human driver would be expected to take over. Machine intelligence would also have to deal with possibilities of hardware failure—not just of the computer itself, but also of the engine, tires, and other parts of the vehicle. Furthermore, the designers of such systems will also have to consider the possibility of people or animals straying onto the road.

---

[16] See John Hilusha's article, "Smart Roads Tested to Avoid Traffic Jams," *New York Times*, October 18, 1988.

Even with all of these complications, from a technical standpoint, intelligent roads represent a substantially easier problem than creating an automatic driver that can cope with traffic situations as they currently exist. One major nontechnical barrier to creating an intelligent road system, however, is that it requires a large measure of cooperation between car manufacturers and the government agencies that manage our roads (and drivers). It is not an innovation that can be introduced to a small number of pioneering users; it needs to be implemented *all at once* in at least some roads and in all cars intending to access such roads. Presumably, cars not equipped with such automatic guidance equipment would not be allowed on intelligent roads. Again, cellular phone technology is similar: it was not feasible until both the portable phone equipment and the overall computerized communication systems were in place. Still, I would expect such a system to be introduced gradually. At first it would be featured on one or a few major highways on an experimental basis. If successful, it would spread from there.

The technology to accomplish this should be available in the first decade of the next century. But because political decision making is involved, it is difficult to predict when it will receive priority sufficient to warrant implementation. Though cellular-phone technology also involved the coordination of a complex system, it has grown rapidly because it created an entrepreneurial opportunity.

The more advanced scenario of the completely driverless car will take us well into the first half of the next century. Another approach might be to forget roads altogether and replace them with computer-controlled flying vehicles that can ascend and descend vertically. There is, after all, much more space in the three-dimensional open air than there is on our one-dimensional roads. There are already plans in place to install a satellite-based collision-avoidance system that will dramatically reduce airplane collisions by the end of the century. The flying vehicles envisioned here would be the size of today's cars and would be even easier to use.[17]

Invisible Credit Cards and Keys

During the 1990s we shall see highly reliable person-identification systems that use pattern-recognition techniques applied to fingerprint scanning and voice patterns. Such systems will typically combine the recognition of a personal attribute (a fingerprint or voice pattern) with a password that the user types in. The password prevents a misrecognition from causing a problem. The recognition system prevents unauthorized access by a thief who acquires someone's password.

Today we typically carry a number of keys and cards to provide us with access to, and use of, our homes, cars, offices, and a broad variety of financial services.

---

[17]Plans are already in place for the development and use of flying vehicles. See, for instance, "Simulation of an Air Cushion Vehicle Microform," final report for period January 1975-December 1976, Charles Stark Draper Laboratory, Cambridge, MA, 1977.

All of these keys and cards could be eliminated by the widespread adoption of reliable person-identification technologies. The acceptance of this technology is likely to be hastened by the loss of confidence in hand-written signatures caused by the explosion of electronic publishing.

Unfortunately, this type of technology is also capable of helping Big Brother track and control individual transactions and movements.

Instant ASICs

One of the remarkable recent innovations in hardware technology is the advent of the application-specific integrated circuit (ASIC), in which an entire complex electronic system is placed on a single inexpensive chip. The advent of the ASIC has provided products that are complex, diverse, customized and highly miniaturized. As Allen Newell points out, one might regard it as an almost magic technology: once an ASIC is developed, it provides enormous computational power at very low cost, takes up almost no space, and uses almost no electricity. The major barrier to greater deployment of this technology is the very long and expensive engineering cycles required to design such chips. The promise of *instant* ASICs is the ability to design an integrated circuit as easily as one writes a high-level computer program and, once designed, to have the actual chip available immediately.

The development of instant-ASIC technology is a major goal of the U.S. Department of Defense. Aside from its obvious military applications, it will also greatly accelerate the availability of innovative consumer products. Just as the difficulty of programming the early computers was quickly recognized as a major bottleneck, so is the difficult design process behind today's advanced chips. Indeed, the latter is receiving intense attention from all of the major players in the semiconductor industry. It is expected that in the early 1990s designers will be able to write chip programs (whose output is a piece of silicon) as easily and as quickly as computer programs.[18] The availability of instant-ASIC technology will eliminate for most purposes what little difference remains today between hardware and software engineering. It will accelerate the trend toward knowledge as the primary component of value in our products and services.

Artificial People and the Media of the Future

Rather than describe the vision I have in mind, I shall approach the idea of artificial people by starting with what is feasible today. Consider the artificial

---

[18] For recent advances in computer and chip design, see James D. Meindl, "Chips for Advanced Computing," *Scientific American*, October 1987, pp. 78–88. An extensive but less current review of the technology may be found in Alan Burns, *The Microchip: Appropriate or Inappropriate Technology?* New York: John Wiley & Sons, 1981.

creatures that we interact with in computerized games and educational programs. An early and prime example is Pac Man, an artificial creature capable of responding and interacting with us in certain limited ways. One might not consider Pac Man to be much of a creature, let alone an artificial *person*. It is kind of a cartoon caricature of a fish with a limited repertoire of movements. Similarly, our range of emotional responses to it is very narrow, but it serves as a useful starting point.

Now consider what is feasible today, about a decade after the first introduction of Pac Man and other computer games. Reasonably lifelike video images of human faces can be completely synthesized and animated. Experiments at such advanced media laboratories as the MIT Media Laboratory have created completely synthetic yet realistic computer-generated images of human faces that can move and express a wide range of responses and emotions.

Let us imagine the next step: computer games and interactive educational programs that use synthetically generated human images. Rather than simply replaying a previously stored animated sequence, such programs would start with knowledge structures representing the concepts to be expressed and then translate each concept into spoken language and articulated facial and bodily movements. We would thus see and hear images—not prestored but created in real time—of people that are reasonably realistic. The motions and speech sounds would be computed as needed from an intent to express certain ideas and emotions. These artificial people would be responding to our actions within the context of the program.

Let us take several more steps. Add speech recognition and natural-language understanding. Add another several generations of improved image resolution and computing power for greatly enhanced visual realism. Add a more sophisticated problem-solving capability and more intelligence to provide greater subtlety of personality. Our artificial person is becoming more like a real person and less like Pac Man.

Applications would include very realistic games, movies that could include the viewer as a participant, and educational programs that would engage the student to learn from direct experience. Benjamin Franklin could take a child on a guided tour of colonial Philadelphia. Rather than a canned visual tour, this artificial Ben Franklin could answer questions, engage the child in dialogue, customize the tour on the basis of the child's own expressed interests, and otherwise provide an engaging experience. One could debate Abraham Lincoln or take Marilyn Monroe on a date. As with any creative medium, the possibilities are limited only by our imagination. As another example, the intelligent assistant could include a persona complete with appearance, accent, and personality. As time went on, such artificial persons would continue to grow in sophistication, realism, communicative and interactive ability and of course intelligence. Ultimately, they would develop a sense of humor.

It should be noted that personality is not an attribute that can be stuck on an intelligent machine. A personality is almost certainly a necessary byproduct of any behavior complex enough to be considered intelligent. People already speak of the personalities of the software packages they use. Shaping the personality of intelligent machines will be as important as shaping their intelligence. After all, who wants an obnoxious machine?

Such artificial persons could eventually use three-dimensional projected holographic technology (a method for creating three-dimensional images that do not require the use of special glasses). Currently, most holograms are static three dimensional pictures, although some use multiple images to provide a sense of movement. The MIT Media Lab has succeeded in creating the world's first three-dimensional holographic image generated entirely by computer.[19] The ability to project a hologram entirely from computer data is an important step in imaging technology. If a computer can project one hologram, then it can be made to project any number. Ultimately, with sufficient computer power, the images could be generated fast enough to appear realistically to move. The movements would not be prestored but rather *computed* in real time to respond to each situation. Thus, our artificial people can ultimately be lifelike, life-size, three-dimensional images with sufficiently high resolution and subtlety of movement to be indistinguishable from real people. These future computer displays will also be able to project entire environments along with the people.

There is concern today regarding the power of television to shape our views and to engage our emotions and attention. Yet television is essentially noninteractive, of low resolution, and flat. A medium that provided nearly perfect resolution and three-dimensional images and interacted with us in an intelligent and natural way would be far more powerful in its emotional impact, possibly too powerful for many (real) people. Harnessing and regulating these media of the future will undoubtedly be an area of much debate and controversy.

Adoption of the advanced media technologies described here will begin in the late 1990s and mature over the first half of the next century. Applications include entertainment, education, conducting business transactions, even companionship.

Another Approach

An entirely different approach to the concept of artificial people lies in the area of robotics. Robots of the first generation, just like the first generation of computer-generated creature images (essentially pictures of robots), were neither intelligent nor realistic. We were as unlikely to mistake an early factory robot for a natural creature, let alone a person, as we were to mistake Pac Man for an image of a real animal. Here again, successive generations of technology have provided greater intelligence, subtlety, and naturalness. The primary drive for robotic technology lies in practical applications in the manufacturing and service industries. Admittedly, for most of these applications, resemblance to humans or to any other natural creature is of little relevance. Yet there will be applications

---

[19] See Stewart Brand, *The Media Lab: Inventing the Future at MIT.* New York: Viking Penguin, pp. 83–91.

for natural robots (sometimes called androids) as teachers, entertainers, and companions. Primitive robotic pets have already created a niche in the toy industry.

Creating a reasonably natural robotic imitation of a person is even more challenging than creating a convincing media image of a person. Any autonomous robot, humanoid or otherwise, has to be able to ambulate in a natural environment; this requires general-purpose vision and a high degree of fine motor coordination. Autonomous robots for exploring hostile environments, such as nuclear reactors and the surfaces of other planets, exist today. Routine use of autonomous robots in more conventional settings is likely to begin by the end of the century. Robots that are reasonably convincing artificial people will not appear until well into the next century.

Marvin Minsky has often said that a good source of insights into the realities of tomorrow's computer science can be found in today's science fiction. Isaac Asimov in his *Robots of Dawn* describes a society two centuries from now in which people live alongside a ubiquitous generation of robotic servants, companions, guards, and teachers. Two of the protagonists are a beautiful female scientist and her lover, a "male humaniform" robot.

Passing the Turing Test

Scientists from the University of Clear Valley reported today that a computer program they had created was successful in passing the famous Turing test. Computer scientists around the world are celebrating the achievement of this long-awaited milestone. Reached from his retirement home, Marvin Minsky, regarded as one of the fathers of artificial intelligence (AI), praised the accomplishment and said that the age of intelligent machines had now been reached. Hubert Dreyfus, a persistent critic of the AI field, hailed the result, admitting that he had finally been proven wrong.

The advent of computers passing the Turing test will almost certainly not produce the above sort of coverage. We will more likely read the following:

Scientists from the University of Clear Valley reported today that a computer program they had created was successful in passing the famous Turing test. Computer scientists reached at press time expressed considerable skepticism about the accomplishment. Reached from his retirement home, Marvin Minsky, regarded as one of the fathers of artificial intelligence (AI), criticized the experiment, citing a number of deficiencies in method, including the selection of a human "judge" unfamiliar with the state of the art in AI. He also said that not enough time had been allowed for the judge to interview the computer foil and the human. Hubert Dreyfus, a persistent critic of the AI field, dismissed the report as the usual hype we have come to expect from the AI world and challenged the researchers to use him as the human judge.

Alan Turing was very precisely imprecise in stating the rules of his widely accepted test for machine intelligence.[20] There is, of course, no reason why a test for artificial intelligence should be any less ambiguous than our definition of artificial intelligence. It is clear that the advent of the passing of the Turing test will not come on a single day. We can distinguish the following milestones:

Level 1 Computers arguably pass *narrow* versions of the Turing test of believability. A variety of computer programs are each successful in emulating human ability in some area: diagnosing illnesses, composing music, drawing original pictures, making financial judgements, playing chess, and so on.

Level 2 It is well established that computers can achieve human or higher levels of performance in a wide variety of intelligent tasks, and they are *relied upon* to diagnose illnesses, make financial judgements, etc.

Level 3 A single computer system arguably passes the *full* Turing test, although there is considerable controversy regarding test methodology.

Level 4 It is well established that computers are capable of passing the Turing test. No reasonable person familiar with the field questions the ability of computers to do this. Computers can engage in a relatively unrestricted range of intelligent discourse (and engage in many other intelligent activities) at human or greater levels of performance.

We are at level 1 today. A wide range of expert systems can meet or exceed human performance within narrowly defined (yet still intelligent) areas of expertise. The judgements of expert systems are beginning to be relied upon in a variety of technical and financial fields, although acceptance in the medical area is much slower. Also, computer success in a variety of artistic endeavors is beginning to be at least arguably comparable.

Level 2 is within sight and should be attained around the end of the century. As expert systems grow in sophistication and achieve more natural human interfaces, we will begin to rely on their expertise as much as (if not more than) human society relies on their idiot savant forebears today.

We will probably begin to see reports of level 3, and newspaper articles similar to the second one given above, during the first decade of the next century, with continued controversy for at least several decades thereafter. The first reports will almost certainly involve significant limitations to Turing's originally proposed challenge. We are close to having the underlying technology (if not the actual program) today if we use sufficiently naive judges and provide them with relatively little time to make their determinations.

Level 4 is what Turing had in mind when he predicted success by the year 2000. Achieving this level is *far* more difficult than any of the other three. It

---

[20] For a straightforward presentation of this famous test, see Isaac Malitz, "The Turing Machine," BYTE, November 1987, pp. 348–358.

requires advanced natural-language understanding, vast knowledge bases of commonsense information, and decision-making algorithms capable of great subtlety and abstraction. Turing's prediction, made in 1950, will almost certainly not be fulfilled by the year 2000. I place the achievement of level 4 sometime between 2020 and 2070. If this turns out to be the case, then Turing will have been off by a factor of between 1.4 and 2.4 (70 to 120 years versus his prediction of 50 years), which actually is not bad for such a longterm prediction. Of course, there is no assurance that *my* prediction will be any more accurate than Turing's.

As mentioned earlier (see *The Debate Goes On*), Hubert Dreyfus has indicated that he will concede that he was wrong (and has been wrong for his entire professional career) if he can be fooled as the human judge in a Turing test. Will this happen? If we assume that Dreyfus is in good health and further that continuing advances in bioengineering technology enable him (and the rest of us) to live longer than today's average life expectancy, then it is altogether possible. Personally, I would be willing to bet on it.

Conclusion

The above scenarios provide only a small sampling of the ways in which intelligent machines of the future can be expected to touch our lives. The computers of today, dumb as they are, have already infiltrated virtually every area of work and play. The bureaucracies of our society could hardly function without their extensive computer networks. If one adds just the sharply focused intelligence of the next phase of the age of intelligent machines to the already prodigious memory capacity and speed of today's computers, the combination will be a formidable one indeed. Our cars, watches, beds, chairs, walls, floors, desks, books, clothes, phones, homes, appliances, and virtually everything else we come into contact with will be intelligent, monitoring and servicing our needs and desires. The age of intelligent machines will not start on a particular day; it is a phenomenon that has started already, with the breadth and depth of machine intelligence growing each year. Turing predicted a time when people would talk naturally about machines thinking without expecting anyone to contradict them or be surprised. We are not there today, but the day will arrive so gradually that no one (except a few authors) will notice it when it does.

Questions

1. What is a scenario? How should managers use scenarios in decision making?
2. Describe how you would use an intelligent assistant in deciding whether or not to market a new product.
3. You will be managing a business in the year 2010. Assume you have become the CEO of a medium-sized firm that year. Write a scenario that describes how you will interact with information systems in your job.

Managing IS Technology

- ◆ 3.1 Assimilating Technology Innovation
- ◆ 3.2 Managing Telecommunications
- ◆ 3.3 Groupware
- ◆ 3.4 Imaging
- ◆ 3.5 Selecting Computer Hardware

Increasingly, managers are recognizing that how technology is managed is at least as important as which technology is being managed. With developments in IS technology occurring so rapidly that their half-lives are now measured in months rather than years, it would be foolhardy to attempt to include articles here on all the forms of technology that are available to support the information processing needs of an organization. Such descriptions would soon be out of date, as new hardware is announced and new software is developed.

On the other hand, discussion of technology is important, if only to establish the areas in which managers should be focusing their attention and to give examples of current practices. Among the many possible technology topics that might have been chosen, five articles were selected that deal with the managing of technology diffusion, four leading-edge technologies (telecommunications, groupware, and imaging) and managing the changing nature of computer hardware.

Issues

Assimilating technology innovation

Every firm is faced with the task of implementing new technology from time to time, whether it is on the factory floor, in the information systems department, or relatively autonomous knowledge workers. James Brancheau and James

195

Wetherbe describe how what we know about innovation diffusion provides guidelines to managers for introducing new technologies into the firm.

Managing telecommunications

Telecommunications and information technology have merged over the years so that it is often not possible to tell where the computer ends and the telecommunications network begins. Telecommunications, by tying people and machines together, increases the tempo in which business is conducted. Randall Tobias describes the confluence of technological and business forces involved and the new capabilities beyond electronic mail and fax which are emerging to create "universal information services."

Groupware

As Peter Drucker tells us in Section 6.1, the 1990s are the era of work teams. A series of developments that started concurrently with the introduction of personal computers makes it possible to provide information support directly to work teams. In David Kirkpatrick's *Fortune* article, he describes the special software, known as groupware, which, together with local area networks, makes this support possible. Started as research and development projects, groupware is now being sold by such major firms as Lotus Development Corporation and IBM. Groupware offers team members the ability to work while separated in space and time, meeting electronically. These software inventions have the potential for changing our very concept of office work.

Imaging

Image processing technology combines photography and computing to replace acres of paper-based records that large corporations and government agencies keep. Think only of the millions of charge receipts that American Express and other credit or charge card companies must handle accurately each month. Imaging allows companies to substitute information flow for paper flow by storing, retrieving, manipulating, and comparing whole documents. Imaging technology, however, is economic only for very large operations. Murray Sherry and Homer Hagedorn discuss the technical, managerial, and people issues managers must resolve in making the decision to implement imaging in their organizations. In reading this article, recognize that the issues discussed apply to many technologies, not just imaging.

Selecting computer hardware

The large mainframe has been the mainstay of information systems from its inception. The clean, large, air-conditioned rooms with raised floors and glass windows containing the whirring machinery from some of the largest companies in the world have been the hallmark of computing in many firms. All this is undergoing change. Many large machines are being replaced by smaller machines and networked PCs in a "client-server" architecture. Bob Violino and Thomas Hoffman present evidence of this trend. Whether the large mainframe will eventually become extinct is still an open question.

3.1

Understanding Innovation Diffusion Helps Boost Acceptance Rates of New Technology

James C. Brancheau and James C. Wetherbe

I f chief information officers understand how certain personality types and other underlying forces will influence the technology diffusion process, they can control end-user acceptance rates of new technology, as well as the effectiveness of new methods.

Recent research on innovation diffusion has created a valuable tool for developing a set of guidelines for managing the introduction of new technology.

Innovation Diffusion Theory

Although a body of knowledge of technology change has not yet developed, a general theory explaining the spread of new ideas and new technologies among people has emerged from research in other fields. For example, rural sociologists have studied the spread of agricultural technology among farmers. The theory developed from the research is known as innovation diffusion theory.

Applying innovation diffusion theory to the study of end-user computing provides a basis for managing the introduction of new information technology. The major components of the theory are:

- ◆ S-shaped adopter distribution.

- ◆ Innovativeness and adopter categories.

- ◆ Individual adoption process.

- ◆ Diffusion networks and opinion leaders.

S-Shaped Adopter Distribution

One of the most salient components of the theory is the notion that the adoption of successful new ideas and products traces an S-shaped curve over time. Research in other fields has shown that the number of individuals adopting per

FIGURE 1 Adopter Distribution for Spreadsheet Software

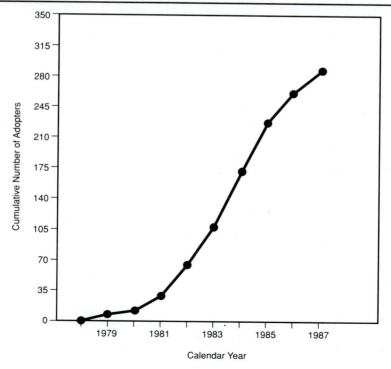

period of time roughly follows a normal bell-shaped curve. Plotted on a cumulative frequency basis, these data describe the traditional S-shaped curve.

The S-shaped curve implies that relatively few people adopt a new idea at first. Then as word spreads and a few pioneers have shown that the idea works, more people are willing to try it. As the idea catches on, it reaches a point where it really takes off and most people will adopt it. Near the end of the cycle, the last few holdouts finally adopt the idea.

Initial research has confirmed the existence of the S-shaped curve for information technology. As shown in Figure 1, actual data on the adoption of spreadsheet software among finance/accounting professionals in 22 organizations conformed closely to the expected pattern. For example, one accounting executive in an educational products manufacturing organization installed a PC on every desk in his controller group during 1984. The department went from less than five percent to 100 percent adoption in a single year. Obviously, the number of adopters did not follow the S-shaped curve in this case. However, in reviewing the utilization data for his organization, he found that the number of hours the PCs were used each week did follow the predicted S-shaped curve. This suggests that even when a new technology is made available early in its diffusion cycle, a learning curve phenomenon may still be at work.

Innovativeness and Adopter Categories

Another major component of the theory is the notion that individuals vary in the time they take to adopt an innovation. One measure of an individual's innovativeness is the relative earliness or lateness that he or she adopts an innovation (Figure 2).

The rationale for the classification is that the people at the head of the curve (pioneers and early adopters) are considerably different than the people at the tail of the curve (majority and laggards) (Figure 3). In discussing how these types of differences affected adoption of spreadsheet software in a specialty manufacturing organization, a group of managers referred to the pioneers and early adopters as "self-starters . . . All you need to do is throw a manual at them . . ." These managers indicated that differences among individuals were apparent well after most of the organization had started to use the software. The self-starters, it turns out, were still more innovative in developing new applications and transferring them to others as appropriate.

Individual Adoption Process

The third major component of the theory suggests that individual adoption is not an instantaneous act, but a process that occurs over time. In making a decision to adopt or reject an innovation, individuals normally go through a series of stages in their thinking; (*e.g.*, knowledge, persuasion, decision, and implementation).

FIGURE 2   Diffusion Curves and Adopter Categories

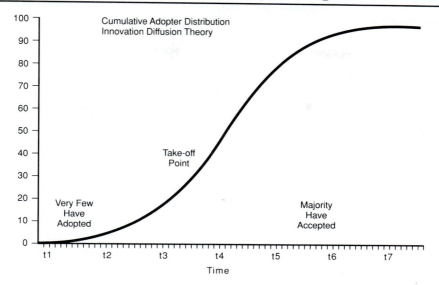

Cumulative Adopter Distribution
Innovation Diffusion Theory

Take-off
Point

Very Few
Have
Adopted

Majority
Have
Accepted

Time

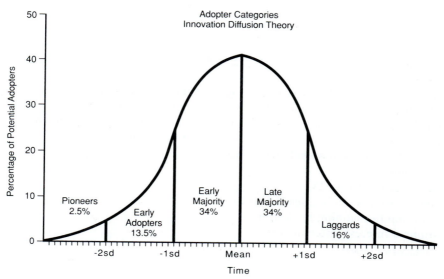

Adopter Categories
Innovation Diffusion Theory

Percentage of Potential Adopters

Pioneers
2.5%

Early
Adopters
13.5%

Early
Majority
34%

Late
Majority
34%

Laggards
16%

Time

The knowledge stage occurs as an individual becomes aware of the existence of an innovation and gains an understanding of its function. Both the need-driven and the technology-driven paths to awareness can operate. The persuasion stage occurs as an individual begins to form a favorable or unfavorable attitude toward the innovation. Attitudes form as additional information is received. Evaluative information from interpersonal networks becomes particularly important. The

FIGURE 3. Initial Findings on Key Adopter Categories for End-User Computing

PIONEERS

Findings
- About average age
- College graduate
- Reads a lot
- Professionally active outside company
- Talks to I/S / I/C frequently
- Usually a computer opinion leader
- Very interested in technology

Implications
- Venturesome
- High tolerance for uncertainty
- Well connected (externally)
- Often acts as "gatekeeper"

EARLY ADOPTERS

Findings
- About average age
- College graduate
- Reads a lot
- Less active outside company
- Rarely talks to I/S / I/C
- Often a business opinion leader
- Less interested in technology

Implications
- Reduces uncertainty for majority adopters
- Well connected (internally)
- Often acts as "boundary spanner"

LAGGARDS

Findings
- About ten years older than average age
- Most likely a clerk or manager
- Holds associate degree
- Reads half as much as pioneers
- About half as much outside participation as pioneers
- Rarely talks to I/S / I/C
- Some business opinion leadership
- No computer opinion leadership
- Minimal interest in technology

Implications
- Traditional outlook
- Suspicious of technology
- Can slow adoption through position in hierarchy

From Brancheau, 1987.

decision stage occurs as an individual consciously decides to adopt or reject the innovation. At this stage, the innovation may be used on a trial basis. Finally, implementation occurs as an individual acquires and makes initial use of the innovation. At this point, an individual is an adopter.

Initial research on end-user computing only partially confirms the prior finding in other fields. While the expected trends in the importance of the various channels (*i.e.*, vendor literature, company newsletters, journals) were confirmed, mass media channels were not as important to adopters as anticipated. As shown in

Figure 4, work colleagues were the most influential sources of information across the stages of decision making. This appears to be an important difference between end-user computing and other contexts. However, consistent with innovation diffusion theory, the influence of local/interpersonal channels increased as individuals' thinking progressed from knowledge, through persuasion, to the final decision.

An information center manager from a large investment products organization relayed his experience with this phenomenon. "Back in 1983 when we started up, the finance people were getting a fair number of ideas from us by way of newsletters, product demos, etc. Now there is very little we know about Lotus that is not already common knowledge in the finance group. They use the software every day and are virtual experts with it. The few novice users left in finance learn more about the technology from their local gurus than they do from us."

Diffusion Networks and Opinion Leadership

The fourth major component of the theory deals with the way information about innovations spreads through a company. In deciding whether to adopt, individuals depend mainly on information from others like themselves who have already adopted the innovation. The interpersonal networks these communications flow through are referred to as diffusion networks.

Closely related to diffusion networks is the concept of opinion leadership. As its name implies, opinion leadership involves informal influence over others' attitudes and behavior. Due to their extensive interpersonal networks and their willingness to experiment with new ideas, opinion leaders can activate the diffusion network in an organization. They affect diffusion to such a degree that the diffusion curve may have its usual S-shape because of the time at which opinion leaders adopt.

One of the early adopters at an energy distribution company echoed these findings. He said that use of spreadsheet software in most departments did not take off until someone inside the department acted as the "seed." Then, others could look over his shoulder and find out what the software could do. "Until enough seeds were planted, most people were very skeptical."

Managing the Introduction of New Technology

Despite strong support for innovation diffusion theory in the context of end-user computing, one research project cannot conclusively establish the validity of the theory as well as the implications that flow from it. Thus, the guidelines offered here are preliminary implications of the theory assuming it is confirmed and further developed through follow-up research.

Tactical guidelines for introducing new technology can be offered in a number of areas.

FIGURE 4   Importance of Communication Channels across Stages of Adoption Decision Making

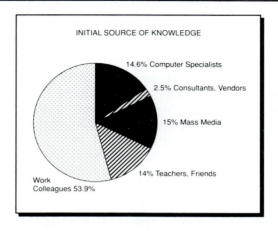

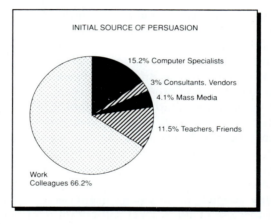

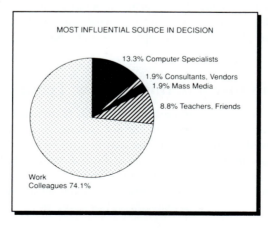

1. Change agents. One of the most effective means for introducing new information technology is to utilize internal change agents in the early stages of the diffusion cycle. Change agents act as intermediaries between the technicians responsible for creating or maintaining the new technology and the users of that technology. In the context of end-user computing, the information systems department normally assumes the change-agent role. For example, most large organizations have set up an information center to help manage the introduction of new technology. But, unless change agents intervene before 10–25 percent of the target population has adopted a new technology, the natural forces within the diffusion network can be very difficult to counteract.

Furthermore, effective intervention requires a great deal of personal contact with users and empathy for their situation to establish credibility. The critical factors are for change agents to establish effective communication channels with potential users and to get involved in diffusion as early as possible. A big problem in the early days of end-user computing was that many companies waited too long before establishing their information centers. As a result, the strength of the diffusion network made it difficult to control users' perceptions of new technology.

2. Opinion leaders are more effective than change agents in influencing new users once diffusion has reached a certain point (estimated at 10 to 25 percent adoption). If opinion leaders are identified in advance in key areas, they can be instrumental in assisting efforts to manage new technology introductions. Of course, the opposite situation can also occur. If opinion leaders reject a new technology, they can stop the diffusion process in its tracks. The key factors are for change agents to recognize potential opinion leaders early and target their efforts accordingly.

3. Communication channels vary in effectiveness across the stages of adoption decision making. For example, mass media channels may be somewhat effective in making potential users aware of new technology, but they are not effective in persuading them to adopt it. In contrast, informal communication with peers who have used the new technology is very persuasive. Because potential users rely almost exclusively on interpersonal channels, change agents should be aware of this and rely heavily upon informal networks to influence adoption decision making.

4. Modeling and demonstration play an important role in spreading new ideas. New information technology is tried "vicariously" when individuals are provided with conspicuous examples of how the technology works. Modeling and demonstration are most effective when they take place in the end user's work environment and are conducted by peers. Opinion leaders are particularly effective in modeling and demonstration.

5. Trial use of a new technology also can increase the adoption rate. Information technology's portability can be exploited in this regard. Change agents can speed diffusion by loaning hardware and software to potential end users. Hands-on experience with the new technology reduces the uncertainty involved in making an adoption decision. This tactic is most effective if aimed at recognized opinion leaders within the organization. Combining trial use with personalized technical support helps to insure successful trials.

6. **Local experts.** Closely related to the issue of influencing individual adoption is the issue of providing support to sustain long-term utilization. Individuals tend to be influenced by others who are close to them in physical distance and relatively alike in social characteristics. Because of this, alternatives to a centralized support organization need to be examined over the long term. One alternative is to use local experts within user departments. Housing technical support personnel inside the functional office areas brings them closer to their "customers." In addition, over time, it will broaden the range of shared experience and improve the effectiveness of communication. If the local expert approach is not taken formally, it will occur informally. And while informal support should be encouraged, it may not meet the long-term needs of the organization. A formal effort to identify and recognize local experts may be required. In the long run, I/S managers must work to close the communication gap and build organizational learning.

An Overall Strategy

A review of what is known about innovation diffusion in organizations suggests an overall strategy for managing the introduction of new information technology. The key points are illustrated in Figure 5 and discussed below.

FIGURE 5   **An Overall Strategy for Introducing New Technology**

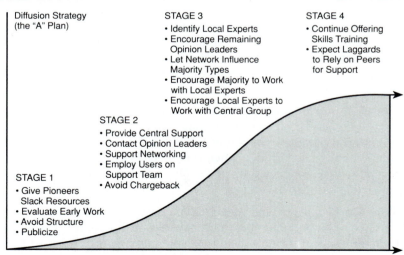

Diffusion Strategy (the "A" Plan)

STAGE 1
• Give Pioneers Slack Resources
• Evaluate Early Work
• Avoid Structure
• Publicize

STAGE 2
• Provide Central Support
• Contact Opinion Leaders
• Support Networking
• Employ Users on Support Team
• Avoid Chargeback

STAGE 3
• Identify Local Experts
• Encourage Remaining Opinion Leaders
• Let Network Influence Majority Types
• Encourage Majority to Work with Local Experts
• Encourage Local Experts to Work with Central Group

STAGE 4
• Continue Offering Skills Training
• Expect Laggards to Rely on Peers for Support

Time

In the first stage, CIOs should encourage pioneers by providing slack resources. No organizational mechanism needs to be established, however, since pioneers work best in an undisciplined structure. The results of pioneer work should be examined for feasibility and organizational implications. Information interchange with early adopters should be facilitated by publicizing the results of the pioneers' experimentation.

In the second stage, when early adopters begin to appear (or when the organization chooses to encourage them), I/S should establish a centralized support center. The potential for the new technology is publicized in general terms through newsletters, bulletins, etc. Where feasible, opinion leaders are contacted personally and encouraged by offers of free trial use. Networking among early adopters and pioneers is encouraged and supported through user groups and focus meetings. The support center should employ user-empathetic support personnel and actively encourage and support early adopters. Charging for support center services should be avoided if possible.

In the third stage, when early adopters have provided solid organizational evidence of the value and feasibility of the new technology, emphasis should shift toward identification and support of local experts. Opinion leaders who have not previously adopted are actively recruited and encouraged. The role of influencing others to adopt is shifted from support center personnel to opinion leaders. The support center provides initial training and consulting but turns over encouragement and on-the-job skill development to local experts. Majority-type adopters are encouraged to seek help from local experts. Local experts work with the centralized support center to solve specialized problems.

In the fourth stage, the diffusion process reaches a stable state as laggards adopt the technology. Laggards can be expected to rely heavily on support systems composed of peers within their functional areas.

This cycle of events can be repeated in a miniversion as new equipment options, new software packages, and new business applications are selected for introduction. The target population necessarily changes with each new technology since it will not be equally useful to all segments of the organization. Pioneers may be willing to try out the new technology during initial technical debugging. Indeed, they are often more adept at this than support center staff. Early adopters may be willing to work through the changes in user and organizational procedures (including training processes). This can help make the new technology operate smoothly in the organization. As the technology diffuses to the remainder of the target population, early adopters will be able to provide the local expertise needed to supplement general training provided by the support center.

The foregoing discussion assumes the managers will lead the introduction of new technology, not react to it. Unfortunately, in day-to-day operations, urgency tends to drive out importance. Even the best managers will not always be positioned appropriately at the beginning of a diffusion cycle. In such cases, an alternate strategy is needed. As might be expected, the strategy calls for staying close to the informal network. Being aware of what pioneers and opinion leaders are doing with information technology will insure that diffusion does not advance too far without an organizational review. In most cases, offering skills training and other basic support services can help get the "late" change agent back into the diffusion network. By offering value-added services, change agents can get pioneers and opinion leaders to work with them instead of against them.

Conclusion

The past half-decade has been a period of rapid change in the role of information systems in the organization. Many I/S managers have found that traditional implementation strategies have not helped them deal with new end-user information technology. Managing the introduction of new technology among relatively autonomous knowledge workers requires a new approach. By understanding what drives the diffusion of technology, managers can work with the natural forces instead of against them.

Suggested Reading

Allen, Thomas J., *The World, Your Company: A Gate for Information! Who Guards the Gate? Innovation*, Volume 8, 1969, pp. 12–19.

Bandura, Albert, *Social Learning Theory*, Prentice-Hall, Englewood Cliffs, NJ, 1977.

Brancheau, James C., Douglas R. Vogel, and James C. Wetherbe, An Investigation of the Information Center from the User's Perspective, *Data Base*, Volume 17, Number 1, Fall 1985, pp. 4–17.

Brancheau, James C., and Gordon B. Davis, *A Model for the Diffusion of End-User Computing*, MISRC Working Paper 87-07, MIS Research Center, Carlson School of Management, University of Minnesota, Minneapolis, MN, November 1986.

Brancheau, James C., *The Diffusion of Information Technology: Testing and Extending Innovation Diffusion Theory in the Context of End-User Computing*, Unpublished Ph.D. Dissertation, University of Minnesota, Minneapolis, MN, 1987.

Brancheau, James C., and James C. Wetherbe, A Comparative Analysis of Higher and Lower Rated Information Centers, *Journal of Information Management*, Winter 1988.

Davis, Gordon B., and Margrethe H. Olson, *Management Information Systems Conceptual Foundations, Structure and Development*, McGraw-Hill, New York, NY, 1985.

Drucker, Peter, *The Age of Discontinuity*, Harper & Row, New York, NY, 1978.

Kanter, Rosabeth Moss, *The Change Masters*, Simon and Schuster, New York, NY, 1983.

Leitheiser, Robert L., and James C. Wetherbe, *Avoiding the Pitfalls of End-User Computing*, MISRC Working Paper 85-09, MIS Research Center, Carlson School of Management, University of Minnesota, Minneapolis, MN, October 1984.

Leitheiser, Robert L., and James C. Wetherbe, Service Support Levels: An Organized Approach to End-User Computing, *MIS Quarterly*, Volume 10, Number 4, December 1986, pp. 337–349.

Peters, Thomas J., and Robert H. Waterman, Jr., *In Search of Excellence: Lessons from America's Best-Run Companies*, Harper & Row, New York, NY, 1982.

Petty, R., and J. Cacioppo, *Attitudes and Persuasion: Classic and Contemporary Approaches*, Brown, Dubuque, IA, 1981.

Rogers, Everett M., *The Diffusion of Innovations*, 3rd Edition, Free Press, New York, NY, 1983.

Rogers, Everett M., and D. Lawrence Kincaid, *Communication Networks: Toward a New Paradigm for Research*, Free Press, New York, NY, 1981.

Tushman, Michael L., and Thomas J. Scanlan, Boundary Spanning Individuals: Their Role in Information Transfer and Their Antecedents, *Academy of Management Journal*, Volume 24, Number 2, June 1981, pp. 289–305.

Wetherbe, James C., and Robert L. Leitheiser, Information Centers: A Survey of Services, Decisions, Problems, Successes, *Journal of Information Systems Management*, Summer 1985, pp. 3–10.

Questions

1. What are the three key adopter categories for end-user computing?

2. Describe the diffusion strategy for introducing new technology.

3. Suppose your company wants to introduce bar code scanners into your inventory management system. What specific steps would you take to make sure this new technology is adopted successfully?

3.2

Telecommunications in the 1990s

Randall L. Tobias

It is an early morning in December 1999, and Dr. Anna Wright, a Chicago based surgeon, is in trouble. What should have been a routine operation has developed nasty complications. No one on staff can help—no one except "Mike."

"Mike, quick, get me a list of the 10 top cardiovascular specialists." As she speaks, a large screen on the wall lights up.

"Yes, Anna," Mike's electronic voice replies. "In the U.S. or the world?"

"World, of course," she snaps.

A list appears. "Get me number one, Dr. Uno, wherever she is." At that, a remarkable sequence of events occurs. Within minutes, Anna gets her specialist on screen. With the help of intelligence in the telecommunications network, Mike has tracked her down. Dr. Uno happens to be in her rental car, on the way back to her hotel from St. Andrews Golf Club in Scotland. But the network could have found her almost anywhere.

Neither doctor speaks the other's language very well, so they ask the network to perform simultaneous translation. Luckily, Dr. Uno has almost reached her hotel, so they are able to use the more powerful information systems available there.

Anna has Mike transfer a copy of the patient's records, including x-rays and motion pictures of the last few minutes of the operation (recorded not on film but electronically). Incidentally, the pictures are displayed on large, flat, high-definition screens that are now widespread. They exhibit colors, shades, and textures with a sharpness and clarity that could be found only in movie theaters 10 years before.

Dr. Uno's expert advice helps Anna save the patient. And Mike records everything—both words and pictures—for the education of other medical people at Anna's hospital.

This scenario is not as futuristic as it may seem. In fact, it almost certainly does not do justice to the more exotic applications of information technology that will appear over the next 10 years in scientific research, engineering, and manufacturing.

But for business managers concerned about the challenges of the next decade, the point here is not whether all aspects of my scenario could really come true by the end of the century. Not all of them will. The point is to see them as logical extensions of powerful trends that are already at work today. One of the first trends to recognize is how much the boundaries between computing and communications are blurring. Today, computers communicate and telecommunications networks compute. It is impossible to consider one and exclude the other.

In what follows, I will focus more on the communications side of the equation, but it should be clear that in the '90s most businesses will need to manage computing and communications as total information systems. How well they manage these systems is certain to become more and more important. Information systems are becoming pervasive and global. They are advancing rapidly, reshaping our home and work environments, and transforming our markets. It is no accident that last year, computers and communications equipment accounted for at least 35 percent of all private investment in the United States—double what it was just 10 years ago.

Increasingly, information systems are becoming strategic. That is, the skill and insight with which they are applied will fundamentally determine a company's performance in the marketplace—by changing its production economics, for example, or its relationships with suppliers, distributors, and customers, or the very nature of its products and services.

The Drivers of Change

The development of computing and communications will be driven by the interaction of two sets of forces—the forces created by technological advances and by the needs, principally, of business users and their customers. (I will mostly ignore here the impact of defense markets.)

The technological forces

The technological forces result from the pace of progress in three fields: microelectronics, fiber optic transmission, and software. In microelectronics, industry has been doubling the number of components on a chip each year for more than 30 years. As a result, the cost per circuit has fallen more than a millionfold. Today a single microprocessor developed by AT&T and Intel concentrates within it the power of the first Cray supercomputer.

The breakneck rate of progress has slowed somewhat—but the industry is still doubling the number of components per chip every 18 months. New generations of computer hardware will come in rapid order, each delivering much more processing power than the previous one for about the same price.

Machine intelligence will continue to become more affordable and ubiquitous. In addition, computing will become much more decentralized, because the economics of this process favor shifting computing loads away from mainframes to mini- and microcomputers networked together.

Fiber optic technology, which transmits information as pulses of laser light through ultrapure glass fibers, will furnish the transmission systems of choice for the 1990s. Industry has doubled fiber capacity each year since it was introduced in the late 1970s, and this rate shows no signs of diminishing through the 1990s. The most advanced system today can transmit information at the rate of 3.4 billion bits per second, or the equivalent of 48,000 telephone conversations on a single pair of fibers. Of course, fiber optics will be important not so much for its role in accommodating voice traffic as for its role in accommodating the explosively growing traffic generated by facsimile, computer networking, and video.

In software, productivity growth has advanced at a much slower rate than in the other two fields. Nevertheless, important advances are occurring. Industry continues to develop more advanced algorithms for solving specialized problems. For example, the Karmarkar algorithm, recently developed at AT&T Bell laboratories, readily solves linear programming problems so huge that they could not even be attempted before on the biggest computers in the world. Other important advances are continually improving the algorithms that enable information systems to recognize images and spoken words. And expert systems are becoming more widely developed and applied; systems that, in well-defined knowledge domains, can make every employee perform nearly as well as the best employee doing a job. And beyond expert systems we are beginning to see software advances enable information systems to learn and think for themselves. This is perhaps the key definition of artificial intelligence. However, as limited as this intelligence may be, it is already proving very useful for specialized tasks like managing the resources in telecommunications networks.

Interestingly, one of the more important uses of artificial intelligence may be in making our information systems less artificial; that is, making them more human, and easier to use. Computers can already recognize a limited vocabulary of spoken words, and sometime this decade they will improve to the point that we will be able to command them and input information more accurately by talking than by keyboarding. But we will need artificial intelligence before machines actually converse with us in natural language and perform simultaneous translation—that is, machines that can go beyond our words and know what we mean, not just what we say.

Achieving this will stretch our abilities, but by the mid-to-late 1990s we will probably see machines that can perform simultaneous translation of vocabularies limited to a few hundred words. A machine with the abilities of HAL, the fully conversational computer in *2001*, could well be possible about the year predicted there or a little later.

Business needs

Technology almost creates more possibilities than industry can ever pursue. The path that a technology actually takes is determined by customer needs. In the 1990s, one of the most critical of these needs will be to increase the productivity of the information workers who make up an ever-increasing share of the work force. These workers are deluged with information, and they contribute to the deluge at their own desks day after day. In fact, according to the U.S. Department of Labor, they file away some 200 billion documents per year in this country at a cost of 55 cents apiece. And they only use about 10 percent of those documents ever again. We all need better ways to exchange, process, and retrieve information.

Businesses also need to exploit ways not only for automating work but also for optimizing the work process. This means creating "just-in-time" environments that minimize inventories and maximize the use of labor, capital equipment, and cash. It means unremitting attention to quality. It means a much more intense and coordinated use of information. This in turn carries with it a need to link disparate information "islands" to form tighter electronic relationships among different parts of the organization and with suppliers and customers. Finally, businesses need more flexibility, control, and reliability. They cannot afford any longer to have information systems inhibit their ability to adapt rapidly to the fast-changing markets that will characterize the 1990s. They will need computing and communications systems that conform to internationally accepted standards, so they will have the freedom to incorporate the latest technologies into their networks without making their present investments obsolete. And, as information systems become so much more central to the day-to-day running of their businesses, they will need systems that seldom or never fail, but that recover quickly if they do.

Telecommunications Networks in the 1990s

Telecommunications service providers will work hard to meet these needs, not least in the highly competitive long distance market in the United States. The biggest challenge will come in meeting their customers' data needs. On AT&T's network alone, data traffic is increasing at the rate of 15 to 20 percent per year; by mid-decade it could account for half of AT&T's traffic. Such growth explains why business customers in the long distance market have signalled their strong preference for digital facilities. Digital facilities deliver higher quality, particularly for data, and they greatly simplify the provisioning of advanced services. What is more, they cost less to operate and maintain, so they contribute to lower pricing. The transition from analog to digital systems has been under way for several years, but business customers' demands have accelerated the process. AT&T, for example, dramatically stepped up its own conversion timetable in 1988, writing down $6.7 billion worth of analog equipment. By 1990, AT&T will carry all of its domestic switched traffic digitally.

The digital revolution has facilitated a steady rise in the intelligence of telecommunications networks. As I indicated, modern switching machines are actually special-purpose digital computers (operating these days on several million lines of code). Yet these switchers represent only the first tier of network intelligence. The switchers can and do interact with other computers in the network and on the customers' premises. This has allowed telecommunications companies to offer a steady stream of new services, including toll-free calling, software-defined voice and data networking, and other services that customers can control for themselves.

As noted, fiber is the digital transmission system of choice for the 1990s and beyond (supplemented importantly by cellular radio in local exchange networks and by digital radio and satellite in long-distance networks). Fiber optic cables already lace the United States, and in the last two years telecommunications companies have laid fiber across both the Atlantic and Pacific. Users now have continuous fiber optic connectivity from Zurich to Tokyo. And that is only the beginning. Many more fiber optic cables are being considered and planned. There is only one segment of telecommunication networks where fiber does not usually exhibit a clear economic advantage—namely, the last mile or so extending from the substation to the residence. However, my scenario assumes that fiber will reach a large number of homes by the late 1990s, driven by soaring demand for High Definition Television (HDTV) services.

HDTV will be a superb entertainment medium—indeed, its advocates say the quality differences between TV and HDTV are at least as great as between black and white and color TV. The entertainment industry has learned again and again that people will gladly pay for such quality improvements. HDTV will probably be introduced in the U.S. around 1992, and if it does in fact take off, fiber to the home is almost a sure thing. With its immunity to electromagnetic interference and its large transmission capacity, fiber is by far the best way to distribute the huge amounts of digital information in HDTV signals. So great is the carrying capacity of fiber that—if a telecommunications company were foolish enough—it could run all its traffic between major population centers on a single cable and have room to spare. But this would only increase the risk of service interruptions at a time when telecommunications has become vital to the everyday health and safety of our society.

As the decade advances, service providers will be competing in many dimensions. Quality will be one of the most important. It can be defined in several critical ways, including transmission clarity, call setup times, and call processing (getting through the first time). But, for more and more businesses, none of these quality dimensions is likely to be more important than reliability. Modern technology is making it possible to build self-healing networks that, for all practical purposes, can make service interruptions a thing of the past. For example, the AT&T network already relies on switching and computing systems that are both redundant and geographically dispersed. If there is a catastrophe in one center, the load moves to the other center without interrupting service. AT&T

has a computer-controlled dynamic routing system that instantaneously provides up to 21 alternative routes for calls when a cable is cut or when unexpected volume builds on a primary route. The fiber optic cable routes are configured in a series of interlocking circles that permit easy routing around a failure. Also, restoration switches are deployed that can sense breaks and divert circuits around failed facilities. Users are rapidly coming to expect precautions like these, and, barring Armageddon, they see no reason why they should have to endure the interruption of a single call or data session. Nor should they.

The Integrated Services Digital Network

One of the most powerful trends in computing and communications today is the trend toward common international standards. The highly integrated services described in the opening scenario will surely prove impossible unless such standards continue to be developed and implemented during the '90s.

For the telecommunications industry in the decade, the most directly important group of these standards is known as the integrated services digital network, or ISDN. Despite its name, ISDN is not a network or service. It is an internationally agreed-upon set of standards for building digital telecommunications networks and delivering integrated voice and data services over them, whether those networks are private or public. ISDN standards will continue to evolve as technology advances. But ISDN services are already a reality. ISDN "islands" exist throughout the United States, and as these become more interconnected, ISDN will be nearly ubiquitous by the turn of the century.

For most users, one of the greatest beauties of ISDN is that it offers them a way to simplify and unify their networks. Business users have typically built multiple special-purpose computer networks. Every time they had a new function, they tended to build a new network. The problem worsened if they happened to choose computers that were incompatible with their existing systems.

By creating an authentic multivendor environment based on international standards, ISDN in most cases eliminates the need for multiple networks, multiple access lines and multiple desktop terminals. It serves all the communications options: voice, electronic mail and other messaging, facsimile, video conference, and PC-to-PC or terminal-to-host data transmission. Users can exercise these options at the same time—for example, they can carry on a telephone conversation while looking at the same computer screen. Moreover, the ISDN signaling system provides a superb means for tying together the machine intelligence on the customers' premises with the intelligence in the telecommunications network. This can in turn be the basis for an array of powerful new services.

ISDN has been a living, evolving reality in the United States since at least December 1986, when McDonald's began a pioneering application of ISDN at its corporate headquarters location in Oak Brook, Illinois. Linked to a switch in an Illinois Bell central office, McDonald's ISDN services were initially used for digital telephones, voice/data terminals, facsimile, and modem pooling. Along with several other kinds of data applications, McDonald's is using ISDN lines to access IBM hosts from 3270-type terminals, which eliminates the need to string costly coaxial cable. One of the most attractive aspects of ISDN for McDonald's is that it will permit consolidation of all or nearly all its 20-odd networks onto a single network. ISDN rollout applications are underway with more than 20 local telephone companies in the United States. AT&T began offering ISDN service last year in the long distance network. Users began snapping up the service so fast that AT&T sped up its timetable and now offers ISDN in virtually every metropolitan area in the country. Outside the United States, ISDN applications are under way or planned in some 20 countries. We are well on the way to delivering globally consistent ISDN services to multinational business.

New Telecommunications Services

We live in a service economy that is certain to create demand for a vast number of new telecommunications services in the 1990s. The telecommunications industry will create these services—but so will business users, who will vie to develop new services for themselves or their customers as a way to achieve an edge in the marketplace. Entrepreneurs will get into the act, too. In fact, ISDN's open architecture could ignite a boom of entrepreneurial activity as great as the PC boom set off when IBM introduced the open MS-DOS operating system in 1980. Here is a sampler that includes services that may emerge, as well as services that exist today but that are likely to become much more widespread in the 1990s.

Home services. Poor results with videotext and in the home-computer market may seem to indicate that Americans do not yet see a great need for home information services. Nevertheless, if HDTV and fiber-to-the-home do materialize, a general-purpose HDTV terminal/entertainment/information center could be the next step. This would be a two-way communications system that could spur dramatic, synergistic growth in pictorial communications, multimedia database services, home shopping, educational services, and the trend toward working at home.

Messaging. Users will be able to create, send, store, forward, receive, file, encrypt, decrypt, and broadcast messages as data, text, fax, or voice. One form will convert readily into another, and natural languages will be translated into another, both for voice and text. For example, people might call their electronic mailboxes and have a speech synthesizer "read" aloud their electronic mail messages. Or they might dictate messages to be broadcast, translated where necessary, and printed out through an international network of fax machines. They will be able to do such things from anywhere in the world, including their vehicles.

Call redirection and handling. Users will be able to forward all calls to wherever they are, and, if they happen to change their plans without informing the network, the network will likely develop the intelligence for searching them out (with permission!).

Users will be able to sort and process incoming calls intensively. To facilitate call screening, with ISDN the callers' telephone numbers, and thus their likely identities, can arrive with the call. A brokerage house might use this feature to trigger retrieval of its caller's portfolio and trading records, and use this information to give its best customers preference before sending both the file and call to designated brokers. Or in a telemarketing center, the procedure might be reversed. Thus, only after an outgoing call to a potential customer is completed would the file and the call be sent to a free agent, relieving agents of the drudgeries of entering call numbers, unanswered calls, and busy signals. Systems such as these already exist today.

Mobile communications. Cellular radio systems will go digital, making mobile communications even more affordable and versatile. Users will be able to receive not just voice and fax, but advanced messaging services and relatively high-speed data.

Fax. Facsimile machines have proven themselves to be tremendously versatile; in combination with the messaging services outlined earlier, that versatility can only grow. People are using fax machines to fill prescriptions, submit insurance claims, place orders, distribute product information to sales forces, and publish newsletters. It will be a very rare location that does not have a fax machine as the next decade advances. And with ISDN, advanced fax machines will print out faster than they do now, on ordinary paper, and with quality that is every bit as good as with the best copying machines. In effect what has happened is that fax standards have created a universal language for transmitting images ("fax Esperanto"). Building on these standards, systems now exist for fax-to-computer and computer-to-fax communications, as do systems for sending paperless fax messages from computer to computer and from computer to file server on a local area network. In this way, messages can be captured, viewed, shared, and filed electronically without the need for paper copies.

Telemarketing. Businesses will use telecommunications to tighten their relationships with customers—both for sales and service. As noted earlier, telemarketers will use sophisticated call-handling techniques to raise the productivity of their agents and reduce lost calls. Speech recognition systems will increasingly take orders and instruct callers to give more information—such as credit card numbers. Business-to-business telemarketing could involve using a central computer to generate price lists, product descriptions, discounts, and promotions. The computer would send this information to a customer's fax or PC and receive orders back from it for processing.

Multimedia teleconferencing. Businesses will have the opportunity to reduce travel costs dramatically with the development of inexpensive and convenient teleconferencing tools. By decade's end, many employees will be able to send video pictures, computer files, and graphics freely to screens at each others' desktop workstations. They will have the ability to open and control windows on their screens that will let them view speakers and graphics simultaneously, or zoom in on either one.

Private networks. Many services I have described will be offered on both public and private network facilities. However, many businesses will discover less need for truly private networks. They will discover that software-defined services will give them virtual private services that combine the flexibility and control of private networks with the economies and reliability of shared public networks. And they will find that they can set up, tear down, and reconfigure their services with less and less delay. They will pay for what they want only when they use it. For example, AT&T's ISDN service already allows users to select among different services—such as data, WATS, and 800 Service—on a call-by-call basis.

Whatever they do, companies can expect better tools for what is now called *network management*. Network management is a complex task that includes not only the ability to manage failures but also provisioning, billing, least-cost routing, and security. Network management standards under development now will play an important role in giving users the unified systems they need to do these jobs in all three domains their networks traverse: the local-exchange network, the long-distance network, and their own multivendor private facilities.

Communications in the 1990s will be dynamic and rich in opportunity. To be sure, the details are impossible to predict. In many cases, it will be hard to tell the sizzle from the fizzle. But if history is any guide, we can look forward to surprises at least as great as the PC and fax revolutions of the 1980s. And we have good reason for expecting that the broad trends I have outlined will persist. Demand for services and transmission capacity ("band-width") will continue to burgeon, as computers exchange larger and larger amounts of information at higher speeds and users rely more and more on graphics and video.

In the last years of our century, such demands will be driving our ISDN networks to evolve toward what AT&T has called an era of "Universal Information Services." In this era, our telecommunications networks will achieve even higher degrees of intelligence. Users will tap into the networks through a small family of universal ports in much the same way we now plug appliances into standard electrical outlets. They will have instant access to a huge range of network resources, because the time lag between ordering and getting services will simply disappear. Users will be able to send and receive information anytime, anywhere, and in any form—voice, data, image, or video.

Using these telecommunications resources effectively will continue to pose complex challenges to business. Equipment vendors, service providers, and users will have to work more closely together than ever before. But together they will have an unprecedented power to make their employees and customers more efficient, productive, and creative.

Questions

1. What new communications services are expected to become universal in the 1990s? With which of these have you had personal experience? Briefly describe your experience.

2. What are the advantages of ISDN?

3. How can ISDN affect the competitiveness of small firms (less than 50 employees)?

3.3

Here Comes the Payoff
from PCs

David Kirkpatrick

Ever been in a meeting where ideas start flowing so fast everybody wants to talk at once? Boeing and other companies have found a radical new way to harness that creative energy. Their brainstormers still sit around a table, but instead of shouting, they type their thoughts on networked personal computers using a new kind of software that keeps track of what everyone has to say. Participants can sift through far more material and act faster than they could in an ordinary meeting.

In fact, after years of complaints that investment in desktop computing doesn't pay off in productivity, this new software—called groupware—has produced dramatic results. Boeing has cut the time needed to complete a wide range of team projects by an average of 91%, or to *one-tenth* of what similar work took in the past. In one case last summer, a group of engineers, designers, machinists, and manufacturing managers used TeamFocus software from IBM to design a standardized control system for complex machine tools in several plants. Managers say such a job normally would take more than a year. With 15 electronic meetings, it was done in 35 days.

Boeing's data come from the largest and most rigorous study yet of the cost-saving impact of groupware—computer software explicitly designed to support the collective work of teams. Productivity gains around a conference table have so far been most obvious. But groupware's ultimate promise is larger—linking departments, or colleagues in different locations, or even entire corporations in ways that vastly improve the efficiency and speed of collaborative projects.

The software has piqued the interest of many company problem solvers

---

because the typical American manager spends 30% to 70% of the day in meetings. The setup that Boeing and others are finding so successful seems absurd at first: a conventional conference room with a computer at every place. "Why can't we just look each other in the eye and talk?" you wonder. The answer: because you seldom elicit all the best ideas, and many potentially valuable contributors remain silent. In many meetings, 20% of the people do 80% of the talking. Those who are shy, junior, intimidated, or just too polite typically shut up.

Meeting software uses several techniques to loosen the lips of the silent majority. Everyone speaks at once, via the keyboard. (In most cases, plenty of out-loud interaction happens too.) As you type in your ideas and comments—hunt and peck is okay—they accumulate on your screen alongside everyone else's. Most people can read much faster than they can listen, so they can deal with far more material in a given period. Says Jay Nunamaker, who helped pioneer the concept at the University of Arizona in the early 1980s and is now CEO of Ventana Corp., a Tucson firm that markets systems based on his work: "In a typical hour-long meeting of 15 people, everybody's got an average of only four minutes of air time. With computer support, everybody's got the potential to talk for 60 minutes. That's a big increase in productivity."

Also important, most systems keep the author of a given comment anonymous. That can be a powerful incentive to speak. Go ahead and disagree with your boss. He won't know it was you. Explains a market researcher at a *Fortune* 500 company who has begun conducting all meetings electronically: "It's generally unacceptable in a culture like ours to say your most private thoughts on a matter. You might be embarrassed or considered silly. But once a thought is on the screen it becomes something to be seriously considered by the group, and otherwise secret thoughts can be very useful. The processes of the mind become open to the group." The software uses a voting system, again anonymous, to rate ideas.

Groupware is already having a major impact on companies willing to move toward the new form of organization futurist Alvin Toffler calls "ad-hocracy," in which individuals decide what needs to be done and form teams to do it. These pioneers—which include Boeing, Dell Computer, GM Europe, IBM, Marriott, MCI Communications, J.P. Morgan, Pacific Gas & Electric, Price Waterhouse, Southern New England Telecommunications, and Texaco—are using technology to push toward flatter, faster, more team-focused organizations.

Proponents believe in what could be called the democratization of data: the flow of knowledge to wherever it is needed. Groupware enables team members to stay abreast of one another's progress whether they are in a meeting room or scattered at PC keyboards from Boston to Bangkok. Companies can more quickly find connections among disparate pieces of information and disparate people whose expertise might otherwise be overlooked.

Many of these companies use a unique product from Lotus Development called Notes, which Robert Johansen, a senior fellow at the Institute for the Future in Menlo Park, California, calls "the bellwether groupware product out there." Introduced in late 1989, Notes is starting to show how the remarkable possibilities of groupware go well beyond meetings. Users type into the system vast amounts of their written work, which creates a set of databases that can be organized and searched in whatever way a user finds most convenient.

Price Waterhouse was Lotus's first Notes customer and now has 9,000 employees hooked up. Sheldon Laube, who has responsibility for all technology in the accounting and consulting firm's U.S. operations, required virtually everyone to have a PC powerful enough to handle the Notes network. Says he: "This is a revolutionary piece of software that will change the way people think about computers."

In many companies, leaders of teams trying to improve customer service have been among the first to embrace groupware. Technology consultants at Boeing used TeamFocus to better identify their customers' needs and to set a strategic direction for themselves. They estimated the process would normally have taken six weeks but with the help of two half-day electronic meetings was finished in one.

At Marriott, human resources executive Carl Di Pietro started using meeting software five months ago. He has run meetings for groups from all across the company, and his enthusiasm is boundless: "In my 30 years, it's the most revolutionary thing I've seen for improving the quality and productivity of meetings. It gets you closer to the truth." A group is able to reach a genuine consensus, he says, and members leave much more committed to decisions than they would have been with conventional methods.

By definition groupware requires groups of PC users wired into a network. That knitting together is happening so fast in the Nineties that Steve Jobs of Next Computer suggests rechristening the machines "*inter*-personal computers." Already 38% of corporate PCs are tied into networks, many spanning whole companies.

Computer networks not only connect machines but also make employees feel connected to the organization. Researchers find that electronic mail users are more likely to feel committed to their jobs than do the unplugged. No similar data yet exist for groupware, but anecdotal evidence so far suggests it creates an even more powerful sense of belonging.

Managers have been frustrated for years by their inability to prove that office computing increases productivity. Morgan Stanley senior economist Stephen Roach flatly asserts that there has been *no* productivity payoff. His primary evidence: While service companies spent about $800 billion on information technology in the past decade, service productivity growth over that period has been a measly 0.7%. One problem, Roach says, is that service companies have not made the staff reductions that the new hardware should have made possible.

Others make a similar point about manufacturing. Economist Gary Loveman at the Harvard business school studied comprehensive five-year cost and productivity data for 60 large manufacturing enterprises and found no evidence that information technology improved productivity.

Neither Roach nor Loveman think computers are the fundamental problem. "I don't blame the machines," says Roach. "It's a managerial problem. Call it ineptitude. They haven't had the guts to trade machines for bodies." Loveman concurs: "I don't think most organizations have thought about what information does to authority, job structures, decision-making and allocation of people's time."

Lotus CEO Jim Manzi agrees that evidence of productivity gains is paltry—so far. "Nobody can demonstrate a return on investment for stand-alone computing," he says. (By contrast, CEO Bill Gates of Microsoft argues that productivity gains do exist but are just extremely difficult to measure.) Manzi thinks progress will come with groupware. Says he: "We think productivity can be improved if we use work group computing to integrate people into team-based organizations." He adds that Notes demonstrates the difference between "information processing" and "information sharing."

IBM was the first company to install an electronic meeting room in a real business situation—a manufacturing and development facility in Owego, New York. A team from the University of Arizona led by Nunamaker designed the software and in the fall of 1987 visited Owego to measure its impact. They found that meeting time was cut by 56%. Subsequent research by IBM itself at a corporate administrative center found similar results.

Boeing's study late last year is the most comprehensive follow-up to the IBM research. It closely replicated the Owego results with a larger sample over a longer period. It also demonstrated cost benefits for the first time. Boeing studied 64 meetings with 1,000 participants, tracking what managers did compared with what they said they would have done without the software. Boeing saved an average of $6,700 per meeting, mainly in employee time. Says TeamFocus project manager Brad Quinn Post, who ran the study: "The data show there are very clear opportunities to use these products to significantly improve business processes, to make our work cheaper, faster, and better."

In 1989, IBM signed a licensing agreement with Nunamaker's Ventana that allowed Big Blue to install more meeting rooms in its own offices and to sell the software to outside clients. IBM now has more than 50 such rooms all over the world. It rents some to outsiders for $2,000 to $7,000 a day, and will license its TeamFocus software—a version of Ventana's system—for one meeting room for $50,000. Ventana charges $25,000 to license its product, called GroupSystems.

One other program is on the market: VisionQuest, developed by tiny Collaborative Technologies of Austin, Texas. IBM has deliberately proceeded slowly, wanting to establish TeamFocus internally and refine the software before pushing it hard on customers. Collaborative Technologies, on the other hand, recently reorganized in order to market its product more aggressively. The company sells a VisionQuest license for $29,000.

All three are elegantly designed and user-friendly. Collaborative Technologies has taken the simplest path: It requires no equipment other than a network of PCs. The competing systems designed and sold by Ventana and licensed to IBM add a big display screen at the front of the room. While a professional meeting facilitator is helpful at any electronic meeting, Ventana and IBM virtually require one. That makes their systems costlier to operate, though they do offer a wider range of features, including a way for groups to collaborate on writing letters or documents.

Some gleanings from the experience of companies already seriously committed to groupware:

- At Marriott's Bethesda, Maryland, headquarters recently, seven executives from one of the company's large Washington-area hotels sat in a room full of PCs equipped with VisionQuest. None had ever taken part in an electronic meeting. A sign at the front warned: "Enter this room ONLY if you believe the ideas and opinions of others have value."

  Their challenge was to find new ways to improve guest satisfaction. After a lot of laughing and a few silly suggestions on screen, the room went silent. Occasionally someone left briefly. The hotel's general manager ate a cookie. After 25 minutes, the group had generated 139 ideas. Then they rated them on a scale of one to five: once according to the likely impact of each idea on guests, and again according to what each would probably cost. A consensus emerged that, among other things, more thorough training of hotel employees was essential.

- A market researcher, who asked not to be identified because he doesn't want his competition to start using groupware, has been running all his meetings with VisionQuest for six months. They typically include scientists, product developers, sales and marketing people, and often ad agency staffers. Says he: "While I thought I was a good facilitator, I'm convinced I was actually missing about 75% of the information I could have got out on the table." He installed the software in a room his company had designed for PC training, where 15 networked PCs often sat unused.

- Southern New England Telecommunications installed IBM's TeamFocus in an electronic meeting room in its New Haven, Connecticut, headquarters in June 1990 and has just added a second. The company used the rooms to develop a new customer relations strategy in seven weeks that it figures would have taken about a year using focus groups or surveys of employees who deal with the public.

- J.P. Morgan installed a handsomely appointed 13-seat room equipped with TeamFocus last March. Since then it has been in almost constant use for meetings devoted to strategic planning, organizational changes, auditing, and employee surveys, among other subjects. Morgan will soon install TeamFocus rooms in its Wilmington, Delaware, and London offices. Says Lynn Reed, a vice president in Morgan's global technology and operations group: "The software works best for a meeting that is going to take more than an hour and that is intended to achieve a group decision. It's not beneficial for status-checking meetings, where each participant has to give a report, or for meetings with a single speaker."

- Dell Computer started using VisionQuest last May for strategic planning meetings. The company found it could include more people in the process and still finish faster. Says Bruce Ezell, manager of business development: "That went so well we've started using it for any type of project that requires groups of people to work together—like product planning and developing marketing strategies."

In one case, Dell used the system to name a new product. In the past, names were developed by asking product team members to send in suggestions by electronic mail. Then meetings were called to consider lists of names on flip charts. "Whoever screamed loudest would be heard," says Ezell. "It was still up to the product manager to make a decision, but there was no way to get consensus." With VisionQuest, a group of marketing and sales managers met for two hours, proposed and rated 75 names, and reduced them to five finalists. It would have taken two months to get there the old way.

Ezell says groupware is a natural for Dell since everyone in the company has good computer skills. More important, the PC industry is experiencing brutal price cutting and going through faster technological change than perhaps any other industry in history. Says Ezell: "When we detect a major change in the market, we need to pull our management team together immediately. We can't tolerate meetings that hash things out all day and end without consensus." Strategic planning meetings that used to last two days now take four hours.

Di Pietro of Marriott is convinced that meeting software can also enhance cultural diversity, a company priority. "It's a room of nondiscrimination," he says. "You don't know if that idea you're reading comes from a woman or a man, part of the minority or majority, or a senior or junior person. People begin to say, 'Hey, we've got a lot in common with each other.' "

Many experts caution, however, that a repressive boss or a dysfunctional group will probably remain so with or without electronic help. Says Bob Bostrom, who teaches at the University of Georgia and consults with companies on using meeting software: "The technology doesn't make people equal in terms of power but in terms of being heard." Some bosses defeat its purpose by walking around the room glaring at people's terminals or loudly bullying everyone to put in ideas that resemble their own, says Gerardine DeSanctis, a professor of information systems at the University of Minnesota. "The group has to decide it wants to get more out of meetings," she observes. "It's like an alcoholic has to want to stop drinking."

The next step is to enable people to meet without being in the same room—or even the same city. The three meeting software products are all designed to work among distant participants, and a few companies, including Dell Computer, are already reporting early success with this approach. Nunamaker, however, says his research has found obstacles. Without the nonverbal cues and other stimuli that come from seeing others in the same room engaged in a common task, people's attention easily wanders.

Groupware has other potential drawbacks. Notes, for example, may prove threatening to some managers because employees can independently identify and connect with others working on similar tasks. These new working relationships may improve efficiency, but they may also upset organizational hierarchies. Says Natasha Krol, an analyst at the Meta Group, a Westport, Connecticut, consulting firm: "You can start your own subculture in Notes. Managers often have very little to do with that, and the process may even help identify which managerial layers are obsolete."

The flip side of Notes is that putting so much employee activity on the network gives management the potential to monitor exactly what is going on in the organization. At Price Waterhouse, some departments use Notes as a kind of electronic filing cabinet, with all written documents inserted in the database. The boss can see every memo anybody writes.

Some new types of groupware on the horizon could increase management control still further. Later this year NCR expects to release an enhancement to Cooperation, its program that ties together office activities now conducted on different computer systems from PCs to mainframes. The new feature can, among other things, keep track of documents that must be passed from person to person for processing. It will alert managers to logjams or other inefficiencies.

The payoff from groupware could be huge. John Oltman, CEO of SHL Systemhouse, a large Ottawa firm that manages computer systems for clients, predicts that some big insurance companies could reduce their claims-processing work force by as much as 50% over the next five years.

Groupware that allows teams to communicate using video will open entirely new productivity horizons. Researchers are already working on various ways to conduct what they call "virtual meetings," in which videoscreens would allow people in various places to interact as if they were face to face. Jay Nunamaker has a plan that calls for groups of four people to sit at terminals in front of giant screens in four different rooms. The screens create the illusion that all 16 participants are in the same room.

At AT&T Bell Laboratories, researcher Sid Ahuja is working on a way to accomplish the same thing from individual offices. His system would display live video images of each participant on a desktop terminal, and allow them to share software, graphics, and other data as easily as if they were all together.

If groupware really makes a difference in productivity long term, the very definition of an office may change. You will be able to work efficiently as a member of a group wherever you have your computer. As computers become smaller and more powerful, that will mean anywhere. Paul Saffo, a researcher at the Institute for the Future, thinks networked computing may well lead to drastic population dispersal. Says he: "For the first three-quarters of the century our cities were shaped by developments in transportation and telecommunications, but now the influence is shifting to computers and communications." And all we really wanted was a little boost in productivity.

Questions

1. What is groupware? Give three examples of groupware.

2. How does groupware reduce the number of meetings in an organization?

3. How does groupware support Toffler's concept of "ad-hocracy" discussed in the article?

3.4

Imaging Systems Replace Paper Flow with Information Flow

Murray Sherry and Homer Hagedorn

I mage processing technology provides significant opportunities for cost containment and competitive advantage. Using earlier information processing technologies, organizations could only extract data from documents. Now, imaging allows companies to substitute information flow for paper flow by storing, retrieving, manipulating, and comparing whole documents or components.

Imaging systems electronically retrieve and transmit pictures of entire documents. Images can be compared on-screen with documents also electronically retrieved and transported, or they can be compared on-screen with stored, digitized data from traditional systems. In more flexible systems, document images can be edited and simultaneously examined at multiple workstations, instantly available wherever the system reaches.

Organizations that implement image-processing technology must restructure work patterns, "removing from the loop" all tasks that deal only with transmittal, rather than content. Much of the productivity gains result from human changes; where the human element has not been considered, the gains have been substantially lower. For real success, top management must lead the profound change.

Changing Work Patterns

Image processing capabilities make it practical to rationalize and simplify work; both information flow and transaction flow can be managed actively. Traditional relationships change dramatically because documents are available almost instantaneously.

Using images leads to significant changes in skills, roles, and relationships among office workers and their supervisors. These changes appear to resemble those already underway in highly automated, information-based factories (*i.e.*, reskilling, deskilling, reducing direct supervision, and offering incentives for people to learn different tasks).

Successfully implementing image processing requires rethinking transactional work flows. Early on, the applications exist within single departments; more widespread organizational change can occur when multiple departments become involved. When broader sets of transactional work are integrated into smooth-flowing processes, opportunities for very basic organization redesign will become apparent (*e.g.*, fewer organizational levels and less restrictive policies and procedures about information sharing).

If imaging truly integrates office work, the opportunities—and headaches—facing large office process-based businesses (*e.g.*, financial services) will soon mirror those being denied or reluctantly examined by manufacturers.

Gaining an Edge in Customer Service

Home Savings of America, San Diego, is a $36 billion institution with most of its assets invested in mortgage loans. The institution services 350,000 retirement-trust accounts.

When Individual Retirement Accounts (IRAs) were introduced in 1975, Home Savings went into the retirement-trust business. As a result of deregulation in 1981, retirement-account volume increased dramatically. Home Savings' need to organize better the growing mountain of paper triggered an evaluation of available technologies.

Three years ago, Home Savings had approximately 150,000 accounts that were being serviced without using an efficient document-storage system. The S&L kept paper files of all accounts and had some difficulty locating misfiled or in-use files. It could answer customer requests and inquiries only after delays, sometimes measured in days. The retirement-trust staff was so frustrated with the working conditions that its turnover far exceeded industry norms. Temporary help had become a permanent expedient.

To manage the situation, Home Savings began microfilming existing and incoming documents. However, this process made documents unavailable during the critical first few days it took to batch, microfilm, review, and key the document indices. Much activity can occur in the first week after an account is opened (*e.g.*, customers may add or change data to correct initial information). If documents were "out" being processed at this time, changes might not be documented and customers' requests not serviced properly.

Three staff members—an officer and two members of Operations Services—started exploring I/T tools and discovered imaging technology in 1984. Home Savings' CEO took a personal interest in the technology, stimulated by his own outside contacts and oriented toward possibilities he saw for the thrift's basic loan-processing business. The next year, File Net Corp. asked Home Savings to consider imaging technology. Since Home Savings had already focused on retirement trust as a problem, it began to consider imaging technology as a solution. An agreement was reached with FileNet, and the three staff members became the core team to implement an imaging pilot.

A combined Home Savings/FileNet team implemented the initial system in late 1985. The team programmed the existing six operational areas into six work streams and made the six operationally independent. It spent two weeks to introduce and train S&L staff for each stream.

All the documents had already been purged and batched for the prior shift to microfilm, so original material was already organized for conversion to optical storage. In addition to the system it purchased, Home Savings leased two additional stand-alone scanning systems and ran them 15 hours per day for four months to complete the conversion. Overall, the cost for document conversion was 11 cents per image.

The first work stream implemented was new-account processing. After only two weeks of operation, Home Savings realized that using old, paper-based processes was limiting the automated system's capabilities. Reexamining the procedures, management realized that the work stream should be broken out into a larger number of smaller flows to use the full system capability. The thrift continued with the implementation, but after the six streams were fully installed, all were reconfigured into a new set of 40 streams during 1986. The initial "payback" milestone justifying the project was a demonstration that IRA applications really could be processed and their documents made available for additional transactions by noon of the day after they came in.

Home Savings also has solved some of its staffing problems:

- Training, even for people with no computer experience, is completed in two weeks.
- Job satisfaction in retirement trust has eliminated the need for temps.
- Turnover in retirement-processing staff has decreased dramatically; in two years, no additional staff has been required even though volume has increased.
- Scanning and indexing new-account documents with imaging doubled productivity.

Management estimates that, with only three or four additional people, it can easily handle the additional 100,000 IRA accounts the Bowery

Savings Bank (which Home Savings acquired in early 1988) needed 21 people to service. In fact, officials directly attribute a 25 percent gain in labor productivity to the imaging system. The remaining productivity gain stems simply from rethinking and modifying the basic procedures.

Home Savings wanted to improve a creaky and out-of-control process; the inevitable result, however, was improved customer service that, in itself, sharpened the bank's competitive edge in retirement-fund processing. Accurate, speedy document retrieval has given Home Savings the edge in customer service. "Like" documents are accessible by multiple users, files are complete, changes can be made immediately online, and images of documents are better than the originals in most cases. This level of control greatly enhances Home Savings' position as a trustee, a power granted in 1984. Home Savings became so efficient that its former trustee for IRA accounts has bought a FileNet system to compete.

Improvement in productivity alone has already paid for the system. Total payoff is much greater than predicted when the system was bought. Home Savings has now embarked on a second imaging project—mortgage loans, its main line of business.

Three Different Approaches

These case studies (see sidebars) explain how diverse organizations have successfully implemented image processing technology for entirely different applications using three separate vendor strategies:

- ◆ Home Savings of America, the largest U.S. thrift in deposits and second largest in assets, implemented retirement-fund processing with a FileNet system.
- ◆ US West Direct, the northwestern regional Bell operating company, implemented Yellow Pages advertising management with a Plexus Computers system.
- ◆ The State of Maryland's Department of Health and Mental Hygiene implemented birth-certificate retrieval with an Eastman Kodak system.

Information executives must answer four principal questions that accompany the early stages of selecting, installing, and implementing imaging systems:

- ◆ When and for what broad purposes should imaging technology initially be introduced?
- ◆ What specific imaging technologies are right for my company and which vendors offer these systems?
- ◆ To what extent and in what fashion does imaging offer potential competitive advantage?
- ◆ How can imaging technology be most effectively implemented by the project team?

All image processing vendors use the same basic technologies, (*i.e.*, data processing, digitized images, compression and decompression of images, laser printing, and very high-speed communications). However, four key differences can significantly affect how an imaging system operates: microfilm or optical storage; relational data base of just images or one that includes text, geometry, and images; converting or not converting existing documents; and an application-programming language or a turnkey solution.

Microfilm or Optical Storage

Optical storage is a crucial technology for image processing. Compared to magnetic storage systems, optical disk drives provide somewhat slower access to much larger amounts of digital information. Most imaging systems use optical write-once, read-many-times (WORM) disks to store documents for intermittent access over long periods—possibly as long as ten years.

Microfilm—a mature, familiar technology—is an option to optical storage for imaging. Today, microfilm offers slower-access, less costly technology. However, the cost of optical storage is dropping rapidly, so it will probably compete on an equivalent cost basis within a few years. Microfilm provides more acceptable legal documentation (potentially an important criterion).

Microfilm images must be created in a batch mode, one film strip at a time; in contrast, optical images are stored individually. It normally takes several days to prepare, film, develop, ensure quality, and index a roll's worth of documents. Documents stored optically can be made available as quickly as they can be individually scanned and indexed.

Speed of retrieval differs for two reasons:

- In both microfilm and optical jukeboxes, mechanical devices retrieve either film cartridges or disks and place them in readers. It takes significantly less time to retrieve a record from a disk rather than sequentially search (on the average, half a strip) to find the desired image.
- Optical-disk images are "cleaned" at time of capture—at retrieval, they require no adjustment for visual quality. In contrast, microfilm images may need adjusting for brightness and clarity since the process usually records images of documents "as is."

Because recording and accessing microfilm documents are more difficult, imaging technology is evolving toward optical storage. A greater rate of innovation is occurring in optical storage than in microfilm.

Relational Data Bases

Since managing images is critical to an image-processing system, a data base program is crucial to its overall performance. The relational approach to managing data bases is more flexible, and it tolerates more freely structured usages than any alternative hierarchical method. A relational data base stores indices of documents and contains addresses that enable the system to locate the documents directly. Plexus, alone among the three vendors in the sidebar case studies, has extended its relational data base to handle textual and graphic data as well as image data.

Cutting Costs While Improving Quality

US West Direct (USWD) publishes The White and Yellow Pages for US West Communications (formerly Mountain Bell, Northwestern Bell, and Pacific Northwest Bell), the operating arm of US West, Inc. USWD produces 300 directories in a 14-state region and generates advertising sales revenues in excess of $600 million.

The operating companies' own directory subsidiaries were merged together to form USWD at the time of the Bell System divestiture in January 1984. As a result of the divestiture, USWD had to develop its own systems instead of relying on its parent company. The firm's charter was to implement "mechanized graphics" that:

◆ Replace an existing, dying technology of 20-year-old printing equipment that was about to lose its vendor support.
◆ Provide a single system to serve all three operating companies.
◆ Create customers' advertising proofs faster and more accurately.
◆ Bring in-house the outside contract work of preparing Yellow Pages graphics.

At the largest of the former companies, this outside graphics work amounted to 50 percent of the workload and cost $5 million per year.

USWD hired a Director of Strategic Systems and Technology Planning from a large microfilm publisher and gave him responsibility for creating the new mechanized graphics process. The Director believed that mechanized graphics (*i.e.*, a phototypesetter) by itself, was "old hat" and that USWD needed more in order to gain a strategic advantage. He wanted to offer computer-accessed, online directories, and he also wanted access to the information contained in existing Yellow Pages ads.

Under his direction, USWD put together a pilot operation in two years (*i.e.*, late 1987). The Director decided that the initial pilot's features would include using scanners to capture graphics for display ads, routing work electronically, and using a retrieval index to identify the status of each ad. The goal was to replace an annual $5 million cost for outside graphics work with a $7 million capital cost for an in-house system. All executives were committed to new technology. For them, the risks lay in failing to introduce new technology. They made it possible to realize image processing much more broadly than just replacing some obsolete phototypesetting equipment, which had been the original intent.

Using a Plexus system, USWD's application runs on a very large relational data base, large-volume storage, and a communications link with software for the phototypesetter. Plexus' "data base engine" is a computer that controls a relational data base of various CAD-like ad elements (*e.g.*, pictures, logos, addresses and telephone numbers, and hours of business). Specifically, copy is stored in machine-readable form; each graphic element is stored individually with its location, size, and orientation.

Plexus designed enough magnetic-disk memory to hold about one-year's worth of ads. It plans to provide optical disk storage on which to store older ads, because producing Yellow Pages involves a tremendous amount of repeat business. Ads are moved to different directories; the same logos are used in different ads; and data has to be saved for more than a year because 60 percent of the ads are reworked annually.

The eight terminals of the new pilot system were placed next to the six terminals of the old production system, so that both could be used. (Initially, productivity with all 14 terminals actually decreased; however, immediately after the supervisor was replaced, productivity increased dramatically.) The new Plexus system forecasts workloads, routes work, tracks ads being produced, and handles file management.

After several months of testing in mid-1987, management elected to turn off the old system and put the new system into production. The project's focus shifted to program tuning and stabilization. Production capabilities such as error checks, backups, and recovery mechanisms were sidelined while the pilot was beefed up into a production system. This enhancement required tremendous efforts by the project team and very vigorous motivation and leadership by top management. USWD canceled its $5 million per year of graphics contracts and brought the work in-house on the Plexus-and-phototypesetter system.

At US West Direct, image processing technology was designed to improve the production process. However, these major benefits may be eventually eclipsed by better customer service and easier follow-on sales—no small matter in a business where competition is heating up. Focus has now shifted to futures: USWD wants to display ads through a terminal in its customer-service area; answer customers' questions quickly, sometimes immediately (it previously took two days just to find the copy); and centrally locate all contracts, ads, and salesperson's notes. It wants to be able to call up signed contracts, notes, and copy sheets and respond quickly to customers' needs. Further in the future are several other features: prepare sales packages electronically, create ads "on speculation," and deliver images and supporting data to remote customer sites and sales offices.

Converting vs. Not Converting

Decisions about converting or not converting existing documents are tied inextricably to the particular applications. Using Home Savings' benchmark cost of

11 cents per document, every million documents to be converted represents an additional cost of more than $100,000, plus the time to convert. In the three case studies, Home Savings and the State of Maryland opted to convert existing data. However, at US West Direct, two-thirds of its ads change annually, so converting historical material offered insufficient benefit to balance cost.

The actual computer programs that read, write, and otherwise manipulate images and their indices are quite complex. Organizations can purchase a high-level, process-oriented programming language that users themselves understand and write, or buy a turnkey solution written in programming language that only the vendor can be expected to manipulate. Operating on the native programs is daunting.

APL or Turnkey Solution

Both Wang and FileNet offer image processing systems that allow users to program their own applications. High-level languages let users with little programming experience tailor their own applications in concise, easy-to-understand ways. These languages automatically handle most data management and operating functions, so users can concentrate on solving business problems. Kodak and Plexus have chosen to tie together image-manipulation programs into meaningful business applications (*i.e.*, turnkey systems).

Short-term personnel requirements must be balanced with long-term needs. Management must answer a series of questions, such as: Can the system be defined in sufficient detail so that only minimal modifications will be required after implementation? What will vendor assistance cost? Will it be available when needed? Does corporate security require that the application be kept in-house? Do users have the skills needed to write their own applications?

Management's Role in Image Processing Implementation

Information executives hold the keys to successful imaging technology. CIOs have the power to:

- ◆ Guarantee the freedom necessary to experiment (*i.e.*, "play") with new technology.
- ◆ Assure continuity of sponsorship and project management during implementation.
- ◆ Select valid justifications and insist on measuring success of the imaging project by concrete standards.

Although it takes a committed cadre of middle-level managers and senior executives to introduce a new technology, CIOs also must:

- ◆ Insist on designing the project so it can justify itself as soon as possible.

- Force rigorous examination of the project team's competence to do the job.
- Assure adequate project team building, particularly if the organization's culture generally lacks emphasis and skill building on teamwork.

High-Level Protection

In addition to senior management commitment, successful implementation requires:

- Committed managers who are senior enough to ensure costs of the new technology project are not financially large in terms of a failure's potential career impact. Managers must be relatively relaxed about the project.
- A concerted effort that communicates management's attitude to the project team. Relaxed managers let team members be more observant, more flexible, and more creative.
- Team members who feel free to "play" with the new technology to find out what—in their setting—it is really good for. Play periods are especially important early on to uncover strategic advantages the technology offers.

"Redundancy" of Sponsorship

Only top management can assure "redundancy" among sponsors and champions. Imaging projects take months to design, implement, and enhance. If converting existing archives is involved, the overall process may take years.

Information executives must ensure that enough enthusiasm exists among project leadership to compensate for the personnel attrition almost certain to occur in a large, long-lived project. It is very risky to rely on only one or two well-informed enthusiasts to sustain a multi-year, multi-million dollar project. They may quit, or as valuable employees, may be promoted. For instance, four of five senior managers recruited by US West were all transferred or promoted to jobs elsewhere within 18 months after they arrived.

Fast Access to Vital Records

The Department of Health and Mental Hygiene (DHMH) of the State of Maryland, Baltimore, is responsible for all state healthcare systems from which citizens can get information. Among these systems is Vital Records, which authenticates claimants' legal status, verifies births and deaths for law-enforcement agencies, and supplies all Maryland demographics data for national records. Vital Records' work includes issuing certificates that verify births, deaths, and marriages.

Birth and death certificates, some dating back to the mid-1800s, are stored in a huge vault. They are bound into books, historically organized by year and by county.

Until the early 1970s, the state had a variety of manual indices to this information. In 1973, DHMH created an index keyed by county, date of birth, name of child, and name of mother, which enabled clerks to find the particular book in which a particular birth certificate could be located. By 1986, 3,400,000 births dating from 1922 were indexed in the data base.

For ten years, this system worked. Calls for birth verifications clustered around three events: retirement, reaching majority, and work permit applications. Requests for birth-certificate copies rose dramatically with two law changes: the recent immigration/work law and the Internal Revenue Service mandate requiring children five or older to have Social Security numbers.

As the number of calls increased, the State had to add "researchers" to find original documents and add the official seal and signature to each copy. Eventually the size of the vault limited the process: only so many people could be inside at one time looking for documents. Citizens had to wait at least two hours to get copies of documents. Those writing sometimes waited four weeks to get responses. As a result, complaints mushroomed.

As fate would have it, in December 1986, Governor-elect William D. Schaefer wanted his birth certificate from Vital Records. His assistant failed to get a response to several telephone calls, so Schaefer decided to get it himself. Choosing to be treated as a regular customer, he suffered through the long wait.

After taking office in January 1987, the governor returned for a "white gloves" inspection and made an official ruckus. He bypassed his Cabinet Secretary and directed the Division Chief responsible for Vital Records to clean up the mess and devise a responsible way to serve the public. The governor's personal interest made all the difference in obtaining funds, making the necessary high-level professional staff available to plan and protect the project, and obtaining more money to accelerate a deliberate conversion process.

Given the official mandate, the Director of Data Processing for DHMH formed a team of senior health professionals to plan the task. These people, relieved of their regular duties to work full time on the problem, were so enthusiastic that they even worked on weekends and holidays.

As much as possible, DHMH wanted to replicate its existing capabilities while reducing turnaround time. The team decided early on to implement an earlier joint study by Data Processing and Vital Records to automate the retrieval process. By mid-1987, it had prepared a system justification and an RFP, obtained proposals, and evaluated the choices.

Based on the proposals, the team identified key imaging system capabilities being offered (*e.g.*, make images of birth certificates a standard size; create long-lasting files; and provide recognizable, secure documents acceptable for public needs) and eventually purchased Kodak's turnkey, mi-